THE JOY OF TREK

LB

THE JOY OF TREK

How to Enhance Your Relationship
With a *Star Trek* Fan

Sam Ramer

A Citadel Press Book
Published by Carol Publishing Group

A Citadel Press Book
Published by Carol Publishing Group
Citadel Press is a registered trademark of Carol Communications, Inc.

Editorial, sales and distribution, rights and permissions inquiries should be addressed to Carol Publishing Group, 120 Enterprise Avenue, Secaucus, N.J. 07094

In Canada: Canadian Manda Group, One Atlantic Avenue, Suite 105, Toronto, Ontario M6K 3E7

Carol Publishing Group books may be purchased in bulk at special discounts for sales promotion, fund-raising, or educational purposes. Special editions can be created to specifications. For details, contact Special Sales Department, Carol Publishing Group, 120 Enterprise Avenue, Secaucus, N.J. 07094.

Manufactured in the United States of America

10 9 8 7 6 5 4 3 2 1

Library of Congress Cataloging-in-Publication Data
Ramer, Sam.
    The joy of Trek : how to enhance your relationship with a
Star trek fan / Sam Ramer.
        p.   cm.
    "A Citadel Press book."
    ISBN 0-8065-1695-X (pb)
    1. Star Trek television programs.   2. Star Trek films.   I. Title.
PN1992.8.S74R36   1997
791.45′72—dc21   '97-34763
                                                                        CIP

To Bonnie,
who needs this book more than anyone

CONTENTS

*I believe that if you put men and women together,
something is going to happen…
Unless you're at a Star Trek convention.*

—*Bill Maher*

PREFACE

"What is it about *Star Trek*?" whined Anthony Lane in the *New Yorker* in his review of the movie *Star Trek: First Contact*. "Why can't it be like any other TV series and stay where it belongs?"

If you've opened this book, no doubt you're asking yourself the same question. What is it about *Star Trek* that causes grown men (and women) to join fan clubs? And go to *conventions*? What is it about a series that has spawned eight movies, four television series, countless books, and a cartoon series? For God's sake, what is it about a series whose fans managed to pressure the government of the United States of America into changing the name of the first space shuttle to match that of their much-beloved *Enterprise*?

What is it, and, more important, is it contagious?

Picture this: You have met a great guy (or gal). Intelligent, a little quirky, but really fun. On the third date, he (or she) says: "I have an idea; why don't we stay in and watch *Star Trek*?"

Oh no, you think. *I'm dating a Trekker.*

This book will help. Now, I can't tell you that this book will cure your Trekker of his addiction. Nothing known to science has been able to stop the inexorable advance of *Star Trek* as a cult. What this book will do is teach you the basics of *Star Trek* and give you ways to cope with someone for whom dressing as a Klingon doesn't seem all that weird. In fact, after you read this book, you may actually enjoy watching *Star Trek* with your addicted friend. Either that or you'll know that it may be best to find another friend.

You should realize, however, that just by picking up this book, you have started down a path. This path will lead you to look at the world as you never have before. You will, for a short time, step into the boots of a Trekker. You will fix the communicator to your tunic. You will place the pointy ears over your own. Have you ever wondered how *Star Trek* fans weathered the scorn heaped upon them by non-Trekkers in high school and college? It's because *they know*. They know the future. They have seen it firsthand. And it's filled with people *just like them*.

WHAT THE HELL IS *STAR TREK,* ANYWAY?

Star Trek began as a television program in the late 1960s. The original (or classic) show chronicled the voyages of the Starship *Enterprise,* registry NCC-1701, a huge spaceship under the command of Capt. James T. Kirk in the year 2264. This program was canceled after three seasons.

Due to popular demand, *Star Trek* was made into a movie called *Star Trek: The Motion Picture*. Subsequently, five more films were made, chronicling the adventures of the crew of the *Enterprise*. The others are *Star Trek II: The Wrath of Khan; Star Trek III: The Search for Spock; Star Trek IV: The Voyage Home; Star Trek V: The Final Frontier;* and *Star Trek VI: The Undiscovered Country.*

In 1986, a new *Star Trek* television program took the airwaves by storm. Set one hundred years after the first series and eighty years after the movies, *Star Trek: The Next Generation* continued the exploration of space. A new, more advanced Starship *Enterprise,* NCC-1701-D, was manned by totally new characters. This show lasted seven seasons and spawned two movies, *Star Trek: Generations* and *Star Trek: First Contact.*

In 1991, the third *Trek* series began. *Star Trek: Deep Space Nine* took place in the same time frame as *Next Generation,* on a space station at the far fringes of the galaxy. Yet a third entirely new crew manned this station, although characters from both the original *Star Trek* and *Next Generation* made appearances.

In 1994, the fourth *Trek* series was produced as an anchor show for the United Paramount Network. *Star Trek: Voyager* also takes place during the twenty-fourth century, but this time a starship is in trouble. The U.S.S. *Voyager* was lost in a remote section of the galaxy. Decades of travel away from anything familiar, the crew of this ship is desperately trying to find its way home.

Star Trek is also the basis for an animated series, comic books, novels, CD-ROMs, video games, and chocolate bars.

I'VE SEEN STAR WARS. DOES THAT HAVE SOMETHING TO DO WITH TREK?

You may not know anything at all about *Star Trek* or science fiction in general. So before we begin, we'll make sure you are able to distinguish *Trek* from the rest of the science fiction world.

Star Trek has *nothing* to so with the following films or television shows:

Star Wars This movie and its sequels, *The Empire Strikes Back* and *Return of the Jedi,* conceived by George Lucas, have absolutely no connection to *Star Trek.* There are differences of opinion among science fiction fans regarding these two universes. Trekkers are usually not diehard *Star Wars* fans. (I know, go figure.)

Star Wars is rooted in the touchy-feely seventies. The main message of *Star Wars* is "Trust your feelings." You've got one chance to save the universe by firing one missile down an exhaust shaft? Turn off your targeting device! Wing it! Want to learn how to fight someone better than you? Put on a blindfold!

Star Trek is quite the opposite: *very* logical. In *Star Trek,* characters are constantly learning to control their feelings and not let them interfere with their goals. Something wrong with your strategy in fighting an enemy? It's due to the fact that you have an unresolved conflict because that alien species killed your family. Something broken on the ship? Run a diagnostic. Whatever you do, don't just trust your feelings. If you do, you'll be asked to see the ship's counselor.

Independence Day This is a movie about aliens invading present-day Earth. Nothing to do with *Star Trek.* The *Enterprise* could kick their ass.

Close Encounters of the Third Kind This is a movie about friendly aliens making contact with Earth. Nothing to do with *Star Trek.* The *Enterprise* could kick their ass.

Aliens   This movie series concerns big nasty aliens in space. Nothing to do with *Star Trek*. They could kick the *Enterprise*'s ass.

Babylon Five   This is a television show about a space station. This is where old sci-fi actors go when they die. Nothing to do with *Star Trek*.

Terminator   Arnold Schwarzenegger and *Star Trek* don't mix. Don't ask me why.

Predator   See above.

2001: A Space Odyssey   The standard-bearer for science fiction movies. A beautiful, unique film. Nothing to do with *Star Trek*.

Terms of Endearment   Jack Nicholson plays an ex-astronaut. Does not concern us.

La Dolce Vita   Fellini's classic, a disturbing neorealist portrait of the Italian bourgeoisie. The *Enterprise* could kick their ass.

WHY YOU NEED THIS BOOK (OR, "I DON'T WANT TO BE SEEN BUYING THIS!")

Maybe you've watched a few episodes of *Star Trek*. You know, the original series, the one with Kirk and Spock and Scotty. Did your brother make you watch it? Did he pull the knob off the old television set so you couldn't change the channel? Maybe, just maybe, you liked the show a little bit. Come on, admit it. Didn't something seem interesting? Didn't the dramatic music composed by Alexander Courage* thrill you deep down?

Okay, it didn't.

But this isn't about you. This is about a show that has millions of fans all over the world. Did you know that *Star Trek* is broadcast in 103 different countries?† Did you know that the *Trek* movies have grossed about a *billion* dollars since the first one? Go to Universal

---

*I swear to God, that's the guy's name. I don't know whether he made it up or not, but if you were going to make one up, wouldn't it be Alexander Courage? "Your table is ready, Mr. Courage," "Here's your dry cleaning, Mr. Courage," "Mother, I'm in love with Alexander Courage."

†All I can say is that you haven't lived until you've seen *Star Trek: The Next Generation* dubbed in German. It's frightening and hilarious at the same time, especially when anyone says "Worf."

Studios and you'll see rides based on the movies. This thing is out of control.

By the way, you should know something before we go on. I am a *Star Trek* fan. I have been one since I first saw the show when I was five years old. To me, Capt. James Tiberius Kirk and Mr. Spock represented the best qualities of humanity. They exemplified the Warrior Code: honor, courage, intellect, compassion. In addition, the show depicted a future in which rationality triumphed over passion and mankind learned to do away with war, poverty, and disease.

Also, they put all the female crew members in really short skirts.*

The vision of the future that Gene Roddenberry created is a positive one. In the world of *Star Trek*, mankind has made tremendous advances. By the twenty-third century, poverty has been eliminated, racism is a thing of the past, and Barbra Streisand doesn't make movies. It's a utopia.

When questioned about their passion for *Star Trek*, Trekkers almost always cite the show's positive, integrated vision of the future. When the show debuted during the cold war, mankind's problems seemed intractable, and an uplifting message was welcome. However, that was not the real reason the show was such a success.

The real reason? The show was cool. A crew of good friends off in deep space in an enormously powerful ship. What could be more compelling? Meeting new alien species every week, trying to be friends, then, when pushed, fighting back. With its polyglot crew, *Enterprise* became a metaphor for America. Out in deep space, our bonds became more important than our differences; we needed to stick together. Every week, the crew brought this message to the country. And every week, in a different form, it still does.

Star Trek is more than just wholesome entertainment. It is hope. Hope for a future that allows us to become our best. *Star Trek*, at its heart, is all the Westerns and adventure movies rolled into one. It is, for lack of a better term, a way of life. And it has been chugging along for thirty years. If you want to know what's going on, you've got

---

*This in no way suggests that this was a good thing. I am examining the possible reasons why the show was so popular with men. I mean it. Really.

a lot of TV watching to do. Or you can hold your head up high and read this book.

So please, keep your hands inside the starship at all times, and if you start to feel nauseated, stare at a nonmoving object in front of you. It's probably a friend of yours.

ACKNOWLEDGMENTS

I owe a great debt to many people who made this book possible. First, I thank my good friend Adam Shrager, whose knowledge of *Star Trek* is exceeded only by his decency. He spent many hours listening to sections of this book without complaint and his contributions were not minor. I also want to thank his wonderful wife, Lisa, for her constant support and advice.

Thanks to Michael Lewis of Carol Publishing Group, without whom this book would never have been completed. His confidence in me and this project spurred me on, and his advice was invaluable. Special thanks go to Margaret Wolf, my editor at Carol. Not only is she an extremely canny editor, but she also made the lengthy editing process a painless one. She helped make this book readable. Colette Russen, my copy editor at Carol, gave this book her all. A tireless cheerleader, she polished the book and used her prodigious *Star Trek* knowledge to double-check my accuracy. She deserves many strips of latinum and her own moon. I also want to thank publisher Steven Schragis of Carol for his support and enthusiasm.

The final form of this book depended crucially on the skills and wisdom of my friend Amanda Gordon, who selflessly gave her time, effort, and enthusiasm above and beyond the call of duty.

Finally, I especially thank the Special Narcotics Prosecutor for the City of New York Robert Silbering for his support and indulgence while I wrote this book. I am indebted to Bronx County District Attorney Robert Johnson and Executive Assistant District Attorney Barry Kluger, who also gave me their support. I particularly want to thank Bureau Chief of 70/80 Peter Kougasian for his encouragement and unflagging enthusiasm. I also want to thank Deputy Bureau Chief Robert Hawkes and the assistant district attorneys who make up the 70/80 bureau. They do a difficult, honorable job every day, and make the Special Narcotics Prosecutor's Office a great place to work.

And Bonnie Kass, whom I cannot possibly ever thank enough.

THE JOY OF TREK

-1-

THE *STAR TREK* PHENOMENON AND WHERE YOU FIT IN

IN THE DESERT

Today, science fiction is a major industry. You can't throw a remote control in a video store these days without hitting a sci-fi flick. *Star Trek* is merely one player in this industry, feeding people's desire to know the future. Keep in mind, however, that *Star Trek* first aired in 1966. To understand the impact the show had on audiences, you have to experience what television was like when *Star Trek* debuted.

The sixties and early seventies were a desert for science fiction fans in terms of films and TV shows. We crawled through the hot sand of *The Invaders, Voyage to the Bottom of the Sea,* and *Land of the Giants,* always seeming to glimpse some sci-fi oasis in the distance. But we would draw close, and we'd find *Lost in Space.*

Director Irwin Allen cut his eyeteeth on a string of science fiction shows in the sixties. Most people would rather be lowered on a fraying cable from a burning skyscraper than watch some of these stinkers. *Voyage to the Bottom of the Sea* started with a good premise, the adventures of a really advanced nuclear submarine, but the crew couldn't find anything to do with it other than fight giant seaweed monsters (they invariably electrocuted the ridiculous things).

Lost in Space was the jewel in the Allen crown and a direct competitor of *Trek.* In fact, CBS asked Gene Roddenberry (otherwise referred to as "The Creator") to pitch *Trek* to the CBS executives, not because they wanted the show, but because CBS wanted to know what kind of competition *Lost in Space* faced. They had cause for concern. *Lost in Space* broke new ground in stupidity. The show chronicled the adventures of the Robinson family, the first family in space. See, the U.S. government decided that a family would be more stable than a nonaffiliated crew on a long space flight, and to prove the point, they sent a young, good-looking male pilot along with Mom, Dad, son, and two teenage daughters. Real stable. You might recall the often-parodied robot. The robot took to crying "Danger, Will Robinson!" repeatedly until someone took out its powerpack, which, thankfully, was positioned for easy removal. The family eventually encountered such menacing creatures as a man-size talking carrot, complete with green leaves sprouting from the top of his head. The guy looked like an extra from an elementary-school nutrition play.

The Allen shows all had a similar feel. For example, if the script called for a spaceship to take off, the actors froze in place and the camera stopped. Then the spaceship was removed from the set. A noise, like a futuristic "boink," was inserted into the soundtrack. The camera rolled, sans ship, and the actors sprang to life, looking around with stunned expressions. They called these sequences "special effects."

Into this void came justice, literally. Gene Roddenberry,* a former police officer, rode out of the Los Angeles Police Department (the only PD in the country where you can bust a perp and pitch a screenplay at the same time) to save the day. This officer had written several scripts for established television shows and dreamed of a space drama that would upstage the Westerns that were so popular at the time. (Westerns were really big in the sixties, God knows why. *Gunsmoke* remains one of the longest-running shows in the history of television. But in one of those great ironies that make living so much fun, *Star Trek* earned millions in syndication, while *Gunsmoke* evaporated. No one knows what *Gunsmoke* even looks like anymore.) This police officer's idea was for a "Wagon Train to the Stars," a program where mankind would journey through outer space the way pioneers claimed the West. He called his idea *Star Trek*.

Roddenberry pitched *Star Trek* hard to skeptical studio execu-

---

* He is referred to by some Trekkers as "The Great Bird of the Galaxy." I kid you not.

tives. They turned him down repeatedly. It is still possible for you to meet some of these executives. The ones who are currently working at McDonald's will spit in your shake if they think you are a Trekker.

You can't really blame the executives.* The concept of *Star Trek* was quite unconventional. Up to that point, science fiction had definite rules, among them that spaceships were the futuristic equivalent of fighter jets or bombers, held a small crew, and answered to the Air Force or some branch of the "Space Force." White men exclusively piloted these ships. Since budgets were small, these ships flew by wire from one Styrofoam globe to another. Alien species came in two varieties: (1) monsters wanting to eat us and (2) monsters wanting to save us.† Either way, we Americans weren't ready for them.

LOOK, A NEW IDEA. KILL IT!

Star Trek didn't follow that blueprint. Set in the far future, it was obvious that the United States of America as we knew it no longer existed. The crew was more international than a New York City subway car. Roddenberry, along with *Trek* pioneer Matt Jeffries,‡ had dreamed up a huge starship, the *Enterprise,* to ferry the crew around deep space. This ship, with 410 crew members, was like nothing ever seen on television or film. It was a beautiful creation (see chapter 9). And with the amount of money Roddenberry was asking to produce each episode, you wouldn't be able to see the wires holding the ship. Trekkers get goose pimples when they hear mention of the *Enterprise,* even if they don't show it. Always speak reverently of this vessel or you'll encounter a long, uncomfortable

---

*Actually, you can. As we will see, there was ample evidence that *Trek* was a success, but they canceled it anyway. Then they created *The Sonny and Cher Show*.

†For example, in the classic film *The Day the Earth Stood Still*, the benevolent alien lands on the White House lawn during primary season. What does he get from peace-loving Earthlings? He gets shot.

‡People who are deep, deep, deep inside *Trek* say that Gene didn't give Matt Jeffries enough credit for designing the look of *Star Trek*—a look that was key to the show's success. He's Trotsky to Gene's Lenin. While it's not important for you to know this, your Trekker will be pleasantly surprised if you throw a mention of Matt into your conversation.

silence as your Trekker tries to figure a way to beam you inside solid matter.

The *Enterprise* followed a naval tradition. Terms used on Earth's oceans, like *port, starboard,* and *amidships,* were the terms for the future of spaceflight. The bridge was the center of command for the ship. With command consoles organized in a circle around the captain's chair, it was reminiscent of the bridge of twentieth-century warships. The *Enterprise* was an explorer in the biggest ocean imaginable. *Enterprise* might have descended from the Apollo program, but her soul reached back toward Magellan and Columbus.

Rather than going out to conquer Mars for the Earthlings, Roddenberry's crew would be charged with the duty to "seek out new life-forms and new civilizations."* During its five-year mission, the *Enterprise* was to expand man's knowledge of the universe, and to incorporate humanity within it. (If you think this is a tired concept for television, remember that at the time *The Munsters* was a hot show.)

Roddenberry's leap of imagination startled network executives. He believed that humans were capable of extraordinary things and that the future would bring the dissolution of national borders. He believed that the exploration of space was mankind's next great endeavor and that it would eventually bring the planet together in ways that made our present wars and skirmishes seem petty. Technology would provide extraordinary energy sources, lifesaving and -sustaining medical techniques, and industrial processes almost beyond comprehension. These advances would permit mankind to evolve as a species. Free from the need to compete for resources, mankind would no longer need money. The concept of work itself would change from a necessity of survival to an expression of a person's drive, talent, and values.

Roddenberry's original plans for *Star Trek* differed from the show we have come to know and love. The first version didn't include Captain Kirk, but centered around Capt. Christopher Pike. Very

---

*This is from the opening monologue of the TV show, and if you don't know this then you need this book more than anyone I know, and should probably buy two copies, just in case somebody borrows the first.

little is known about this captain as compared with other *Trek* captains. For example, we do not know which alien species Pike liked to sleep with. Pike's first officer was an icy female referred to only by the ancient nautical term "Number One."*

Making a woman second in command was a daring move in 1966. The studio executives probably wondered if the earth would open up and swallow them whole for even thinking about it. Another first for *Star Trek* was the presence of an alien as part of the crew. Before *Trek*, aliens and humans cooperated as often as Republicans and Democrats. Yet here, on the bridge of this new starship, the science officer was from the planet Vulcan. Lieutenant Commander Spock is the only character to have remained basically intact through the preliminary versions of the show.† This is an indication of how critical he was to Roddenberry's vision of the future.

This first version of *Star Trek* was rejected by the networks, but they took Roddenberry's phone number and promised to call. *Star Trek* had potential, the executives thought, but was probably too unusual for the American public to embrace. They may have been right. Quite a few elements of this first *Trek* were woven into later *Trek* programs, and even in the eighties it took some time for diehard fans to get used to them.

But *Star Trek* was saved by another TV program—*I Love Lucy*. Desilu, Lucille Ball's production company, was looking for a new concept. They needed one, because the only properties they had were the *Lucy* shows, and without Ricky they were never the same. Desilu liked Roddenberry's ideas and they contracted him to write three pilot episodes.

Roddenberry's first *Trek* pilot resembled his original concept. Spock kept the pointy ears, and Roddenberry found the man to play the part: Leonard Nimoy. Nimoy was the first and only choice,

---

* It's no surprise that Number One wasn't happy. To find out why, try calling your wife or girlfriend "Number One." After a while, she will begin to think there's a Number Two, Number Three, and Number Four, and then you are in deep trouble.

†Spock originally sported both pointy ears and red skin, giving him a demonic appearance. I can only imagine the look on the studio execs' faces when Gene suggested putting Satan on prime time.

according to the Creator. Nimoy became known to Roddenberry by starring in *The Lieutenant*, a previous Roddenberry vehicle. Like other promising actors, Nimoy was a veteran of *The Twilight Zone*, but also appeared in the talking-mule movie *Francis Goes to West Point*.* For Roddenberry, Nimoy's calm screen presence was perfect for his half-Vulcan, half-human officer. The female first officer, the cold and dispassionate Number One, stayed on. A cantankerous doctor with the nickname "Bones" was an integral part of the crew, going with the captain on away-team visits to new worlds. (In the future, HMOs authorize doctor visits to home planets.) Add a few expendable crew members to be killed by the alien of the week and a brave new show was born.

This pilot episode, "The Cage," never aired. It was later cannibalized and used in a *Star Trek* episode called "The Menagerie." (Take the pilot, frame it with a half hour of current characters, and *poof!* a two-hour episode!) It's cool to watch because "The Cage" is almost *Star Trek*, like an artist's sketches before a final rendering. With wooden acting and a crew without chemistry, it was an example of a failure common to science fiction: the sacrifice of genuine human drama for the sake of a big "concept." "The Cage" is sort of like dormitory food: It looks like *Trek*, it's supposed to be *Trek*, but it gives you a queasy feeling.

Undeterred by the rejection of his first pilot, the Creator labored on his second. A new captain was needed, and Roddenberry based this character on C. S. Forester's heroic Horatio Hornblower. James Tiberius Kirk would be the type of leader to explore deep space. Fiercely independent, with great reservoirs of strength, Kirk's only vulnerability was the dedication he showed to his ship and crew.† Roddenberry tapped Canadian William Shatner to play his new captain. Shatner wasn't well known, but he had experience in television. Although Shatner appeared in several TV shows and plays, his most famous pre-*Trek* work was on *The Twilight Zone*. (If

---

*One imagines that after doing a talking-mule movie, when a producer asks you to put on pointy ears, you do it.

†Well, he had another one, but we'll get to that shortly.

your Trekker is making you watch *Star Trek*, you should probably get used to watching *Twilight Zone*, too.)

Shatner's heroic screen presence made him perfect to play James T. Kirk. His evident strength and his pauses in speech convinced legions of Trekkers that he was indeed commander of a starship. The same qualities also made him easy to parody and created work for dozens of comedians, who never even sent him a thank-you note.

After the first pilot network executives gave Roddenberry a choice. They couldn't stomach the idea of both an alien and a woman on the ship; someone had to go. (In the sixties, to television executives, women *were* aliens.) Roddenberry chose to keep Spock.* He gave the alien the qualities originally exemplified by the female Number One: logic, efficiency, and the position of first officer. But Roddenberry firmly believed that women were to be equal partners with men in the future. He insisted on putting a woman on the bridge. Lieutenant Uhura, an African American, took the post of communications officer shortly after the series aired. Nichelle Nichols, the first black actress to portray such a serious character in a television series, was mindful of her historic role. Because Uhura remained a character with few lines besides "Hailing frequencies open, sir," Nichols often thought of quitting the show. Martin Luther King Jr., however, implored her to stay on television as a role model for young African Americans. It's fortunate that she did, as we will see later.

With the arrival of the ship's doctor, Leonard "Bones" McCoy, the winning chemistry of the original *Star Trek* was achieved. Played by DeForest Kelley, the doctor meshed perfectly with the rest of the characters. Something remarkable occurred when DeForest Kelley joined the cast. The three leading actors developed a camaraderie that was visible on the screen. Suddenly, the show didn't seem so silly anymore. They created a sense of drama and a sense of family.

As for what happened when the show took the air, please

---

*The actress who played Number One, Majel Barrett, didn't take it too hard, it seems. She remained married to Roddenberry, and went on to play several roles in *Star Trek* features.

remember that *this is a television show.* Keep saying that to yourself as you read further. *This is a television show, with commercials and station identifications and actors and greasepaint. That's all it is.*

THINGS GET FREAKY

The first *Star Trek* episode was broadcast on September 8, 1966. Lyndon Johnson was president. Mankind was three years away from walking on the moon. Madonna got her first pointy bra. NBC, the network airing *Trek,* was deeply concerned about the show's prospects. Science fiction was not generally popular, despite America's obsession with the space race (or perhaps because of it). NBC was so concerned that they convinced *TV Guide* to list the program as an "Action Adventure" instead of "Science Fiction." *Variety* reviewed the new series and pronounced it a failure.

Television shows live and die by their ratings. However, in those days, the Nielsons didn't break audiences down into demographic groups. (The ability to determine the reactions of specific groups separated by factors such as age and income was a wonderful development that later made things like Urkel and the Lifetime channel possible.) The type of audience that *Trek* was attracting was just the type of audience that the networks wanted: highly educated, male, between the ages of eighteen and forty-five, and willing to spend money on things for which they had absolutely no use. But without demographics, the only question answerable by the Nielsons was "Are families tuning in?" With the results of this crude instrument, executives at NBC were hamstrung, because the answer for *Star Trek* was no.*

At the end of the first season, the cast and crew of *Star Trek* could read the writing on the wall. NBC wanted to cancel the series. Word of this broke out in the science fiction community, and Harlan Ellison, the famous sci-fi author, organized a write-in campaign to

---

*After *Trek* was canceled, it was rumored that Nielson executives came to NBC and basically said the following: "We've done a thorough analysis and found the perfect television show. It appeals to the demographic group you most want to target, and isolates them exceedingly well." "What's the name of this show?" the executives asked. "*Star Trek,*" they replied.

save the show.† Famous authors Poul Anderson, Theodore Sturgeon, and Lester Del Rey joined the "Committee," as the group was known. They persuaded thousands of *Trek* fans to write to NBC, to beg them to keep *Trek* on the air. It worked. *Star Trek* was authorized for a second season, and NBC executives immediately tried to secure unlisted phone numbers.

In the meantime, the actors of *Star Trek* had to come to grips with the sudden attention fans bestowed upon them. Nimoy got the worst of it. He hosted a small parade dressed as Spock—ears and all—and hundreds of fans mobbed him. Shatner received attention, too, but Spock seemed to be the favorite, and this fact complicated their off-screen relationship. ("I have more groupies!" "No, I do!")

As Hollywood actors are wont to do, the cast tried to cash in on the popularity that they honestly believed would be short-lived. Leonard Nimoy recorded and released the album *Mister Spock's Music From Outer Space*. Not to be outdone, Shatner recorded an album called *The Transformed Man*, on which he sang "Lucy in the Sky With Diamonds." (Shortly thereafter, the Beatles broke up. I'm not saying one has anything to do with the other, but it's spooky, isn't it?) Macy's in New York City declined to have Nimoy make an appearance to promote his album: The store felt it could not guarantee the actor's safety. Model kits of the *Enterprise* were authorized, even a kit of Mr. Spock himself pointing a phaser toward a three-headed serpent. Never mind that there were no serpents on *Star Trek;* a mythology about the show was forming, and only a very few people at the epicenter had figured out what the tremors meant.

James Blish wrote novelizations of the episodes, which sold like hotcakes. On college campuses, groups formed to watch the show, and small fan organizations began to accrete. As the show gained strength in the second season, NBC executives couldn't help but notice the surging popularity of the characters, but the ratings

---

*Well, Roddenberry did ask him to get involved, so it wasn't exactly spontaneous. But he did like the show, and genuinely wanted it to survive. Ellison later wrote the script for one the best episodes, "The City on the Edge of Forever," but it was altered so much in preproduction that Ellison resented it for years. Ellison later wrote a comprehensive book about the entire episode.

remained lousy. Again NBC planned to cancel *Trek*. And again fans
came to the rescue.

THE BEGINNINGS OF THE MOVEMENT

Spearheading this new campaign was someone who would become
legend. Bjo (pronounced Bee-Jo) Trimble, a *Trek* fan, was tipped off
by Roddenberry about the cancellation. She alerted the science
fiction underworld to the demise of the show. She distributed
leaflets and spread the word at fan clubs and science-fiction
conventions, as well as organizing a write-in campaign that dwarfed
the first one. By the time she was done, it is estimated that one
million letters found the besieged NBC executives who planned to
kill the series. One million letters! The executives must've thought
these people were nuts.

Imagine that you are an executive at a network and you have a
series with ratings near the bottom of the list. You can't charge as
much as you would like for advertisements because the advertisers
have seen the same ratings numbers you have and they refuse to pay
a lot for ads they think won't be seen. And the show costs a lot to
make. So you cancel it. Then you find out that the series' creator has
helped orchestrate a letter-writing campaign that pressures you to
keep the show on the air. So you extend it another season, what the
hell. Then the new numbers come in, and they are just as bad as
before. You think, well, this time the show has to go, but now you
receive a blizzard of letters, many of them threatening to beam you
inside solid matter. What do you do?

In hindsight you'd figure there must be something wrong with the
numbers. But that's not what happened. NBC authorized *Star Trek*
for another season but cut its budget severely. In addition, they cut
the legs out from under the series by moving it to Friday nights at 10
P.M. At that hour, the show had virtually no hope of growth. The only
people who would be home at that hour to watch it were, well,
Trekkers.

Roddenberry was furious. NBC was taking revenge for the write-
in campaign! He threatened to quit the show if the old slot wasn't

returned. They called his bluff, so Roddenberry quit. Actually, he quit the way baseball managers get thrown out of games: by going to the locker room and phoning in directions. He retained the title of executive producer and monitored the show from afar. However, the writing and the production values started to decline. The worst episodes were produced during this third season. In the end, NBC got its way. The *Enterprise*'s five-year mission ended on June 3, 1969. In all, seventy-nine episodes of *Star Trek* had been filmed.

They dismantled the bridge. *Mission: Impossible* took over the set and hired Leonard Nimoy. Shatner made margarine commercials. A bleak mood overcame the intense, connected science-fiction world. Even *Lost in Space,* the sci-fi addict's methadone, wasn't on the air anymore. James Blish wrote a new *Trek* book entitled *Spock Must Die!* Fans picked it up and walked to the cash register with the weight of the world on their shoulders. It was a dark time.

THINGS GET REALLY FREAKY

In the early seventies, television was so bad I can't even remember what was on. No cable. No pay-per-view. The one bright spot was the survival of *Star Trek* in syndication. Local stations bought the program and aired it opposite whatever the networks were offering. Some stations, like WPIX in New York, aired *Star Trek* six days a week—and it picked up in the ratings.

Around this time the *Star Trek* cult began to gather steam. The depression fans felt began to be displaced by something else: a certain self-righteousness and anger. But underneath, pride reared its head. Because the series could be seen again and again, NBC's mistake was evident to all. Fans had demonstrable proof of the quality of the show. Bumper stickers sprouted on the backs of Volkswagen Beetles: STAR TREK LIVES. BEAM ME UP, SCOTTY, THERE'S NO INTELLIGENT LIFE DOWN HERE. SPOCK FOR PRESIDENT.* At some college campuses professors rearranged their schedules so that classes wouldn't conflict with the airing of the

---

*Dr. Benjamin Spock, the famous baby doctor, ran for president around this time. Don't be confused, though. *Spock for President* meant Mr. Spock.

show. Whether this benefited the students or the professors is something you can decide.

In 1972, the first international *Star Trek* convention took place in New York City at the Statler-Hilton Hotel.* The planners expected one thousand people to attend. Five thousand showed up. To put this in proper perspective, try planning a party in your home or apartment for twenty people. Now imagine a hundred people attending. Get the idea? It was a mob scene.

Photocopied newsletters created by fans, called fanzines, proliferated. These fanzines discussed every aspect of the show. Some searched for hidden meanings in each episode. Some described erotic encounters between Kirk and Spock. Besieged night and day, the actors wondered whether they had made a mistake. It was difficult for them to get work because they had been typecast as members of the *Enterprise* crew. Eventually Shatner landed the role of T. J. Hooker, a police officer who always seemed to be clinging to the hood of a speeding car. Nimoy found work on a show called *In Search Of…* Each week Nimoy would narrate an episode investigating some sort of weird phenomenon, such as extraterrestrial visitors and ancient Mayan temples.

Leonard Nimoy rocked the *Star Trek* world when he wrote a book about his experiences with fans and made the mistake of calling it *I Am Not Spock.* Fans wrote angry letters that basically said, "Yes, you are Spock, and you're going to keep on being Spock until we say so. Nyah." Nimoy took revenge by continuing to host *In Search Of…*, thus forcing Spock-starved Trekkers to learn even more about ancient Mayan temples.

In 1973, *Star Trek* became an animated Saturday-morning cartoon. The entire cast of the original show reunited to provide the voices for the cartoon's characters. It didn't last long, and it wasn't very good, but some of the episodes stayed with fans because they were written by great *Star Trek* veterans such as D. C. Fontana.† In

---

*I attended this convention, as I will explain in chapter 11, and my poor mother will never forgive me for forcing her to take me.

† If your Trekker tries to make you watch the cartoons, leave him and don't look back.

the end, though, it was a poor substitute for what fans really wanted: the return of *Star Trek*.

Star Trek made so much money in syndication that Paramount (the new owner of Desilu Productions) didn't want to create a series that would take viewers' attention away. Ironically, the efforts of fans to promote the show kept them from getting what they most wanted.

Yet the power of the *Trek* lobby could not be denied. *Trek* fans infiltrated the technology class, the scientists and professors who kept America at the forefront of scientific advancement. When the first space shuttle was ready for testing, another letter campaign sprang up demanding that the ship be named *Enterprise*. The government acquiesced (even though there was no evidence that Trekkers actually vote), and this country's first reusable spacecraft was named after the famous starship. The actual TV model of the Starship *Enterprise* found its way to the Smithsonian, and was hung only a few feet away from the real *Mercury, Gemini,* and *Apollo* capsules that explored space. Momentum for a new *Trek* continued to build. Fans seemed ready to film the damned show themselves.

Paramount prepared a television series called *Star Trek: Phase II.* They called back the old crew (minus Spock) and added a few characters. Roddenberry helped write the new scripts. Word spread that the show was gearing up. Fans held their breath. Yet fate had another plan for the crew of the *Enterprise,* and it came from a long time ago, in a galaxy far, far away.

HEY, THAT GUY LUCAS IS MAKING MONEY

On May 27, 1977, *Star Wars* premiered in New York City. Lines formed around the block at the Ziegfeld Theater. *Time* and *Newsweek*, which some people consider to be the same publication, ran nearly identical articles about this movie and its runaway popularity. For the first time, movie executives realized (get this) *there was money to be made in science fiction.*

Paramount made a jump to light speed: *Star Trek* would be made into a movie. They picked the inspired title *Star Trek: The Motion*

*Picture**** and rounded up the entire crew, including Spock. Robert Wise, the director of *The Day the Earth Stood Still* and *West Side Story*, signed on as director. A $15 million budget was authorized (it would later climb to $45 million, and believe me, it wasn't worth it).

In December 1979, Trekkers the world over nervously took their seats. I am not ruining anything by telling you that the movie was bad. Critics, who definitely were not Trekkers, panned it. However, Trekkers were so eager to see the film that it made a substantial profit.

Nimoy didn't enjoy filming the movie or its results. Gossip crackled through conventions that he would never make another. Although the hunger for more *Trek* had been satiated, the movie was not what fans wanted. They wanted what it seemed they couldn't have. They wanted the old show.

Luckily, Paramount felt they could milk some more money from Trekkers. A second film took shape. *Star Trek II: The Wrath of Khan* was produced, this time on a much stricter budget. Nicholas Meyer, a former television director, was brought in to direct. Minimizing the budget and using a TV director seemed to bring *Star Trek* back to its roots.

The big issue surrounding the release of *Wrath of Khan* was the death of Spock. It seems that the only way the producers of the film could get Leonard Nimoy to sign on was to offer him a great death scene. Of course, this upset Trekkers a great deal, and much mail was sent begging them not to kill Spock. They killed him anyway, and very well. *Wrath of Khan* was a great success. Fans finally received their due. It captured the old spirit of *Star Trek*. When Spock died, there wasn't a dry eye in the house.

With the success of *Star Trek II* there was no doubt that new movies would be made. Spock was resurrected in *Star Trek III*, but the *Enterprise* was destroyed. The *Enterprise* was resurrected in *Star Trek IV*, but the franchise itself was jeopardized by the poor quality of *Star Trek V*. To this writing, there have been eight *Trek* films, with no end of the story in sight.

**Gives you chills, doesn't it?

THE CRITICS: GEEKS VS. GEEKS

It's understandable that movie critics refused to accept *Star Trek: The Motion Picture*. After all, it wasn't a good movie. *Wrath of Khan*, however, was much better. Trekkers all over the world loved it and made it a box office smash. To this day it is considered one of the first *Trek* films. Even some critics point to it as the best. The *New York Times,* for example, gives the movie its "recommended" star symbol. But when the movie debuted, virtually all the critics panned it. Generally speaking, all *Trek* movies are panned by critics when they are released. Why?

Well, it goes back to high school. Most Trekkers were, at some point, geeks.* That is, they were passionately interested in science fiction and intellectual pursuits, and this earned them the temporary scorn of their classmates. (Until, of course, geeks founded software companies and took over the Western world.) Today's journalists were also geeks in high school—newspaper geeks. They devoted themselves completely to the *Daily Meshuganneh* or whatever the high school paper was called. Although they didn't know they were geeks, they sensed it subconsciously, but repressed it, calm in the assurance that they were at the center of the school's social life. But they weren't. They developed a permanent dislike of other geeks, simply because they could not come to grips with their own latent geekiness.

Take Jeffrey Lyons, the movie reviewer, on the day *Wrath of Khan* was released. "Does Spock die?" he asked rhetorically. "Do you really care?" he answered. He seemed almost personally offended that people could care about such things. Even after thirty years, the resentment by the critics continues unabated. Take Janet Maslin, the *New York Times* movie critic. Not only did she pan *Star Trek: First Contact* so viciously that you can still see bite marks in the newspaper, but her ire also spilled over into other reviews. In her piece about the rereleased *The Empire Strikes Back,* she wrote, "And when [Darth] Vader declares, 'It is useless to resist,' he anticipates the 'Resistance is futile' line that [*Star Trek: First Contact*] borrowed."

---

*A geek, technically, is someone who focuses on one pursuit to the exclusion of everything else, unless he is an athlete.

See? It all makes sense. Because a character in a movie fifteen years ago said "It is useless to resist," *no one can ever use any of those words again in any combination in any science fiction movie. So don't even try.* Maslin and company aren't satisfied by simply panning a *Star Trek* movie. They must humiliate the Trekkers, deride them, and falsely accuse them of plagiarism. Trekkers bear this rain of insults stoically, as they have always done. But inside we wonder, When will they realize that they are us?

THESE GUYS ARE GETTING OLD

As the films stacked up on the shelf, one appearing every three years, fans began to notice something. Scotty couldn't fit in the turbolift anymore. Shatner aged, but his hair didn't. The crew began to look like victims of a virus that made them age really fast. Producers began to ask themselves the key question: If these guys keep growing old, how can we keep making money?

It was time for a new *Star Trek*. A series with new characters, new actors, a whole new generation of Trekkers to grab hold of. This time, however, producers were ready to let Roddenberry take the wheel. Roddenberry didn't have much to do with the movies and he was ready to regain control of the *Star Trek* universe he created. A new series would enable him to do everything he wanted to do the first time, to thumb his nose at the conventional wisdom of the networks. They were ready for Gene and his weird future society. If Roddenberry builds it, the networks thought, they will come.

The old cast didn't cotton to the idea of a new cast. Nimoy said you couldn't capture "lightning in a bottle" again. Trekkers worried. Would it be a disaster like the first movie? How could *Trek* exist without the original cast? How would fans afford all the new *Trek* merchandise that would be produced?

MEET THE NEW GUARD,
SAME AS THE OLD GUARD

Roddenberry decided to set the new series farther into the future than the first one. The ship would be called the *Enterprise* but would be larger than the old one and the crew would come complete with families. This would open up the prospect of a "mother-in-law in space" episode.

The new crew bore striking similarities to the old crew. The "Number One," Comdr. William Riker, had sexual interludes with members of alien species, a key Kirk feature. Commander Data, an android, was a machine striving to be human, clearly Spock in reverse. Again women were on the bridge of the *Enterprise,* this time without the tiny skirts. (But one of them had posed in *Playboy*—the more things change, the more they stay the same.)

Still, the new show had profound differences. The captain, Jean-Luc Picard, was a diplomat and a scholar, more intellectual than Kirk (if you can believe *that*). A teenager was added to the crew, and Trekkers soon began devising interesting ways to kill him.

The new show did pretty well considering that even toying with the old concept was considered treason by a bunch of fans. The first two seasons were awkward, and fans still have some difficulty watching the reruns. But ratings were good and the writers kept devising interesting plots. Kids who'd been too young for the original series became fans. However, older fans still bore a torch for the movies, in which the original cast was defining the events in the *Star Trek* universe.

In 1990, during the show's fourth season, *Star Trek: The Next Generation* came into its own. A two-part episode called "The Best of Both Worlds" transformed *Trek* fandom. The end-of-season cliffhanger, fueled by rumors of the death of Picard, haunted Trekkers. Focus shifted from the old crew to the new. Not only was the series the best it had ever been, but it was also earning the loyalty of the older fans. The *Star Trek* universe shifted perceptibly; when you thought of *Star Trek,* you thought of Picard and his crew. ("The Best of Both Worlds" proved to be so popular that the Museum of Television and Radio in New York exhibited the two-part episode in a theater as a full-length movie.) It certainly didn't hurt *Next Generation* at all when *Star Trek V: The Final Frontier* was released and gave everyone stomach cramps.

Next Generation caused a steady rise in the number of Trekkers. The show was rated number one in syndication. New novels and comic books were written based on the new characters. Conventions welcomed the new crew, as they once did the old. *Star Trek* was no longer an underground phenomenon: It was a full-fledged industry.

ANOTHER SERIES? SURE, WHY NOT?

By 1991, the final chapter of the original crew's film series had been written. And *Next Generation*, though strong, was in jeopardy due to contract squabbles between cast and management. A new series was needed to keep the franchise healthy and growing, and it would prove to be the biggest challenge of all—because in 1991, we lost the Creator.

Gene Roddenberry died that year, before a third *Trek* series could emerge. Fortunately for fans, Roddenberry was ably followed by Rick Berman and Michael Piller. These producers, longtime *Trek* fans, kept Roddenberry's spirit alive and created *Star Trek: Deep Space Nine*.

Deep Space Nine differed greatly in concept and design from*Trek* as we know it. *Deep Space Nine* is a space station, built by an alien race, the Cardassians, but is now occupied by Starfleet. The dynamic first episode wowed Trekkers with a new cast of characters. At the time of this writing, *Deep Space Nine* is the *Trek* standard-bearer: it's where the fate of the *Star Trek* universe is decided on a weekly basis.

With the creation of the third series, the pressure on *Next Generation* was reduced. The cast had worked hard for seven years and wanted to move on to film. The last film with the original crew, *Star Trek VI: The Undiscovered Country*, had been a huge success. It was time for *Next Generation* to make the jump to the big screen.

The seventh film, *Star Trek: Generations*, combined the old crew and the new. (Spock didn't sign on, but the meeting of the two famous *Enterprise* captains was enough of a draw.) The film earned $130 million at the box office. The new crew looked great on the big screen, and the *Enterprise* got destroyed again. What more could you want?

HERE WE GO AGAIN

Paramount, the company that is the fount of all things *Trek*, had longed to become a television network. In fact, that *Star Trek: Phase II* show we learned about earlier was actually going to be an anchor for a fourth network. After twenty years of planning, Paramount finally got its network, a string of independent stations united in programming and appearance. The United Paramount Network (UPN) was launched in 1994, and its cornerstone was a new *Trek* series.

Star Trek: Voyager is an attempt to get back to the roots of the franchise. Over the years, as we will see, *Star Trek* became very complicated. There are dozens of species, interweaving story lines, and more alternate history time-line stuff than you can shake a Denebian Slime Devil at. Trying to keep them all straight is a daunting task. *Voyager* removed this problem by flinging its starship to a far corner of the galaxy.

U.S.S. *Voyager* is in a region of space so distant that even at full speed it would require seventy years to reach home. The crew must find a way home or live out the rest of their lives in this unknown reach of space. Thus the standard alien species (Klingons, Cardassians, Romulans, and Ross Perot supporters, for example) will not be present.

Of course, this new show spawned novels, comic books, models, and action figures, as had *Deep Space Nine*. If this all sounds like too much to keep track of, it is. *Deep Space Nine* was not the ratings powerhouse that people expected. Some producers think it's because the show takes place on a space station. Some Trekkers think that since the Great Bird of the Galaxy died, the shows haven't been the same. Some people think that there's just too damn much *Trek*.

Well, it's not that simple. The eighth film of the series, *Star Trek: First Contact*, released in 1997, was perhaps the most successful and critically acclaimed movie of all (I use the term *critically* loosely). The *Next Generation* cast, together again, boarded a new *Enterprise* and successfully defended Earth from the evil Borg. The film took in approximately $30 million in its first *weekend*. *Time* and *Newsweek* once more sent the same reporter to watch it, and he liked it.

GREAT. SO WHERE DOES THIS LEAVE ME?

For the *Star Trek* novice, this is both the best of times and the worst of times. With the *Next Generation* crew now making movies, fans can expect a new high standard in science-fiction films. *Deep Space 9* has entered a dangerous and dramatic phase. *Voyager* is geared up and moving and promises exciting developments. But, frankly, you've got thirty years of *Star Trek* history to catch up on.

Well, lots of the old episodes have been released on videotape, and repeats of *Next Generation* are in the video stores. The novels are always there, and the comic books. And, of course, your Trekker would always be happy to tutor you in the basics of *Trek* history. But unfortunately, when they do, it always sounds like this:

"Okay, there are the Kazon, right? They are this alien species that used to be dominated by the Trabe, and they lived above the Ocampa, but then they separated into different sects, using the Trabe's technology, and so the Kazon Nistrum wants *Voyager's* technology, but the Prime Directive won't allow the dissemination of that technology, so the Kazon persuade Seska, who's really a Cardassian, to betray the crew. Get it?"

This is no help. This doesn't communicate the dread that should come over you when you first see a cube-shaped Borg ship on the main scanner. This doesn't cause your heart to swell, as it should when Spock and Data finally meet. This doesn't communicate the annoyance you feel when Counselor Troi states the blatantly obvious. (Well, maybe you'll be able to pick that up on your own.)

What will help is meeting the *Star Trek* crews face to face, finding out what basic events have occurred in their lives, and what makes them tick. The key to coping with this stuff is to get a better understanding of it. It's not as wacky or nerdy as you might think. It's just a new mythology, with modern heroes instead of ancient ones. Well, okay, maybe it's a little nerdy. But it's not *Lost in Space*.

CHAPTER ONE QUIZ

1. What was Gene Roddenberry's nickname?

    a. The Great Bird of the Galaxy
    b. The Great Gildersneeze
    c. The Great Gatsby
    d. There are some who call him...Tim

2. Who was the original Number One?

   a. Jonathan Frakes
   b. Michael Jackson
   c. Nichelle Nichols
   d. Majel Barrett

3. What TV show was a competitor of *Star Trek*?

   a. *Gunsmoke*
   b. *Lost in Space*
   c. *My Favorite Martian*
   d. *Space: 1999*

4. How many seasons did the original *Star Trek* last?

   a. too many
   b. 3
   c. 7
   d. 4

5. How many people attended the first *Star Trek* convention?

   a. too many
   b. not enough
   c. none
   d. 4000, and 20 are still there

6. What book did Spock write that upset Trekkers?

   a. *Trekkies, Get a Life!*
   b. *Trekkies, What Are They Good For?*
   c. *I Am Not Spock*
   d. *Ich Bin ein Trekkie*

7. Who told Nichelle Nichols to continue playing Lieutenant Uhura?

   a. AT&T
   b. Whoopi Goldberg
   c. Martin Luther King Jr.
   d. Robert Kennedy

8. What *Star Trek: The Next Generation* episode stole the fans from the old *Trek*?

   a. "The Best of Both Worlds"
   b. "QPid"
   c. "Please Watch Our Show, We Have Families to Feed"
   d. "Elogium"

9. Why do movie critics hate *Star Trek*?

   a. They're paid to
   b. They are "latent geeks"
   c. "Well, I didn't actually *watch* the movie…"
   d. They're *Lost In Space* fans

10. Who is "The Woman Who Saved *Star Trek*"?

   a. Janet Maslin
   b. Bjo Trimble
   c. Bjo Tribble
   d. Jeffrey Lyons

ANSWERS

   1, a; 2, d; 3, b; 4, b; 5, a; 6, c; 7, c; 8, a; 9, b; 10, b.

-2-

How to Live With a Trekker;
or,
"Must We Have a Full-Size Poster
of Worf in Our Bedroom?"

At this point you must be wondering: What sort of people get into all this? I mean, are they normal? Do they have screws loose? Did something terrible happen to them when they were children? Or you may be wondering: What's wrong with me that I was not a fan of this show? Was I stupid? Did I have my head in the ground? Was I reading Janet Maslin too much?

Well, let's find out. Let's take a look at the psychological profile of a Trekker and see whether the person in your life meets the stringent requirements of Trekker status. And if he or she does, let's find out what *kind* of Trekker you're dealing with.

A few years ago, the Smithsonian Institution in Washington arranged a special *Star Trek* exhibit. They displayed starship models, a few of the uniforms, and some exhibits on the science of *Star Trek* and whether it would be possible to attain its level of technological development. I went to the exhibit. I didn't get to see it, of course. All the tickets had been sold out days before. *Days before!* This wasn't a Broadway show or a football game. This was a *Star Trek* exhibit. I live in New York City. If, after work, I want to go see an original Renoir, I can go to the Metropolitan Museum of Art and have the whole room to myself, except for one security guard. So how come I couldn't get a ticket to the *Star Trek* exhibit?

Well, I took a look at the line of people waiting to get in. I would have said it was 50 percent children, 50 percent adults, right down the middle. And not your freaky, live-long-and-prosper-wearing-a-communicator-pin adults. These people looked as though they knew the meaning of the words *open-plan gourmet kitchen*. They looked like they owned property. There were some college kids there, but they were normal-looking college kids. I mean, they would've been up for a game of ultimate Frisbee, but they didn't look like Courtney Love was their role model in life. And there was another thing: These people looked smart.

How can someone *look* smart? I don't know, but there seems to be a quality of expression that some people perceive as an indication of intelligence. Doesn't make it true, mind you, but it's there nonetheless. (Take Peter Jennings, for instance.) Well, these people had it. They were the kind of people you wouldn't mind having around if you were in an accident. They looked like they'd be able to dial 911 correctly.

Well, maybe this was a fluke. Maybe the real nerdy Trekkers would emerge in a darker place, say, the inside of a movie theater. So I decided to see the latest *Star Trek* movie, *First Contact,* on the very first day it opened. To protect myself, I went with a bunch of friends. I was able to purchase tickets a few days before (you really do learn things at the Smithsonian) and I met my friends at the theater. Although it was a packed house (all the shows were sold out), the crowd was orderly and friendly. There were an unusual number of groups of friends there.

Usually movies play to certain demographic groups: When I worked at a movie theater, I could tell who was going to which movie. (Those of you who think I am generalizing a little bit should go to a multiplex and watch who walks out of the latest Jackie Chan movie and who walks out of *The First Wives' Club*.) But *Star Trek* pulled in a surprisingly diverse crowd. When the lights dimmed and the credits started, a good mood pervaded the audience. We cheered at certain actors' names, and laughed when some actors' names got no reaction. No one yelled at the screen, threw anything, or got into a fight. (So what? you may ask. Well, this was a New York crowd.) Basically, the audience comprised members of a Federation, and it was as peaceful as the one we were watching on the screen.

I suppose I should have been nauseated by the warm, fuzzy

feeling this experience gave me, but I wasn't. It was nice not to feel cynical. It was nice to worry about characters I felt I knew. It was nice not to be concerned with issues of whether the movie was "important" enough, or whether it glorified drug use, or whether it exemplified bad morals. This was no guilty pleasure. It was fun. Wasn't this what movies used to be?

Star Trek, in the end, is about fun. It's about letting your imagination run wild and fantasizing about the kind of world your children will inherit. It's about faith: faith in our ability to solve our problems and go out and do cool things, like achieve world peace, build cities in space, and make out with strange aliens.

Why, then, do Trekkers get such a bad rap?

For what it's worth, here's what I think. *Star Trek* fans like to set themselves apart. They feel what they have is unique, so special that they don't especially like sharing it with people who don't appreciate it. They would rather meet someone who also has grown to love *Trek* on his own, not because someone exposed him to it.

Also, Trekkers are often technologists, people who love gadgets and pure scientific research. Individuals like these seldom made up the in crowd at the local high school. Whoever heard of students climbing over one another to get into the astronomy club? Also, *Star Trek* is about the *big* picture. You know, "What is mankind's place in the universe," yada, yada, yada. Someone who thinks about the big picture is generally not the life of the party. Nobody wants to hang out at the beach house with the guy who keeps saying, "You know, in four billion years the temperature on this beach will be two thousand degrees Kelvin."

But the real reason Trekkers get grief is because of what Trekkers used to be: Trekkies. The term itself sounds derogatory, because it is. (I prefer the term "Trekster" myself.) The first *Star Trek* fans were a little over the edge. They had to be, as we saw earlier, because nobody else cared enough to keep the show going. Some people are still self-described Trekkies, but you don't want to go down that road.

As we will see in chapter 11, the original *Star Trek* fans were gung ho, and people just did not understand what the big deal was. They didn't understand the attraction of what Roddenberry was selling.

The "nutty *Star Trek* fan" image stuck over the years, even making it to *Saturday Night Live*. Remember William Shatner telling fans at a *Star Trek* convention to "Get a life!"

In thirty years, however, the face of the *Trek* fan has shape-shifted, and now people will actually walk into their offices and not think twice about asking, "Hey, did you catch *Star Trek* last night?" They are everywhere, and even the worst condemnations of society cannot stop Paramount from making a mint. In thirty years, different types of fans have appeared, all Trekkers, but with different loves. What type of fan do you know?

THE BABY-BOOMER ORIGINAL SHOW
TORCHBEARER

To some people, *Star Trek* was Kirk and Spock and Scotty and the original three seasons. That's it. As Scotty once said, "Show me the bridge of the *Enterprise* NCC-1701. No bloody A, B, C, or D." These people tend to be older members of the baby-boom generation. They discovered *Star Trek* in their high school and college years, and by the time *Next Generation* appeared, they were in their forties and found Picard to be a little too much, or not enough. They couldn't adjust. These may be the saddest of all the Trekkers. The old show just doesn't play anymore on TV. And although the movies kept them going for a while, the old crew's phaser banks are depleted. However, these were the people who helped *Trek* become the phenomenon it is, and we owe them gratitude.

THE PICARD BRIGADE

A large group of fans took to the seven-year *Next Generation* series but were never big fans of the original show. These people are generally members of Generation X, but there are a few who are older. These fans tend to be more analytical in outlook, and appreciate Picard's preference for thinking his way out of a problem rather than shooting first, the way Kirk would. A police officer I know said it best: "I like *Next Generation* because they make mistakes. The original crew, with Kirk and Spock—they were perfect. Picard, he's more human. You root for him because you know he can fail. I always knew that Kirk and Spock would win by the end of the episode. Not so with *Next Generation*. You really felt they were doing their best in a difficult situation."

These fans are the most unlike traditional Trekkers. They do not feel loyalty toward any of the other shows. They are the least likely to go to a *Star Trek* convention.

THE RODDENBERRY ELITIST

Probably the most interesting type of Trekker, these strict constructionists are only fond of *Trek* shows with a heavy influence by the Great Bird of the Galaxy, Gene Roddenberry. They are also likely to feel that the shows produced since his death, *Deep Space Nine* and *Voyager*, are not authentic *Trek* because Roddenberry had so little to do with them. They are also skeptical of the movies. These people are similar to the Baby-Boomer Original Show Torchbearers, but they are more fanatical. They are the big devourers of *Star Trek* novels and fanzines. They are probably the least fun to talk to about *Star Trek*, because their standards are so high. Don't even mention *Voyager* to them.

THE *DS9*/*VOYAGER* ENTHUSIAST

The fans of the two newest shows in the *Star Trek* pantheon are generally young and like to focus on *Deep Space Nine* and *Voyager* almost exclusively. This is because they were too young to appreciate *Next Generation*, and for them *DS9* and *Voyager* are the future of the franchise. These fans are among the most likely to go to conventions because their shows are so vibrant. *Star Trek: Starfleet Academy*, which is rumored to be the next concept show, would probably be aimed at this market.

THE *STAR TREK* JUNKIE

These people were fortunate (or unfortunate) enough to have had *Star Trek* impressed upon them at an early age. Diehard fans, they are most interested in the success of the *Star Trek* universe rather than any single show. They will watch almost anything having to do with *Star Trek*. They will root for shows to get better, they will argue about how they could improve them. I suspect that *Star Trek* producers get more unsolicited scripts from this group than any other.

These are the people who most often credit *Star Trek* with changing their lives. (And I don't mean cult members either.) They are scattered throughout the professions, and they probably spend more money on *Star Trek* products than any other. They are also quite likely to attend conventions and to follow other science-fiction programs and movies. And they are the most likely to be disappointed if a *Star Trek* program makes a mistake of *Star Trek* fact or if the quality sags. If you are trying to get along with one of these people, you have your work cut out for you. They like to dress up as the Borg for Halloween.

Whatever your brand of Trekker, keep in mind that *Star Trek* is not something that people can just quit. A psychologist in London studied Trekkers for four years and reached the conclusion that 5 to 10 percent of the fans met the psychological criteria for addiction. This means that if they miss an episode they may show withdrawal symptoms such as frustration and agitation. They also develop higher tolerance levels, so they need increasing doses of *Star Trek*. Be very careful when dealing with your Trekker: He or she may be in that 5 to 10 percent that needs Trekkers Anonymous.

WELL, I LIKE ONE OF THESE GUYS OR GALS. WHAT DO I DO?

Don't panic. There are ways to cope. The first thing *not* to do is ridicule them. Don't say things like "We're not going to have to watch that stupid *Star Trek* show again, are we?" Try to be interested in the program. *Ask questions.* Trekkers love answering questions about the show, unless they are blatantly obvious ones like "Are they in a ship?"

The important thing for you to know is that you do not have to allow *Star Trek* to take over your life like the Borg. It can be contained, and in that measured form it can be enjoyed by both of you. First of all, you will need the following:

This book
A videocassette recorder
A second television set
A TV guide from a major paper
A small curio cabinet or out-of-the-way shelf

Step 1: Read this book. This book provides you with more than enough information and jokes to relate to your Trekker. You do not need to consult encyclopedias or compendiums, and besides, your Trekker probably owns them already.

Step 2: Study the TV guide. Become aware of when these programs are on TV. Because *Star Trek* is a syndicated program, times vary from city to city. *Star Trek* episodes are often repeated late at night later in the week. It's important to be familiar with these second-chance times, because they allow the Trekker to catch a program he may have missed.

Step 3: Watch the VCR. I don't mean look at it. I mean monitor it. Be careful about turning it on or off, because your Trekker may be taping *Star Trek*. If it's running, watch the other TV for an hour. Trekkers love to tape *Star Trek* because it gives them the opportunity to rewind and study references a nonfan would dismiss. I personally watched the scene where the Klingons attacked *Deep Space Nine* about five times. That's nothing compared to the amount some of my friends watched it.

Step 4: Designate the "*Star Trek* Shrine." If your Trekker is above the age of twenty-five, it is likely he or she did not have many *Star Trek* toys while growing up. Today, marketing and films go hand in hand. Back then, the only *Star Trek* toys available were some plastic models you had to glue together. And they sucked, because the engine nacelles were too heavy and sagged, making the whole ship look a little depressed. Trekkers longed for accurate models and toys they could admire. As *Trek* has gained momentum, more and more toys have been released. I know precious few Trekkers who have been able to resist the siren call of owning their very own *Enterprise*. (Some of these can be quite expensive. The Franklin Mint offers several versions of the Starship *Enterprise* cast in pewter for $200. The nacelles still sag, though.)

Some of these toys are quite small and come with their own display stands. In short, they are dust traps. They will drive you nuts if you let them proliferate. Ask your Trekker to select four that he or she likes, and put the rest away. Then display the favored four in the designated *Star Trek* Shrine. Don't bother to dust them. They won't look any better, you might break them, and true Trekkers don't care if they are a little dusty. Find something more important to do.

Step 5: Cover your Trekker. Every *Star Trek* fan has had the experience of missing an episode. After weeks of repeats, a new episode sneaks into the lineup, complete with a fundamental change in a favorite character's life. Your Trekker will have to wait for the show to repeat, which could take months. But two heads are better than one. If you are aware of *Trek*, the chances are better that you'll catch a new episode and turn on the VCR for your Trekker. Nothing makes a Trekker happier than finding the episode he thought he lost.

I Hate *Star Trek*. I Can't Help It. What Do I Do?

If you are involved with a Trekker, you should recognize that the person you adore was a bit nerdy in school. You should be a little sympathetic. Even if your Trekker is suave and sexy now, most Trekkers still feel a remnant of that high school shame. And that's okay. Just don't be vocal about your hatred. Encourage your Trekker to share his hobby with friends. Try not to make a face when he or she comes back from a great *Trek* film. If it gets to be unbearable, ask yourself, "Why do I hate *Trek*? Do I have any issues with *Star Trek*?" It may turn out that the problem is more deep-rooted than you think. Remember what Shakespeare said: "The fault lies not in our stars, but in ourselves."

-3-

The Story So Far;

or,

"How Did Scotty Get So Old and Fat?"

One of the daunting obstacles for the *Star Trek* novice is the water that has already passed under the bridge. After thirty years and four TV series, the story line has grown to mammoth proportions. How can anyone possibly catch up, especially with Trekkers out there studying the program like Talmudic scholars?

Well, fear not. Let's take a quick tour of the history of the future as predicted by *Star Trek*. After this chapter, you'll be able to hold your own at a *Star Trek* convention—if that's your goal in life.

The Near Future: We Are All Doomed

To begin with, the future is now. Because the original *Star Trek* aired in the 1960s, many of the "far future" references were set in the unimaginable 1990s. If *Star Trek* were fact and not fiction, we would be in the midst of the Eugenics Wars right now. In 1992 the genetically engineered dictator Khan Noonien Singh (Ricardo Montalban) seized control of one-quarter of Earth. After Khan's defeat, he gathered eighty of his fellow genetic supermen and blasted off into space onboard the S.S. *Botany Bay*. There they lay in suspended animation for centuries until they were thawed out by Captain Kirk like a twenty-third-century Swanson turkey dinner.

World War III broke out in the mid-twenty-first century. A nuclear war, it devastated much of Earth and killed millions. Society reverted to a barbaric state, during which brutal, tyrannical regimes ruled—and all the lawyers were killed. (I don't know if nuclear weapons were used on the lawyers, but it seems likely.) Human society fell stagnant and people suffered under the oppressive weight of the corrupt governments and alliances. We also lost both television and baseball, thus ending Joe Garagiola's career.

ZEFRAM COCHRANE AND FIRST CONTACT

Star Trek as we know it began in the year 2063, when scientist Zephram Cochran made the first faster-than-light trip in his spaceship, the *Phoenix*. The warp field that Cochran created attracted the attention of a passing Vulcan ship, which landed in Montana, of all places. This event, known forevermore as First Contact, ushered in the true space age and forever changed the way mankind thought of itself.

First Contact could not have occurred without the help of Captain Picard and the crew of the *Enterprise*-E. The evil Borg had traveled back in time and tried to stop Cochran from completing the warp test but the *Enterprise* followed the Borg into the past and defeated them. Commander Riker and Engineer Geordi La Forge rode along on the maiden voyage of the *Phoenix*.

Now equipped with warp engines, mankind began to explore the universe, encountering friendly and not-so-friendly alien species. This exploration had the added benefit of unifying all of humanity to finally achieve the dream of one global government. (Unfortunately they put the World Capital in France.)

THOSE PESKY ALIENS

Of course, war broke out soon after we got into space. In the twenty-second century, Earth forces clashed with those of the Romulan Star Empire (those are the Vulcan offshoots with the big shoulder pads). The Romulans didn't have warp drive and the combatants couldn't even see one another because interstellar video communication had not yet been invented. After the Romulans suffered a stinging defeat, peace negotiations were conducted over subspace radio and a neutral zone was established to keep Romulan and Earth forces apart.

After this war the United Federation of Planets was formed among Earth and her friendlier neighbors. Starfleet was established to protect the Federation and explore deep space. As starships became faster, more alien races were contacted. Unfortunately some cross-cultural infection occurred. For example, one race, the Iotians, based their entire society upon *Chicago Mobs of the Twenties,* a book left behind by a visiting crew member from Earth. (All I can say is thank heaven we didn't leave a copy of *The Bridges of Madison County.*)

In the early twenty-third century Starfleet encountered the Klingons, but this "First Contact" was a disaster. The Klingon Empire and the Federation became bitter enemies, skirmishing over the control of dozens of star systems. From then on Starfleet adopted a more careful stance based on the Prime Directive, which forbids starship crews from interfering in the development of a planet or a planet's culture. A frustrating restriction, it wreaks havoc with crews faced with the deaths of civilizations and interplanetary massacres.

THE KIRK YEARS

In the latter half of the twenty-third century, Capt. James T. Kirk took command of the Starship *Enterprise.* He embarked on the famous first five-year mission, and his exploits have become required reading for all Starfleet cadets.

Just after Kirk took over the *Enterprise,* the Romulans unleashed a new plasma-based weapon on the Federation outposts along the neutral zone. The Romulan ship was also equipped with a cloaking device that shielded the ship from detection. With several wrecked outposts as evidence of the Romulans' violations, Kirk pursued the alien ship into the neutral zone and destroyed it. This encounter convinced the Romulans to stave off plans for further invasions.

The explorers aboard the *Enterprise* were a tight-knit group whose close bonds were a potent defense against hostile forces. Case in point: Khan, the twentieth-century dictator who was found in suspended animation. Khan tried to take over the ship, threw Kirk into a decompression chamber, and asked the crew to mutiny and accept Khan as their leader. They refused and regained control of the *Enterprise.* Kirk gave Khan a choice: imprisonment by the Federation or abandonment on an empty world. Khan chose the latter and he took one of Kirk's crew members with him as his wife. Kirk forgot all about Khan, which later came back to haunt him.

Meanwhile, relations between the Klingon Empire and the Federation had deteriorated. Before war could begin, a peace treaty was imposed on them by the Organians, a race of beings composed of pure energy. Conflicts over star systems were to be decided in favor of who could develop the planet more efficiently. The Federation liked this arrangement because they were far more likely to bring prosperity to new planets than were the warlike Klingons.

Perhaps as a result of this forced economic competition, the Klingons entered into an alliance with the Romulan Star Empire. The Romulans began using Klingon starship design and now both of the Federation's worst enemies had cloaking technology which could make their warships invisible. The Federation gained access to this secret technology when Kirk sneaked into Romulan space and stole a cloaking device while disguised as a Romulan. (As a result of this, Starfleet could make its starships invisible as well, but a current interstellar treaty forbids them to do so.)

After the *Enterprise*'s five-year mission, it was refitted with more modern equipment. The warp nacelles were slimmed down, the secondary hull was enlarged, and the crew received new uniforms that looked like pajamas but were not as stylish.

STAR TREK: THE MOTION PICTURE AND THE COMING OF V'GER

The *Enterprise* crew reunited to save Earth from an alien probe known as V'Ger. Immensely powerful and all-knowing, V'Ger liked to zap and store as digital information everything it encountered. It took our intrepid Captain Kirk two and a half hours to realize that V'Ger was really *Voyager VI*, an old Earth space probe altered by an alien race of machines. (He discovered this by rubbing some dirt off of the NASA nameplate.) Before it could destroy Earth the *Enterprise* crew made contact with V'Ger and helped it become a new energy life-form. (Trekkers, who love trying to figure out what mysteries new characters are responsible for in the past, believe that the race of machines that enhanced the probe was none other than the Borg.)

THE GENESIS DEVICE, THE *WRATH OF KHAN,* AND THE *SEARCH FOR SPOCK*

Federation science complicated everyone's lives with the creation of the Genesis Device, which could transform a dead planet into a living one in a matter of minutes and could destroy a planet just as quickly. Its dangerous potential was made clear by Khan, who escaped from the planet Kirk had marooned him on. Khan stole the Genesis Device and came after Kirk for revenge. With the Genesis Device ticking away, the crippled *Enterprise* seemed certain to be caught in the blast. Spock, in a stunning act of sacrifice, exposed himself to lethal radiation to fix the warp drive and save the ship. Spock died and his body was ejected into space. It somehow soft-landed on a new planet formed by the Genesis Device called, strangely enough, the Genesis Planet.

Once the Klingons heard about the new weapon, they wanted one for themselves. Kirk and crew, while trying to find Spock's body on the Genesis Planet, were waylaid by a Klingon Bird-of-Prey. The Klingons boarded the *Enterprise,* and Kirk was forced to steal the Klingons' ship and order the *Enterprise* to self-destruct. Trekkers everywhere wiped away a tear as their beloved ship exploded.

For this, the Klingon government branded Kirk a terrorist and sought his extradition. Luckily for Kirk, Earth needed to be rescued from the threat of yet another weird alien probe.

STAR TREK: THE VOYAGE HOME

This time the probe in question was seeking to make contact with whales, all of which had long since been extinct. The transmissions from the probe were so strong that they started vaporizing Earth's oceans—which wouldn't have benefited the whales, if there were any.

Kirk took the Klingon ship back in time to Earth's twentieth century and succeeded in bringing back two humpback whales, who spoke to the alien probe and sent it on its way. The Federation honored Kirk for his heroism by presenting him and his crew with a new Starship *Enterprise,* designated NCC-1701-A. Needless to say, the Klingons were not happy about this.

THE UNDISCOVERED COUNTRY: PEACE

Trekkers have long observed that the alien cultures in *Star Trek* seem analogous to nations on Earth: Klingons are the Soviets, Romulans are the Chinese, Vulcans the Japanese, and so on. Thus it came as no surprise that as the Soviet Union collapsed, the Klingon Empire found itself facing dissolution. In the sixth *Star Trek* feature, the Klingon's main energy-producing facility on the moon Praxis exploded, plunging the Klingons into an environmental crisis that threatened their existence. Since the peace treaty with the Romulans had collapsed years earlier, the Federation was the only game in town. Before peace talks could begin, a conspiracy among Starfleet, Klingon, and Romulan officers succeeded in assassinating the Klingon Chancellor, and pinning the blame on Kirk and McCoy. Spock was able to rescue the captain and expose the conspiracy, and the long peace process with the Klingons began.

NEW GENERATIONS, AND A NEW *ENTERPRISE*

To replace the outdated *Enterprise*-A, Starfleet commissioned the *Enterprise*-B, based on the longer *Excelsior* design. Responding to a distress call, the *Enterprise*-B sought to rescue two El-Aurian refugee ships caught in a time rift known as the Nexus. (The El-Aurians were most likely fleeing the Borg, who had destroyed their homeworld.) One of the refugees saved by the *Enterprise*-B was Guinan (who would later become the bartender on the *Enterprise*-D). During the rescue, Kirk was lost in space and presumed dead. In reality, he had been drawn into the Nexus, a dimension where all you desire becomes reality.

THE *ENTERPRISE*-C SAVES THE KLINGONS

At the beginning of the twenty-fourth century, the Federation and the Klingons were still trying to hammer out an alliance. Again a ship named *Enterprise* played a pivotal role. The *Enterprise*-C, the fourth ship to carry the honorable name, responded to a distress call from a Klingon outpost. The Romulans had staged a sneak attack, and the *Enterprise*-C came to the Klingons' defense, taking on four

Romulan Warbirds. Although the *Enterprise*-C was destroyed, the Klingons viewed the sacrifice as an act of honor, and it brought the Federation and Klingons closer together, ushering in a new era of peace.

Unbeknownst to anyone, during this battle the *Enterprise*-C was blown through a time-rift into the future. The disappearance of the ship from battle changed the time line and created...

THE "YESTERDAY'S *ENTERPRISE*" ALTERNATE TIME LINE

Now try to follow this, because it's very cool and integral to *Star Trek* history. The immediate predecessor to our ship, the *Enterprise*-C, while rescuing a Klingon settlement from Romulan attack, encountered a time rift and journeyed twenty-two years into the future. Because the *Enterprise*-C disappeared from that time, it missed its appointment with destiny and created an alternate time line. History was altered. The *Enterprise*-C found the future was now a dark one.

The Klingons never made peace with the Federation, and war soon broke out. Our ship, the *Enterprise*-D, was instantly transformed by the changing time line into a battleship. The crew of the *Enterprise*-C found that because they had journeyed into the future, the Federation had been at war with the Klingons for twenty years. And Starfleet was losing. *Enterprise*-C had to go back through the time rift and face certain death at the hands of the Romulans in order to restore the course of history.

In this alternate time line, Tasha Yar was still alive. Guinan, whose alien senses knew that the alternate "war" time line was incorrect, told Tasha that in proper reality she should be dead. A shaken Tasha asked Picard to transfer her to the *Enterprise*-C so that her death would have meaning. A conflicted Picard reluctantly agreed.

Enterprise-C went back into the rift, fought the Romulans, and corrected history. However, that wasn't the end for Tasha. Now twenty-two years in the past, Tasha was taken prisoner by the Romulans. A Romulan commander found her attractive and took her as his wife. She bore a daughter, named Sela (who was played by the same actress who played Tasha). When Sela was four, Tasha tried to escape from her Romulan captors. Sela, loyal to her Romulan father, cried out, and Tasha was caught and executed. Sela grew up to look just like Tasha (plus pointy ears), and became a powerful officer in the Romulan military.

Needless to say, this shocked the hell out of Picard. Because the time line had been changed, Picard had no memory of sending Tasha back in time. Sela turned out to be a major pain in the ass for our crew, and almost succeeded in turning the Klingon Empire into an enemy of the Federation. If Denise Crosby's agent is any good, you should expect to see Sela in upcoming features. (Keep in mind, Tasha Yar was killed by a slimy alien during the first season and in the "Yesterday's *Enterprise*" alternate time line, she survived to go back in time and was captured and killed by the Romulans. In either universe Tasha's dead.)

MORE FIGHTING, ANYONE?

If things were hunky-dory with the Federation, Klingon-Romulan relations couldn't have been worse. With the help of a Klingon traitor, the Romulans attacked the planet Khitomer. Thousands of Klingons were murdered. One of the survivors of the Khitomer Massacre was a small boy named Worf, who was adopted by human Starfleet officers.

Meanwhile, the Cardassians, a smaller, equally hostile civilization, attacked and annexed the planet Bajor. They oppressed its peoples and stripped the planet of its wealth. The Cardassians built a mining station called Terok Nor in orbit around Bajor. They also attacked a Federation colony and killed hundreds of civilians. The Federation responded and a prolonged conflict with the Cardassians ensued.

THE *ENTERPRISE*-D TAKES FLIGHT

A new Starship *Enterprise*, under the command of Capt. Jean-Luc Picard, took up where the last one left off: mainly, saving the Federation. Q, a powerful new entity, put humanity itself on trial to determine whether it was worthy of continued existence. Picard succeeded in convincing Q to spare humanity, but Q's obsession with the *Enterprise*-D brought about the most serious threat to the Federation.

In a fit of pique, Q transported the *Enterprise*-D seven thousand light-years away into a region of space controlled by the Borg, who attacked the ship, causing severe damage and loss of life. Although Q saved the ship at the last minute by returning it to Federation space, the Borg had already gained access to the *Enterprise*'s computer banks. The Borg knew where the humans lived and came running. Starfleet Command, scared out of its wits by reading Picard's reports late at night, ordered a team to develop a defense strategy against the invincible Borg. (Of course, nobody figured out the obvious way to defeat them: to beam over with a huge bomb and blow them into little self-starting charcoal Borg-ettes.) The dreadnought U.S.S. *Defiant*, later stationed at *Deep Space Nine* under Worf's command, was designed during this effort.

THE BATTLE OF WOLF 359

Less than a year later, the Borg invaded Federation space. Starfleet was not prepared, and one Borg cube sliced through Federation defenses toward Earth. The Borg abducted Captain Picard and assimilated him into their collective. Using Picard's knowledge of Federation tactics and capabilities, the Borg destroyed thirty-nine starships at the Battle of Wolf 359. William Riker and the *Enterprise*-D crew recovered Captain Picard and used his connection to the Borg collective to destroy their ship. However, the Battle of Wolf 359 exacted a heavy toll on Starfleet in lost ships and officers.

At some point after this experience with the Borg the Federation and the Cardassians signed a peace treaty ending years of conflict.

WORF AND THE KLINGON CIVIL WAR

Worf, the first Klingon to serve as a Starfleet officer, became embroiled in a Klingon political crisis on his homeworld. Worf's father, Mogh, was declared by the Klingon High Council to be the traitor who had betrayed the Khitomer outpost to the Romulans. This guaranteed that Worf would be considered a traitor for the rest of his life, as would his children. Worf discovered that the traitor was actually the father of Duras, a powerful member of the Klingon High Council. Worf was trapped: revealing Duras to be a traitor would cause a civil war, and not challenging the Klingon High Council's declaration would result in Worf's excommunication from the empire. Worf chose discommendation and accepted his status as a traitor in order to preserve the empire.

This matter could not remain closed. The Klingon Chancellor, K'mpec, soon learned that he was dying of slow poison. He suspected one of the two candidates for his soon-to-be-vacant office: Duras and Gowron. The Chancellor asked Picard to determine who the murderer was because a Klingon who kills "without showing his face" is considered without honor and would lead the empire to ruin. Picard was thus forced to become the Arbiter of Succession.

During this process, Duras, whose father was the true traitor of the Khitomer massacre, killed K'Ehleyr, the Klingon ambassador, when she became suspicious of him. Worf, enraged at the death of his beloved, killed Duras in ritual combat, thus paving the way for Gowron to become leader of the Klingon Empire.

After Duras's death, his sisters, Lursa and B'Etor, vowed revenge. (It's tough to keep these sisters straight, so just keep in mind that B'Etor is the good-looking one.) They continued Duras's alliance with the Romulans. They sought to install Toral, Duras's twelve-year-old son, as the Chancellor instead of Gowron. Civil war broke out within the empire, and Duras's forces, aided by the Romulans, began to overwhelm forces loyal to Gowron. Picard discovered that the person behind the Romulan alliance with the House of Duras was none other than Sela, a Romulan who claimed to be the daughter of dead *Enterprise* Security Chief Tasha Yar. Sela told an astonished Picard how he had, in an alternate time line, sent her mother back in time on the *Enterprise*-C. (See how this is all tying together? We're having some fun now.)

To stop Sela, Federation forces were deployed across the Romulan-Klingon border in an attempt to expose the Romulans. They deployed a tachyon detection grid that was successful in revealing the locations of the cloaked Romulan supply ships, and

Sela abandoned her support of the Duras sisters. Without the Romulans' aid, the sisters were defeated by Gowron and he gave Worf the opportunity to kill Toral, the twelve-year-old son of the man who had falsely proclaimed Worf's father a traitor. Of course, Worf, being a Good Guy, could not kill a child, and spared his life. (Why do we get the feeling we're going to see this kid again?)

VULCAN-ROMULAN UNIFICATION

The Romulans were not the only ones conducting covert operations at the time. The now-Ambassador Spock had smuggled himself into Romulan territory to advance the unification of the Vulcan and Romulan people, a movement gaining strength among the Romulans. He disappeared, and Picard borrowed a Klingon Bird-of-Prey to sneak into the Romulan Empire and find him. Although Spock was alive and well, the "unification movement" was a ruse designed by Sela to conceal an invasion of the planet Vulcan. Starfleet foiled the invasion, and Spock elected to remain on Romulus to encourage a genuine reunification effort.

THE BORG RETURN

Shortly afterward, a crashed Borg scout ship was found on a planet in Federation space. An adolescent Borg had survived, and he was treated for his injuries by the crew of the *Enterprise*-D, who named him Hugh. They developed an invasive computer virus that, if downloaded into the captured Borg, would destroy the collective and Hugh as well. However, Picard chose not to sacrifice Hugh when it became evident that he had developed his own personality. Hugh was allowed to return to the collective. Hugh's experience of individuality had a devastating effect when downloaded into the Borg hive mind.

A group of Borg infected by the idea of individuality formed around Hugh, and they separated from the Borg collective con- sciousness. During this time of confusion, they were found by the evil Lore, Data's brother, who became their leader. Lore brought them back to Federation space, and they attacked the *Enterprise*-D, trying to help Lore to fulfill his dreams of revenge. Data briefly joined Lore, but Hugh was able to overcome Lore's influence and help the *Enterprise* crew defeat him.

THE CARDASSIANS LEAVE BAJOR

Meanwhile the Cardassians, weary of terrorist activity on Bajor, left the planet. Retreating troops poisoned the fields, destroyed the cities, and abandoned Terok Nor, the orbiting mining station. A provisional Bajoran government took over.

As the Cardassians prepared to attack a star system in Federation space, Picard became an undercover intelligence agent, but was captured and tortured extensively by Cardassian agents. The Federation charged into the Cardassian forces, pushing them back and freeing Picard.

The Bajorans asked the Federation to take possession of Terok Nor and establish a presence in the Bajoran system. Benjamin Sisko took command of the station, now named *Deep Space Nine*.

Commander Sisko discovered the first stable wormhole, a tunnel in space from the Alpha Quadrant to the Gamma Quadrant. Sisko found that the aliens who lived within this artificially generated wormhole exist outside our space-time continuum. Sisko made friends with the aliens, and the wormhole was opened to interstellar traffic. The Bajorans decided that Sisko was the Emissary, a religious figure prophesied for millennia. Bajor instantly became a major center for interstellar commerce to the Gamma Quadrant.

DNA PROVIDES AN ANCIENT MESSAGE AND AN ANCIENT KLINGON LEGEND

Around this time, scientists around the galaxy raced to solve a mystery: it seemed that the combined DNA from dozens of races contained a coded message. Working together, the Cardassians, Klingons, Romulans, and humans discovered that the message was implanted by an ancient race that spread humanoid life throughout the galaxy. That race hoped that the mission to find their message would foster harmony among the many races, who would now realize that they were brothers. (Yeah, right.)

Meanwhile, working in secret, Klingon scientists created a genetic copy of Kahless the Unforgettable, the father of Klingon society. They programmed him to think and act like Kahless, and then sought to install him as Emperor. Chancellor Gowron bitterly opposed this as a direct challenge to his power. However, Gowron, recognizing that the empire required the spiritual uplift Kahless would provide, agreed to allow him to become Emperor, but only as a figurehead.

A STARFLEET CONSPIRACY, AND A FEDERATION REBELLION

A secret cabal at Starfleet Command developed a phase-cloaking device for Federation ships. This device, besides rendering a ship invisible, could enable it to move through solid objects, such as a planet. The Treaty of Algeron with the Romulans had proscribed the Federation from developing cloaking technology. Captain Picard exposed and defeated the conspiracy, and Trekkers finally learned why Federation starships can't cloak.

Finally, after years of conflict, the Cardassians and the Federation reached a peaceful resolution. A demilitarized zone would be created between them, and colonists living in the area would have to be removed to make room for the Cardassians. Several colonies were dissatisfied with this arrangement and formed a rebel group called the Maquis. The Maquis believed that the Federation had abandoned them, and they relinquished their Federation citizenship. They acquired ships and weapons, and began to raid Cardassian outposts. Many of the Maquis were later killed off when the Cardassians joined the evil Dominion.

On Bajor, Vedek Winn, a conservative religious cleric, became the Kai, the spiritual leader of Bajor. This development was seen as a negative one for Bajor's future.

THE DOMINION THREAT REVEALED

Meanwhile, *Deep Space Nine* had become the stepping-off point to the Gamma Quadrant. During a routine expedition, the violent Jem'Hadar took Benjamin Sisko and his son hostage. This was the first contact with the Dominion, the empire on the other side of the wormhole. The Dominion threatened to destroy all Federation ships in the Gamma Quadrant, and demanded that all traffic through the wormhole cease. The Starship *Odyssey*, a sister ship to the *Enterprise*-D, conducted a rescue operation. Although they saved Sisko and his crew, the *Odyssey* was destroyed by the Jem'Hadar with a loss of all hands.

Sisko was able to convince Starfleet to station the U.S.S. *Defiant*, a prototype warship designed to combat the Borg, at *Deep Space Nine*. Using the powerful ship, Sisko and crew investigated the Gamma Quadrant, searching for the mysterious rulers of the Dominion, the Founders. The Founders were discovered to be changelings, shape-shifters who can assume any identity. Although they allowed the *Defiant* to return to Federation space, the Founders made it clear that they planned to impose order, *their* order, on the rest of the galaxy.

THE HOUSE OF DURAS
DESTROYS THE *ENTERPRISE*-D

The *Enterprise*-D, while investigating the activities of the El-Aurian scientist Dr. Soren, came under attack by the Duras sisters, eager for revenge for the role that the ship played in their defeat in the Klingon Civil War. Although the sisters were killed, the *Enterprise*-D was destroyed. A dramatic planetary landing by the ship's saucer section saved the crew.

U.S.S. *VOYAGER* DISAPPEARS

While looking for a Maquis raider ship in the Badlands, the U.S.S. *Voyager* was abducted to the Delta Quadrant by a powerful alien force. *Voyager* would now be cut off from all Federation contact for years. Shortly after being transported, the crew discovered a microscopic wormhole connecting the Delta Quadrant to the Alpha Quadrant. *Voyager* contacted a Romulan ship in the Alpha Quadrant, and the crew hoped to beam themselves back to the Alpha Quadrant through the wormhole. But the wormhole was also a time rift, and the Romulan ship they had contacted existed twenty years in the past. Capt. Kathryn Janeway elected not to evacuate the crew to the past but did record messages from the crew to their families on a computer chip. They gave this chip to a Romulan, who promised to deliver it to Starfleet in twenty years. However, it was discovered that this Romulan died shortly after contacting *Voyager*, and the crew never found out whether he completed his task.

THE DOMINION GETS SERIOUS

In an unusual alliance, the Romulan secret intelligence service, the Tal Shiar, and its Cardassian equivalent, the Obsidian Order, moved a massive fleet into the Gamma Quadrant to destroy the Founders. But the Founders had anticipated the sneak attack and had moved their civilization to another world. Suddenly, hundreds of Jem'Hadar ships swooped in and destroyed the Romulan and Cardassian invaders. This loss of ships and officers significantly weakened both the Romulan and Cardassian governments. On Cardassia Prime, a civilian government overthrew the military dictatorship.

THE KLINGONS ATTACK CARDASSIA

The Klingon Empire, fearing that the Cardassian government had been infiltrated by changelings, declared war on Cardassia. The Federation was invited to join them, but refused. Gowron, offended, revoked the Khitomer Treaty. A fleet of Klingon warships invaded the Cardassian Union; the Cardassian fleet was defeated, and several worlds were annexed by the Klingons.

The U.S.S. *Defiant* rescued the Cardassian civilian government to shield them from the Klingons. Enraged, Gowron opened fire on *Deep Space Nine*. In a pitched battle, *Deep Space Nine* held off dozens of Klingon battle cruisers until reinforcements could arrive. A tentative truce was reached with the Klingons, but the situation was more tense than ever.

STARFLEET GETS PARANOID:
EVERYONE'S A CHANGELING

Meanwhile on Earth, a political conference was bombed. Evidence revealed that Founders had reached Earth and were assuming human guise. Martial law was declared. Fortunately, the threat was determined to be minimal. If that wasn't enough, the Federation was having difficulty controlling the Maquis. The Maquis did not stand still during Cardassia's troubles. Using Maquis sympathizers in Starfleet as secret agents, the Maquis staged several daring raids and stole several industrial replicators.

Odo, the changeling aboard *Deep Space Nine*, suddenly became ill. Taken to the Gamma Quadrant, he visited the Founder home-world and was joined in the Great Link. While in contact with his people, Odo was led to believe that Gowron, leader of the Klingon Empire, was a changeling. A Klingon attempt to annex the Archanis Sector provided further disturbing evidence of the Founders' manipulation of the Klingon Empire.

On a secret mission to the Klingon homeworld, several Starfleet officers disguised as Klingons attempted to expose Gowron as an impostor. However, it was General Martok, the second in command, who was actually the Founder operative pressing Gowron to attack the Federation. This Dominion infiltration was the prelude to an invasion of the Alpha Quadrant.

Worf and Garak, while responding to a Cardassian military signal on the other side of the wormhole, discovered that Dr. Bashir on *Deep Space Nine* was also a changeling: The real Dr. Bashir was imprisoned with the remnants of the Cardassian and Romulan fleets. At the same time, a large fleet of Jem'Hadar warships came through the wormhole and headed straight for Cardassia. Gul Dukat, the provisional civilian leader, allied the Cardassian Union with the Dominion. With the Dominion adding its muscle to that of the Cardassians, Klingon warships came under heavy attack and lost significant ground.

In response to the threat of a combined Dominion-Cardassian attack, the Klingons reactivated the Khitomer Accords, once again making allies of the Federation. A combined Federation, Klingon, and Romulan fleet waited while sensors showed dozens of incoming enemy ships, but the forces never materialized. The "attack" was a ruse, designed to gather the forces of the Alpha Quadrant together while the alien Dr. Bashir blew up the Bajoran sun, destroying Bajor,

Deep Space Nine, and the fleets. The *Deep Space Nine* and *Defiant* crews stopped him. In the wake of this hostile act, it was agreed that the Klingons would establish a permanent presence on *Deep Space Nine,* and that General Martok would serve as the Klingon-Federation liaison.

THE CARDASSIANS SEIZE *DEEP SPACE NINE*

To stop Dominion forces from streaming through the wormhole toward Cardassia, Starfleet mined the entrance using cloaked explosives. The Dominion and Cardassia responded with a massive attack against *Deep Space Nine.* Starfleet chose not to send reinforcements and instead mounted a surprise attack on the Cardassian-Dominion shipyards, destroying them. However, Dominion ships pierced *Deep Space Nine*'s defenses, and Gul Dukat made good on his old promise to reclaim Terok Nor.

Commander Sisko, drawing on his credibility as the Emissary, talked the Bajorans into signing a treaty with the Dominion to keep them out of a conflict that would destroy their still-fragile world. The Romulans, who are never to be trusted, signed a nonaggression pact with the Dominion, keeping themselves out of the fighting. Meanwhile, a combined fleet of Federation and Klingon warships massed and set their course toward *Deep Space Nine* and the precious wormhole....

THE BORG MAKES ITS MOVE

While the Federation had its plate full with these jokers, the Borg returned, and again one single ship reached Earth, although this time it sustained significant damage. Before being destroyed by Captain Picard, who knows the weak points of Borg vessels from his time in the collective, the Borg launched a time-ship, which succeeded in altering Earth's past. Earth changed suddenly, becoming colonized by the Borg. In an attempt to correct the past, the new, upgraded *Enterprise*-E followed the Borg ship to the year 2063. The crew of the *Enterprise*-E helped Zefram Cochrane complete the first test of warp drive, and secured the proper flow of history.

VOYAGER AND THE BORG

Far from Federation space, U.S.S. *Voyager* traveled deeper into the unknown. The Delta Quadrant, home of the Borg, can be a dangerous place for one lone ship, as the *Voyager* crew learned when they encountered a derelict Borg cube. The crew beamed aboard and found that the ship had been deactivated by a massive electrical disturbance. Perhaps there was something more powerful than the Borg?

The crew of this Borg ship was stranded on a nearby planet, partially recovered from their Borg implants. Without their ship to electronically connect them, they were fighting among themselves. They mentally forced Commander Chakotay to activate the Borg ship's neural network to create a benevolent Borg society.

Voyager soon found itself wandering into Borg space, with hundreds of Borg star systems ahead of them. However, a "Northwest Passage" devoid of Borg presence beckoned. Before they could take advantage of it, the *Voyager* crew observed a large number of Borg ships racing toward them. The crew said their prayers, but, uncharacteristically, the Borg were not interested in them, and raced by at high warp. *Voyager* discovered that the Borg fleet had been wiped out by strange squid-shaped vessels. The aliens piloting these organic ships, called Species 8472 by the Borg, could somehow disable Borg ships and resist Borg efforts to assimilate them. These new aliens emerged from an artificially generated quantum singularity (a black hole) originating in another continuum, and this hole in space was in the Northwest Passage. *Voyager* was caught between a rock and a hard place.

In a fateful decision, Captain Janeway contacted the Borg and proposed a temporary alliance and exchange: *Voyager* could help the Borg learn to assimilate the new species, but only if the Borg would safely escort them through their space. With Species 8472 chasing them both, Janeway hung on the Borg's answer....

There, now you're up to speed.

But wait! There's still....

THE MIRROR UNIVERSE

Late in the twenty-third century, Captain Kirk, Scotty, Dr. McCoy, and Uhura, while beaming up from a planet during an ion storm, found themselves in an "alternate universe," a dimension like our own but twisted. On this dimension's *Enterprise,* the characters had demonic personalities. The Federation was an oppressive empire, and starships kept the local systems in line through a reign of terror. Promotions came from the death of superiors: you rose through the ranks by killing your boss. (Trekkers love that part.)

Our "good" officers had changed places with their "evil" counterparts. Spock was logical as always, but an efficient officer in this cruel system. The only thing noticeably different about him was a goatee he wore, making his look "Vulcan beatnik." The officers from the "good" universe faked being madmen, but the "evil" officers in our universe couldn't carry off the nice act, and the "good" Spock threw them into the brig.

Scotty found a way to beam the away team back to the "good" universe, but before he did, Kirk gave a speech to the "evil" Spock. In one of the most inspiring speeches ever written for *Star Trek,* Kirk encouraged the "evil" Spock to become captain, and change the nature of the evil empire. When Spock said he could not do it alone, Kirk retorted with an answer that still gives Trekkers goose pimples. As the music swelled, Kirk stood on the transporter pad and said, "In every revolution, there is one man with a vision."

Spock activated the transporter and replied, "Captain Kirk, I shall consider it."

This dialogue changed an entire universe.

Eighty years later, on *Deep Space Nine,* Major Kira and Dr. Bashir were accidentally transported to the mirror universe. The evil Human Empire had fallen, due to a revolution organized by the mirror Spock years earlier following Kirk's speech. The new friendly empire was quickly destroyed by a Cardassian-Klingon-Bajoran alliance, and humans were now slaves. Kira and Bashir met their counterparts, the evilest of whom was Kira, who dressed in black leather and kept sex slaves. Kira and Bashir talked the mirror Sisko and Miles O'Brien into becoming freedom fighters for humanity, and left the mirror universe.

The saga continued when Benjamin Sisko was abducted by the mirror O'Brien. O'Brien wanted Sisko to talk Sisko's wife (who was still alive in the mirror universe) out of designing the ultimate weapon for the Cardassian-Klingon alliance. He succeeded and returned to his own universe. The mirror Jennifer Sisko took Benjamin's words to heart and joined the human resistance.

In yet another mirror universe episode, the mirror Jennifer Sisko came to our station and kidnapped Jake Sisko to the mirror universe. Benjamin Sisko followed, as he was supposed to. The human resistance wanted his help building a version of the *Defiant* for them. Sisko completed the ship and piloted it against the mirror Worf, stopping him from retaking *Deep Space Nine*. The mirror Kira, still in black leather and still seductive, killed Jennifer Sisko, but spared Jake. She told him that she intended to collect on this debt.

Now you're really up to speed.

THE STORY QUIZ

1. How did the Borg seek to destroy humanity?

    a. By coercing everyone to start wearing khakis and blue denim shirts (oh, I'm sorry, that's how the *Gap* tried to destroy humanity)
    b. Two words: *Melrose Place*
    c. By traveling back in time to destroy the *Phoenix*
    d. By putting liberal bias into every Sunday edition of the newspaper (oh, I'm sorry, that's how the *New York Times* tried to destroy humanity)

2. In the evil mirror universe, how do we know Spock is evil?

    a. He smokes
    b. He wears a black hat
    c. He votes Republican
    d. He sports a goatee

3. What was the name of the genetic superman who detonated the Genesis Device?

    a. Kang
    b. Khan
    c. Conch
    d. Irving

4. After the moon Praxis exploded, what did the Klingons do?

   a. Partied like it was 1999
   b. Sought counseling
   c. Went on *Jenny Jones*
   d. Sued for peace

5. Who gave secret codes to the Romulans at Khitomer?

   a. Duras's father
   b. Worf
   c. Worf's father
   d. The Rosenbergs

6. Who is Tasha Yar's daughter?

   a. Sela
   b. B'Etor
   c. Lursa
   d. Madonna

7. Which sister ship of the *Enterprise* did the Dominion destroy?

   a. The U.S.S. *Odyssey*
   b. The U.S.S. *Defiant*
   c. The U.S.S. *Minnow*
   d. The *Andrea Doria*

8. What happened to the Tal Shiar and the Obsidian Order when they attacked the Founders?

   a. They succeeded
   b. They were turned into charcoal briquettes
   c. They were turned back
   d. They were invited to join the Dominion

ANSWERS

   1, c; 2, d; 3, b; 4, d; 5, a; 6, a; 7, a; 8, b.

4

THE CHARACTERS—
STAR TREK: THE ORIGINAL SHOW

When talking about the original show, Trekkers say "TOS."

JAMES T. KIRK (WILLIAM SHATNER)

In a Nutshell

- ❏ Kirk is a passionate man of action, dedicated to his ship and crew. He is a risk-taker, and hates to lose. He is *muy macho.*
- ❏ Kirk's relationships with women are unstable but numerous.
- ❏ He hates and is hated by the Klingons, the alien race he has defeated on many occasions.

The man in command of the original Starship *Enterprise,* the flagship of Starfleet, is James Tiberius Kirk. He's the alpha male of the show; the one who gets the girl and saves the universe. During the first TV show, Kirk was thirty-three years old, the youngest captain of a starship in history. Kirk is a swashbuckler, a man of passion and action. Because other men, for some strange reason, could resent a man like this, Kirk was given one key weakness: his dedication to his ship and crew. Kirk's devotion was so deep that it precluded many chances he had to hook up permanently with gorgeous women or more prestigious careers. Don't be fooled, though. Jim Kirk was a ladies' man and never passed up an opportunity to beam down to a planet for "cultural studies."

ABOUT JAMES T. KIRK

Kirk was born in the year 2233 in Iowa of all places. He had an older brother, George Samuel Kirk, whom he called Sam. (This caused me a brief thrill when I first heard it.) By the time he was thirteen, Kirk was out in deep space on a planet called Tarsus IV. There he witnessed the massacre of four thousand colonists. The man who killed them, Kodos the Executioner, would later visit the *Enterprise*. Of course, Kodos didn't come to a good end. This would be a common fate for many of Kirk's acquaintances from the past.

Jim Kirk was a standout at Starfleet Academy, but deeply hated an upperclassman named Finnegan. (Later, on a planet where fantasies became reality, Kirk got to beat the living daylights out of him. Imagine being able to beat up anybody from your past you didn't like. I think that could be the basis for a game show.)

All Starfleet Academy cadets must endure something called the *Kobayashi Maru* scenario, which is a test of command abilities. It's supposed to be unwinnable and its purpose is to test the character of future officers. Kirk, alpha male that he is, was the only cadet to beat the scenario. He did it by changing the computer program to make it possible to win—which was cheating. However, he won a commendation for original thinking.

Kirk served on two ships before being awarded the *Enterprise:* the *Republic* and the *Farragut*. We know more details of his time on the *Farragut*. Captain Garrovick, his commanding officer, was killed by a gaseous creature, and Kirk blamed himself. (Even this early in his career, Kirk must have noticed that people near him met unfortunate ends.) Several times, Kirk risked his command and his career to save his friends and his ship.

He has been known to quote "All I ask is a tall ship and a star to steer her by."

KEY KIRK EPISODES

Certain episode plots affected Kirk's life more than others. We learn a great deal about his character from these. What follow are not necessarily the best episodes, but they're important to the development of our captain.

"**Where No Man Has Gone Before**" The *Enterprise* journeys to the edge of the galaxy, where it encounters an unknown energy barrier. A crew member, Gary Mitchell (an old friend of Kirk's), begins to develop godlike telepathic powers, and tries to seize control of the ship. Kirk attempts to maroon his friend on a deserted planet, and is forced to kill him when he resists.

"The Naked Time"   A strange virus infects the crew of the *Enterprise*, causing them to reveal hidden feelings and act out fantasies. Kirk reveals his deep love for the ship and its crew. We learn how far Kirk will go to protect his ship.

"The Enemy Within"   A transporter malfunction splits Kirk into his evil self and his good self. His evil self sweats a lot; his good self agonizes over routine decisions and would probably have voted for Ralph Nader for president. It seems that Kirk needs both aspects of his personality to function. We learn how far Shatner will go to overact.

"Amok Time"   Spock, appearing to lose his sanity, must return to his home planet to mate. Kirk takes him there against orders and is forced to fight Spock in an ancient ritual. The depths of his friendship with Spock were first made clear to Trekkers in this episode.

"The Paradise Syndrome"   Kirk, his memory damaged, lives on a primitive planet with a tribe of natives who bear an eerie resemblance to Native Americans.* He falls in love, gets married, and conceives a child. His wife gets stoned to death by the end of the episode. We learn how dangerous it is to get romantically involved with Kirk.

"The City on the Edge of Forever"   Dr. McCoy accidentally goes back in time and saves a woman who should have died (played by Joan Collins). This alters the future, destroying society as we know it. (See, Joan Collins was a peacenik who, if she had lived, would've talked the U.S. out of going to war with Germany. Hitler would have won and history would have been changed.) Kirk and Spock must journey back in time to stop McCoy. Kirk falls in love with the woman but lets her die anyway. See above lesson.

---

*Kirk thinks his name is Kirok and shouts "I am Kirok!" at anyone who will listen.

THE MOVIES

After the five-year mission of the *Enterprise* on television (which, as we know, lasted only three seasons), Kirk became an admiral. After saving Earth in *Star Trek: The Motion Picture,* he taught at Starfleet Academy. Kirk lost his best friend when Spock died in *Star Trek II: The Wrath of Khan.*

Wrath of Khan was a stressful movie for James Kirk. He was reunited with Carol Marcus, an old girlfriend, and finally met his now-grown son by her, David Marcus. David didn't care much for his space-cowboy father, preferring to develop the dreaded Genesis Device.

Admiral Kirk disobeyed orders and stole the *Enterprise* in order to help Spock back to life in *Star Trek III: The Search for Spock.* During this mission, Kirk's son was killed by Klingons. Kirk repaid this debt by killing the Klingon commander who had ordered David's death and by stealing the Klingon's ship. In order to save his crew, Kirk finally made good on a long-time threat: he destroyed the *Enterprise.*

After saving Earth yet again in *Star Trek IV: The Voyage Home,* Admiral Kirk was demoted to captain for stealing and destroying the *Enterprise* in the last movie. Starfleet built a new *Enterprise* and gave Kirk command of it. (Starships, it seems, are like rental cars: if you wreck one they give you another.)

Starfleet Command ordered Kirk to take part in negotiations for a peace treaty with the Klingons in *Star Trek VI: The Undiscovered Country.* Kirk hated the Klingons, blaming them for the death of his only son. As a result of a conspiracy between hawkish elements in Starfleet and other empires, Kirk was captured by the Klingons and sentenced to a penal colony on an inhospitable world. However, Kirk was freed and made the peace treaty possible by exposing the conspiracy. Kirk reexamined his hatred of the Klingons and, as a result, began to recover a lost sense of optimism about the future.

Kirk was presumed dead when, on the first cruise of the third ship called *Enterprise,* he tried to save the ship and was caught in a section of the hull exposed to space. In *Star Trek: Generations* we learned that Kirk was actually trapped in a dimension known as the Nexus, where anything you dream can come true. Kirk's vision of paradise was living on a ranch with a woman named Antonia. He gave up this fantasy life to team up with the *Next Generation*'s Captain Picard in order to save a populated planet (this time not Earth). James T. Kirk died on a barren planet after a small bridge collapsed. His last words were "Oh, my." Picard placed Kirk's body in a small cairn upon a mountain on this dead world. With Kirk's demise, the transfer of *Star Trek* from the old crew to the new was complete.

SPOCK (LEONARD NIMOY)

In a Nutshell

- ❑ Spock is half human and half Vulcan, an alien race. He was raised on the planet Vulcan and considers himself a Vulcan.
- ❑ Spock, like other Vulcans, has renounced emotion and lives a life ruled by pure logic. Spock struggles with his human half, constantly on guard against human emotions and feelings.
- ❑ Spock's intellect has made him renowned throughout the universe. His nature is peaceful.
- ❑ He frequently collides with the more emotional Dr. McCoy, but is close friends with him as well as Kirk. Spock is dedicated to Kirk.
- ❑ Spock has died and come back to life. This, understandably, has affected the way he views the universe and funeral parlor prices.

Spock, the first officer aboard the original *Enterprise,* is constantly trying to come to terms with his half-human, half-Vulcan identity. Spock possesses superhuman strength and all sorts of biological advantages over humans. These appear when necessary, like an inner eyelid that protects against blindness. In addition, Spock has all sorts of healing techniques he can use to survive beyond the last commercial break. (See "Vulcans" in chapter 8.) He can mind-meld with others, learn secrets, and all sorts of intimate stuff.

ABOUT SPOCK

Spock was born on the planet Vulcan in 2230. His mother, Amanda, was human, and his father, Sarek, a Vulcan diplomat. His dual nature caused him difficulty as a child. Torn between the two cultures, this struggle has defined his life.

At the age of seven, Spock was "telepathically bonded" to a Vulcan girl, T'Pring, who was to be his mate. (Evidently, it's harder to get out of that than it is to get a divorce in Italy.) Spock is forced by his body chemistry to return to Vulcan and mate, or die trying, once every seven years. Spock had a pet sehlat (like a big dog) named I'Chaya, that died when he was young. The death of his pet helped Spock decide to follow the Vulcan path of logic. Spock is the first Vulcan to join Starfleet. He worked with Christopher Pike, the prior captain of the *Enterprise,* for eleven years before becoming Kirk's first officer.

Spock joined Starfleet over his father's objections: Sarek wanted his son to be a scientist, and the two wouldn't speak to each other for eighteen years over the matter. (Spock had a half-brother, named Sybok, who rejected logic as a way of life. He later got his in *Star Trek V: The Final Frontier.*) Eventually Spock and Sarek were reconciled.

Spock became devoted to Kirk and McCoy during his tour of duty aboard the *Enterprise.* The bond among these three is so strong that they are, in many ways, a family. Many enemies have tried to divide them, and all have failed.

KEY SPOCK EPISODES

"The Naked Time" A virus infects the crew of the *Enterprise* and Spock reveals the pain he carries due to not being able to display emotion. We learn that Spock looks weird when he cries.

"Amok Time" Spock experiences *Pon farr,* the Vulcan drive to mate. Because of the treachery of his betrothed, Spock must fight Kirk and apparently kills him. When it turns out Kirk is not dead, Spock displays joy and surprise, an uncharacteristic reaction for a Vulcan. We learn that even Vulcans get horny.

"The Galileo Seven" Spock commands a shuttlecraft mission that crash-lands on a planet populated by hostile giants. Spock must find a way off the planet, and learns about his ability to command.

"The *Enterprise* Incident" Kirk apparently loses his sanity, ordering the *Enterprise* into the forbidden territory of the Romulan Empire. Intercepted by the Romulans, it appears that Spock has killed the irrational Kirk and become emotionally stirred by the beautiful Romulan commander. But our boys Spock and Kirk were faking in order to steal Romulan technology. Psych!

"Journey to Babel"   Spock's parents, Ambassador Sarek and Amanda, appear on the *Enterprise* for an interstellar conference. Sarek has a heart attack, and Spock donates his own blood for the operation. Sarek recovers and reconciles with his son.

"All Our Yesterdays"   Spock and McCoy go back five thousand years to a planet's ice age. Spock begins to revert to the barbaric ways of his ancestors, and he gets lucky with the only woman on the planet. However, McCoy ruins it by making him come back to the present.

THE MOVIES

After the five-year mission of the original show, Spock returned to Vulcan to pursue the Kolinahr—a ritual through which Vulcans can achieve pure logic. However, the V'Ger space probe headed for Earth disturbed his emotions, and he rejoined the crew of the *Enterprise*. After saving Earth (again), Spock remained at Starfleet headquarters and was promoted to Captain. (The first time the words "Captain Spock" were uttered on-screen, you could hear the muted laughter of Trekkers in the audience.)

Spock was killed in 2285 while saving the *Enterprise* from the explosion of the Genesis Device. Spock's killer, Khan Noonien Singh, a tyrant from the late twentieth century, was on a vendetta against Kirk. Spock received a military funeral, and his body was ejected into space in a torpedo tube. Somehow the tube soft-landed on the Genesis Planet (which had been formed by the above-mentioned Genesis Device), and Spock's body came back to life (hence the term *genesis*).

Around this time, McCoy began acting logical, suspiciously like Spock, and it was soon discovered that, right before his death, Spock had placed his *katra* (spirit) into the doctor's mind. Kirk stole the *Enterprise* to get to the Genesis Planet, and was successful in bringing both Spock's mind and body to Vulcan. There, Spock was reunited with his mind by the *fal-tor-pan* (refusion) process. Spock suffered no ill effects except that for a short time he became a liberal. Spock entered a period of reeducation, and was better able to reconcile his human and Vulcan halves. He remained devoted to Kirk and the crew of the *Enterprise.*

THE NEXT GENERATION

Spock's work grew more diplomatic as time went on. As a special envoy to the Klingon government, he helped develop the peace treaty between the Klingons and the Federation. Much later, Spock secretly infiltrated the Romulan Empire, working toward reuniting that empire with the planet Vulcan (see "Romulans," "Vulcans" in chapter 8). Spock's father, Sarek, died without saying goodbye to his son. But before Sarek died, he mind-melded with Picard. Spock later met Captain Picard and mind-melded with him, experiencing Sarek's emotions for his son. (As you can tell, Picard has had almost as many extrasensory episodes as Shirley MacLaine.) As of this writing, Ambassador Spock's whereabouts are unknown.

LEONARD H. "BONES" McCOY
(DeFOREST KELLEY)
In a Nutshell

- ❏ McCoy is the *Enterprise's* chief medical officer, and is a deeply emotional man. He is well loved by Trekkers for uttering such emphatic lines as "He's dead, Jim," and "I'm a *doctor,* not a (bricklayer, soldier, seamstress, etc.)."
- ❏ McCoy is a self-proclaimed "old-fashioned country doctor." He distrusts technology, transporters in particular.
- ❏ McCoy and Spock bicker endlessly. McCoy finds Spock's reliance on logic infuriating. However, deep down he feels great affection for the Vulcan.

ABOUT LEONARD H. McCOY

McCoy was born in 2227, making him only three years older than Spock. At some point, he became romantically involved with a woman named Nancy Crater. (Years later, on a distant planet, he believed he encountered her. It turned out to be a salt-sucking monster merely imitating her. This is an example of how truly bad this guy's love life is.) McCoy's father, David, suffered from an incurable disease, and McCoy mercifully ended his father's life. Shortly afterward, a cure for his father's condition was discovered, and McCoy felt guilty about his death for years.

KEY MCCOY EPISODES

"The Man Trap"   McCoy is reunited with an old girlfriend on a distant planet, but she turns out to be a salt-sucking monster. He kills the creature, who was on the verge of killing Kirk.

"For the World Is Hollow, and I Have Touched the Sky"   McCoy is diagnosed with an incurable disease and finds he has one year to live. At the same time, the crew of the *Enterprise* discovers a civilization living inside a spaceship disguised as an asteroid. McCoy falls in love with Natira, the leader of this civilization. He marries her and decides to resign from Starfleet and live out his life with the Queen Babe. However, Spock finds a cure for the disease in the alien spaceship, and McCoy rejoins the crew.

"Spock's Brain"   Aliens steal Spock's brain. An alien computer turns McCoy into a superdoctor, and he puts Spock's brain back where it belongs. Before McCoy can resign and open up a Park Avenue practice, he forgets all the knowledge he gained. (Most graduate students find this to be their favorite episode, for obvious reasons.)

THE MOVIES

After the five-year mission, McCoy resigned from Starfleet and grew a beard. He came back to the *Enterprise* at Kirk's behest in *Star Trek: The Motion Picture*. He didn't have much to do until Spock stuck his *katra* into McCoy's brain before his death. McCoy retained Spock's spirit until he took part in the Vulcan ritual for transferring Spock's consciousness. It is unclear whether there was a rental fee for the use of McCoy's body.

McCoy didn't have much to do after that either until he and Kirk were convicted falsely by the Klingons for murder and sentenced to a penal colony on an inhospitable planet. Eventually he became an admiral, and lived to be at least 137 years old. He appeared on the very first episode of *Star Trek: The Next Generation,* when he toured the fifth Starship *Enterprise* and united the old crew with the new. Given his advanced age, it is unlikely his love life will improve in future episodes.

MONTGOMERY "SCOTTY" SCOTT (JAMES DOOHAN)

In a Nutshell

- ❑ Scotty is the chief engineer aboard the original *Enterprise.* He was so resourceful in the position he became famous as a "miracle worker." He is well-loved by Trekkers for proclaiming "I can't change the laws of physics. I've got to have thirty minutes!" and "I've got to have more power!"
- ❑ Scotty is Scottish. He loves to drink, especially Scotch.
- ❑ If there is a technological trick that needs to be pulled off so the plot can proceed, Scotty's the one to do it.
- ❑ Scotty loves the *Enterprise.* I mean, really *loves* it.

Scotty's personality is well defined but hasn't grown much during the years (as opposed to his weight, which has grown considerably). Basically, he's in love with the ship, maybe even more than Kirk is. He knows the *Enterprise* inside out, and he is always capable of tweaking a little more warp speed out of her, or fixing the transporter at the last minute. For example, once, when the ship's engines were pushed too far, Scotty cried "My bairns, my poor bairns." (*Bairns* means "children" in Gaelic.)

Scotty was once tried for murder on a distant planet. He remembered nothing about what happened, but it turned out he was possessed by an alien being who had been none other than Jack the Ripper. He fell in love once, with a woman named Mira Romaine, but that woman ended up being possessed by an alien entity. Later, in the movie series, he seemed to be falling for Lieutenant Uhura, but that was because their minds were possessed by Sybok, Spock's half-brother. Whoever said that falling in love messes with your mind was thinking about Scotty.

He made a pretty smooth transition to *Next Generation*. On his way to a retirement colony, his ship crash-landed on a huge alien construct called a Dyson sphere. He survived by jury-rigging the transporter to keep him in suspended animation for over seventy years until Picard's crew found him. He annoyed the *Next Generation's* crew for a whole hour before they gave him a shuttlecraft to call his own. As we last saw him, he was out there somewhere in a faster-than-light minivan, probably hopping from one interstellar trailer park to another.

HIKARU SULU (GEORGE TAKEI)

In a Nutshell

- ❑ Sulu was a helmsman of the original *Enterprise*.
- ❑ He has a lot of hobbies, including botany and old handguns. (Yeah, like those go together.)
- ❑ He displayed great loyalty for Kirk, often risking his career for his captain.

Sulu didn't do much on the *Enterprise* but steer the ship. He was very loyal to the captain, but spent most of the time staring at the viewscreen, gaping at the weird outer space phenomenon of the week.

After the series, Sulu's big claim to fame is that he became captain of the *Excelsior*, a more advanced starship than the original *Enterprise*. In *Star Trek VI: The Undiscovered Country* he played a key role in saving the peace negotiations with the Klingons. In addition, Sulu is the only member of the original crew that has made an appearace on *Star Trek: Voyager*. That's got to be worth something.

PAVEL A. CHEKOV (WALTER KOENIG)

In a Nutshell

- ❑ Chekov is of Russian descent. You can tell by the strong Russian accent he has. For example, "vessel" becomes "wessel."

❏ But strangely enough, "warp" becomes "varp."
❏ "Captain" becomes "Kepten."

Chekov was an ensign aboard the original *Enterprise,* which was his first assignment in Starfleet. He took great pride in being Russian, often claiming something was invented in Russia even if it wasn't.

After the series, Chekov became a lieutenant. He was assigned to another ship, then returned to the *Enterprise.* I can't think of anything else to say about him.

LIEUTENANT UHURA (NICHELLE NICHOLS)

In a Nutshell

❏ Uhura is the communications officer for the original *Enterprise.* Basically, she was the office secretary.
❏ Her name means "freedom" in Swahili.
❏ Her mind was once completely erased by a space probe and she had to learn how to say "hailing frequencies open, sir" all over again.

Uhura is a cool character, but unfortunately the writers never knew what to do with her. She has great strength and screen presence. (On a separate historical note, Uhura and Kirk were once forced to kiss by beings who controlled them telepathically. This was the first interracial kiss on television. The fact that they did it against their will was one of those tricks writers use to bring progress to television.)

After the series, Uhura and Scotty had some kind of fling. Thankfully, it was never fully exposed. Trekkers didn't want to know about it.

SECONDARY CHARACTERS

These are people who appeared from time to time, but didn't affect the series.

NURSE CHRISTINE CHAPEL (MAJEL BARRETT)

Chapel was the nurse aboard the original *Enterprise,* and was in love with Spock. She became a physician aboard the *Enterprise* in the first movie, but then moved to Starfleet Command and did something there regarding emergency operations. (Chapel was played by Majel Barrett, Roddenberry's wife, who was Number One in the first Trek pilot. She later played Lwaxana Troi on *Next Generation,* and was the voice of the computer on that show.)

YEOMAN JANICE RAND (GRACE LEE WHITNEY)

Rand was Captain Kirk's gorgeous blond assistant. After the series, she became Sulu's communications officer on the *Excelsior.*

HARCOURT FENTON "HARRY" MUDD (ROGER C. CARMEL)

An interstellar trader, Harry Mudd was a con man, liar, and thorn in the side of the crew. He once gave a drug to women to make them seem more beautiful (the Venus drug) and tried to sell the women as wives to space settlers. He also commanded a race of androids for a short time. He had a big handlebar mustache and an unctuous personality.

TOS CHARACTERS QUIZ

1. James Kirk received a commendation for original thinking in the Academy for what reason?

   a. He slept with the dean's wife
   b. He slept with the president's wife
   c. He slept with his professor
   d. He cheated on his final exam

2. An enemy possesses knowledge of a secret plan to sabotage important peace talks. How does Spock obtain this knowledge?

   a. By tickling him
   b. By asking politely
   c. With the Vulcan mind-meld
   d. By pretending he doesn't care

3. Every seven years, what must Spock do?

   a. Clean his quarters

    b. Write his parents
    c. Get a date
    d. Study for exams

ANSWERS

    1, d; 2, c; 3, c.

5

THE CHARACTERS—
STAR TREK: THE NEXT GENERATION

When talking about *Star Trek: The Next Generation*, Trekkers say "TNG."

Although the crew of *The Next Generation* obviously paralleled the crew of the original *Enterprise*, obvious differences make *Next Generation* an altogether different (and some say better) program. Primarily, it is the captain of the new *Enterprise* who stands out as a departure from the classic series. Capt. Jean-Luc Picard is as different from James T. Kirk as you can get. (Well, Woody Allen as commander of a starship would be even more different, but you'd still have the problem with female aliens.)

JEAN-LUC PICARD (PATRICK STEWART)

In a Nutshell

- ❏ Picard is a renaissance man. He is an intellectual, and less of a risk-taker than Kirk. Picard has never been married, has no children, and does not enter into relationships with women lightly. He likes to say "Make it so" when giving orders. Maybe that's why he's not married.
- ❏ Picard has had a long smoldering affection for Dr. Beverly Crusher.
- ❏ Picard's hobbies are archaeology, horsemanship, music, and anything else you can think of. He knows everything about everything.
- ❏ The greatest tragedy in Picard's life was his abduction by the Borg. The Borg transformed Picard into Locutus and used him as their spokesman. They assimilated him into their collective and forced him to help the Borg destroy much of Starfleet.

Played by Shakespearean actor Patrick Stewart, Jean-Luc Picard is the captain of the *Enterprise*-D, the fifth starship to bear the *Enterprise* name. Noted throughout the universe as a scholar, scientist, and diplomat, Picard started out on *Next Generation* as a stern, intellectual, aging captain, and ended up in the seventh season as a stern, intellectual, aging sex symbol. The popularity of Picard's character is remarkable considering what a hard-core intellectual he is. A member of a proud family, Picard has an aristocratic, elite air about him, as opposed to Kirk, the boy from Iowa. While Kirk would be willing to destroy the *Enterprise* to keep some alien from getting ahold of *his* ship, Picard is more willing to destroy the *Enterprise* to make a philosophical point.

ABOUT JEAN-LUC PICARD

Jean-Luc Picard is from France, yet he speaks with a distinctly British accent. No explanation has yet been provided for this incongruity.* He was born on Earth, in France, in the year 2305. Picard's family has owned an extensive vineyard for generations, and Jean-Luc was raised on this family property. His father eschewed technology and disapproved of Jean-Luc's intention to join Starfleet. Jean-Luc's brother, Robert, was very old-fashioned, and he took over the responsibility for running the farm while Jean-Luc went gallivanting around the universe. Robert deeply resented Jean-Luc for this. They did, however, make peace before Robert died. (He was killed along with his son in a fire at the vineyard.) Your Trekker will love you if you use the pretentious French pronunciation that Jean-Luc does: Ro-Bear.

Jean-Luc applied to Starfleet Academy when he was seventeen but was rejected. He applied again a year later and was accepted. Of course Jean-Luc excelled, winning top academic honors.† He was the only freshman to win the Academy marathon on Danula II. At

---

*I can guess at one, however. It would sound really stupid for a captain to have an outrageous French accent.

†I wonder what happens to those cadets who graduate at the bottom of the academy's class. Do they run tour starships and ferries? "Over here on your left you'll see where the infamous Khan tried to kill Admiral Kirk. Now over here…"

the academy, Picard committed some serious offense of an unknown nature, and his career in Starfleet was saved by Boothby, the Academy groundskeeper. Boothby is a wise man of some sort, and supposedly knows everything that's going on at the Academy. Of course, he's not smart enough to get a better job than groundskeeper, but that's another story.

Tragedy struck Picard shortly after graduation. During a fight with some Nausicaans (a particularly aggressive alien species), one of the combatants stabbed Picard in the back. The blade went through his torso, piercing his heart and coming out his chest. Picard received an artificial heart, and it's fairly reliable. (It requires service once in a while, and one time it nearly killed him.) This brush with death changed Picard irrevocably. Before being skewered, Jean-Luc was an arrogant, promiscuous man, much like Jim Kirk. Afterward, however, he became more responsible and logical. (Nothing like a good stake in the heart to remind you of your priorities.)

Picard eventually rose to lieutenant on the U.S.S. *Stargazer*. The ship's captain was killed in action, and Picard took command, saving his ship. Starfleet made him captain. He remained in command of the *Stargazer* for twenty years and looks back on these years fondly. The *Stargazer* experienced what turned out to be the Federation's first contact with an alien race known as the Ferengi. A Ferengi Marauder (a type of ship) attacked the *Stargazer*, damaging it severely. Picard saved the day through an inventive technique which later became known as the "Picard Maneuver." (Wipe that dirty smirk off your face.) His heroism became legend through the Federation. When the *Enterprise*-D, a *Galaxy*-class starship (one of the largest and most advanced in Starfleet), was commissioned, she was given to Picard.

KEY PICARD EPISODES

"The Naked Now"   Basically, the same episode as "The Naked Time" from the original show. The same disease causes the new crew to lose control of their emotions. Picard's feelings for Beverly Crusher are strongly hinted at.

"The Best of Both Worlds"   In this two-part cliffhanger, Picard is kidnapped by the evil Borg, who assimilate him and use his knowledge to bring the Federation to its knees. They even gave him a name, Locutus, which they sometimes use when they refer to him.

"Family" Picard goes home to France to recuperate from his terrifying experience with the Borg. He breaks down during a fight with his brother Robert. Picard, in tears, confesses that he was helpless to stop the Borg. *Star Trek* fans everywhere cry with him.

"Reunion" The dying Klingon leader chooses Picard to arbitrate who will be his successor. Picard becomes an alien umpire and is thus linked to a growing civil war within the Klingon civilization.

"Unification" In this two-parter, Picard and Spock meet. Picard allows Spock to mind-meld with him, granting Spock knowledge of his father's love for him. (Sarek and Picard mind-melded before Sarek died.) *Star Trek* fans kvell at seeing Picard and Spock link minds.

"The Inner Light" One of the big ones. An alien probe knocks Picard unconscious. Although only a few minutes pass, Picard is experiencing an entire life as a man named Kamin. The probe turns out to be from a long-dead planet, and this was the dead civilization's way of preserving the memory of their lives. So Picard lives thirty years in the space of a few minutes. At this point, fans are asking, how much more can this guy take?

"Chain of Command" Yet another two-parter in which Picard is captured and tortured by Cardassians. The lead interrogator wants to break Picard's will, and tries to force Picard into admitting that he sees five lights before him when there are only four. Picard screams, "There are four lights!" thereby frustrating his interrogator. In the end, he admits to Riker that he did indeed see what he was told to see: five lights on the wall. Picard, our man of action, is only human.

"Tapestry" The omnipotent Q allows Picard to re-live his life, and Picard chooses to avoid being stabbed in the heart in a fight as a cadet at the Academy. When Q returns him to his "new" present, Picard learns that the circumstances of his life have changed. As a junior lieutenant in Astrophysics, he doesn't have the character necessary for command. It seems that Picard's impetuous youth formed an essential part of his personality, without which he would not have been the same. Picard asks for, and receives, his old life back. This is *Star Trek*'s homage to *It's a Wonderful Life,* and Trekkers imagined Picard running through the decks shouting "Merry Christmas, Mr. Potter!"

PICARD'S RELATIONSHIPS WITH WOMEN: FEW AND FAR BETWEEN

Picard's a tough character. What type of woman could keep up with him? She's got to be beautiful, intelligent, accomplished, aloof, and completely devoted to him. In short, she's that girl your mother's been telling you she wants to fix you up with. Over the years, Picard has fallen for a few women, and when he has he's fallen hard.

In the first season we learned of a woman named **Jenice Manhelm**. She and Picard were in love a long time ago, and their relationship ended when Picard stood her up in Paris to sign up with Starfleet. She later married a scientist at a distant outpost, where she and Picard ran into each other again. They reminisced, and finally kept their date in Paris via the holodeck (see chapter 9).

Dr. Beverly Crusher and Jean-Luc have had a smoldering affection for one another for a long time. Picard fell in love with Beverly when they met early in their careers, but he never revealed it to her, because she was in love with, and married to, Jack Crusher, Picard's best friend. (You see, another example of the difference between Picard and Kirk. What would Jim Kirk have done in this situation?) Jack Crusher was killed, and Picard continued a platonic relationship with Beverly out of respect. Beverly later learned of Picard's feelings, and it turned out that they were mutual. However, the two are now just close friends.

Vash (her name sounds like she's a pretentious supermodel, doesn't it?) is a beautiful archaeologist-renegade whom Picard fell for on Risa, the pleasure planet. Vash is a female Indiana Jones and there is something untrustworthy about her. Picard and Vash had a brief fling and parted friends. Vash later joined Q in his travels across the universe.

Kamala wins the "Most Difficult Woman to Get Over" award. An alien humanoid, Kamala was an "empathic metamorph." This means that she was able to find out which type of woman a man likes the most, and then take on those characteristics. Oh, man, was this breakup tough. Picard spent a lot of time with her and as a result she permanently became the kind of woman Picard most desired. Ironically, it was only because she had become noble and duty-driven, like Picard, that she was able to enter into a loveless marriage in order to end an interplanetary war. If Picard ever stays up late at night thinking about a woman, my guess is he's thinking about Kamala.

Lt. Comdr. Neela Daren, a stellar cartographer and music enthusiast onboard the *Enterprise*-D played duets with Picard, she on piano, he on Ressikan flute. Picard gradually fell in love with her. When he was reluctant to send her on a dangerous mission, he realized that his objectivity as captain was jeopardized by their relationship. Neither wanted to abandon their careers, so Neela transferred off the ship.

Of course, for pure type-A personalities, it's hard to beat the **Borg Queen.** The leader of the evil, powerful Borg, the Queen had a thing for Picard (Locutus) and was extremely angry that he rejected her by fighting the Borg. She was most notable for being half woman, half machine, but without her lower mechanical half, she's sort of a drag to have around.

The Movies

Picard, who thought his brother would be able to carry on the family name, must now come to terms with his brother's death and the fact that there will be no more Picards after him. Picard's decision to pursue his Starfleet career and not marry has weighed heavily upon him. In *Star Trek: Generations,* his deepest longings were fulfilled when Picard was pulled into the Nexus. While in the Nexus, Picard experienced how it would feel to have the perfect family, all happily devoted to him. It took great strength of character to reject this fantasy.

It was in the Nexus that Kirk and Picard met. Picard rejected the perfect fantasy the Nexus created for him and helped Captain Kirk reject his. They teamed up to fight the evil Dr. Soren, and Kirk died as a result of that struggle.

Picard is haunted by his experience with the Borg. In the eighth film (the first to exclusively showcase the new crew), *Star Trek: First Contact*, Picard sensed the coming Borg invasion, and realized he still has a telepathic link with Borg. Picard's hatred for the Borg is so deep that at times his judgment suffers. When the Borg seized control of the *Enterprise*-E, he refused to admit defeat by ordering the ship to self-destruct, preferring to continue fighting them in a quixotic attempt at revenge. Luckily, Picard recovered his wits. He used his intimate knowledge of the Borg Queen (who wanted Locutus-Picard as a mate!) to defeat her. (And thankfully before she was able to realize her ultimate plan: to assimilate Pauly Shore and use him to destroy Earth's civilization.)

WILLIAM THOMAS RIKER
(JONATHAN FRAKES)

In a Nutshell

❏ Riker is Kirk of *The Next Generation*. *Quien es mas macho*, Kirk or Riker? *No se.*
❏ He is very popular with women. He likes to tell jokes and plays the trombone. His trombone playing is a joke in and of itself.
❏ He had a long-time, heavy affair with Counselor Troi.

Riker is an officer who likes to do things in an unorthodox fashion. He is the first officer, the "Number One" under Jean-Luc Picard on the *Enterprise* D and E. Devoted to Picard, he has repeatedly given up chances for a command of his own in order to stay on the *Enterprise*. He raises his voice frequently. Emotional and impulsive, he is the anti-Picard. (During the second season, Riker grew a beard. This beard is a clear signal to *Star Trek* fans: if Riker has the beard, the episode is worth watching. If he doesn't, it's a first-season episode, and you should change the channel.) Riker is a man of action, a man whose good sense of humor contributes to his popularity with the crew.

ABOUT RIKER

Born in Alaska, Riker comes from a damaged family. His mother died when he was two, and his father abandoned him when he was fifteen. Riker's bitterness toward his father helped push him into a Starfleet career. Riker graduated near the top his class from the Academy, and upon graduation was assigned to a ship called the *Pegasus*. That ship suffered a mutiny because the vessel was testing a top-secret cloaking device. (Remember, it's a violation of the Federation's treaty with the Romulans for a Federation ship to have a cloaking device.)

Early in his career, Riker was stationed on the planet Betazed, where he met Counselor Deanna Troi. They fell in love and she was disappointed when he chose to make his career a priority.

Riker's biggest crisis, strangely enough, *is* his career. He has been the first officer on the *Enterprise* for the entire seven years of the TV show and in two movies. He is highly regarded within Starfleet, especially since he defeated the Borg. In fact, they want to give him his own ship. Starfleet has pulled out the captain's chair for him at least three times, but he won't sit down. They are starting to wonder about him. It's likely he's holding out for command of the *Enterprise,* but it's also likely that Jean-Luc will continue to be the captain for at least another three movies. Who knows? Maybe Riker's personality will undergo some kind of rebirth. It's happened before. Actually, there are now two Rikers floating around the *Star Trek* universe.

During a mission to an alien world an exact "copy" of Riker was created. This copy was found years later, living alone on the same deserted planet. Neither the copy nor the original knew about the other. The copy Riker was beamed up and immediately started sleeping with Deanna. The original Riker was perplexed. Could he be jealous of himself? Should he punch himself out? Shouldn't he at least be allowed to watch? Calling himself Thomas Riker, the copy went off on his own and joined the Maquis, a splinter resistance group within the Federation. (Thomas Riker later stole the U.S.S. *Defiant* and attacked the Cardassians. He was sentenced to life in prison on Cardassia.)

You might think that Riker's copy has a more interesting life than Riker does. You're absolutely right. (However, Jonathan Frakes has had plenty to do: He was the director of *Star Trek: First Contact.*) Look for future events concerning Riker's twin.

KEY RIKER EPISODES

"Hide and Q"   The omnipotent Q tempts Riker by giving him godlike powers. Riker offers the crew their fondest wishes, but they turn him down, affirming their humanity.

"11001001"   Riker falls in love with Minuet, a holodeck character. Her program gets erased, and he feels the same dejection your Trekker would feel if you erased his only copy of "Bikini Vixens From Outer Space."

"A Matter of Honor"   In an interstellar exchange program, Riker becomes the first officer on a Klingon vessel. He gets to eat live worms and beat up a Klingon.

"The Best of Both Worlds"   Riker takes command of the *Enterprise* in the fight against the Borg. He outmaneuvers Locutus (Picard under the influence of the Borg), and saves the galaxy. Riker gives up his three hundredth chance for a ship of his own, and everyone thinks he's nuts.

"The Outcast"   Riker meets Soren, a member of a race with no gender. Riker's sexuality is so compelling, however, that Soren admits to having feminine feelings toward him, which is a crime, since her race has outlawed gender identification. Her feelings are discovered by her people, and they force her to undergo "reeducation." She asks Riker if they can just be friends. Riker loses her phone number.

THE MOVIES

Commander Riker shows up for the movies, and that's about it. In *Star Trek: Generations,* he was in command of the *Enterprise* when it was destroyed. In *Star Trek: First Contact,* he got to go along on the first successful warp-drive-powered ship. However, because Frakes directed several *Next Generation* episodes as well as *First Contact,* Riker remains a loved character.

DATA (BRENT SPINER)

In a Nutshell

❑ Data is an incredibly advanced android (robot), so sophisticated that he is regarded as a sentient life-form with full human rights. He has tremendous strength and speed, and doesn't require rest, food, or drink. He has a "positronic brain," which is based on positrons, the opposite of electrons. He is "fully functional," meaning he can have sex. His life span is measured in millennia.

❏ Much of Data's effort throughout the series has been directed toward becoming more "human." He mimics human behavior as closely as possible in order to help himself reach this goal. This means he can have sex.

❏ Data has recently acquired emotion and is still learning how to cope with it. Emotion has interfered with Data's ability to carry out his duties, but luckily he is able to turn it on and off at will. This means he can have sex.

ABOUT DATA

Data was built on a distant planet by the brilliant scientist Noonien Soong in the year 2336. (Of course he's a brilliant scientist; sentient androids are rarely created by mediocre scientists.) Data was underground when the population of the planet was destroyed by a creature called the Crystalline Entity, and he was found later by a starship crew. (The Crystalline Entity looks like a huge malevolent snowflake that sucks all the life out of a planet. It sounds funny until you see one of these things.) Since Starfleet officers rescued him, Data showed his gratitude by attending Starfleet Academy.

Data was the second android built by Soong. The first, Lore, was unstable and had to be dismantled. This "brother" of Data's returned several times to cause trouble for the crew of the *Enterprise*. Data and Lore are identical in appearance: that is, they both look just like Dr. Soong, who built them in his image. Because Data is a machine, he is susceptible to alien computer programs that rewrite software. Because he has biological components, some viruses can affect him.

On the *Enterprise*, Data mans the position at Operations (Ops) that coordinates the various departments of the vessel. The *Enterprise* is Data's first assignment.

KEY DATA EPISODES

Data's evolution has taken many turns. More episodes have involved Data than any other member of the crew. However, some stand out as benchmarks in the development of this favorite character.

"Datalore" Data's evil brother Lore appears for the first time. A really evil guy, Data beams him out into space.

"The Measure of a Man" A scientist from Starfleet wants to dissect Data to find out how he works. Data doesn't like the idea. A hearing commences to determine whether Data can refuse to be dismantled. Picard argues for Data, claiming he's a life-form, and Riker is forced to try to prove that Data is simply a machine. You don't need me to tell you how this one turns out.

"The Most Toys" A ruthless collector, Kivas Fajo, kidnaps Data and places him in his collection of rare valuables. He forces Data to submit by threatening to kill his own assistant, whom Data has befriended. Data is saved, but so is the collector, because Data was about to kill him. We learn that Data is capable of murder.

"Brothers" Data malfunctions and hijacks the *Enterprise* to a distant planet. He was responding to his creator, Dr. Noonien Soong, who sent a recall signal. Lore, Data's brother, returns as well. Soong had designed a computer chip for Data that would give him emotions, but Lore secretly takes Data's place and fools Soong into giving the chip to him. Lore attacks Soong and kills him.

"The Offspring" Data creates Lal, a female android based on his structure. Lal (a Hindi word for *beloved*) is his "child." Lal begins to develop emotions, something Data was never able to do, but Lal malfunctions and dies. Data absorbs Lal's memories into his positronic brain, letting her "live" forever as a part of him.

"Redemption, Part II" Data takes command of the U.S.S. *Sutherland*, a really cool *Nebula*-class starship. He encounters anti-android bigotry from his first officer, but wins the crew over by thinking on his feet.

"Descent" Lore returns in this two-part episode commanding a contingent of renegade Borg. Lore uses the stolen emotion chip to give Data little bursts of emotion and tempt Data into joining him. After Lore is defeated and disassembled, Data obtains the emotion chip. Data wants to destroy it, but his friend Geordi convinces him to keep it.

"Birthright" Data finds he has the ability to dream. His creator designed a "dreaming program," to be activated at a certain point in his development. Data dreams of Dr. Soong as a blacksmith forging a metal bird, and Soong whispers, "Data, you are the bird." Fans all over the world get goose pimples.

THE MOVIES

In *Star Trek: Generations,* Data decided to implant the emotion chip into his brain. It worked. However, Data was overcome by the flood of emotions, and it interfered with his ability to do his duty on the *Enterprise.* (Picard actually called Data on the carpet for it.) By the time *First Contact* was released, Data was able to turn the emotion chip off at will.

Data was captured by the Borg in *First Contact.* The Borg Queen tempted Data with humanity by grafting human skin onto his android exoskeleton. Data told the captain later on that he had been tempted to join the Borg for .069 seconds, which, for an android, is an eternity. However, Data fooled the Borg Queen into believing that he would join her, then turned on her, thus saving Earth from being assimilated by the Borg.

WORF (MICHAEL DORN)
In a Nutshell

❏ Worf is a Klingon (a hyperaggressive alien race). Take Kirk Douglas, subject him to testosterone injections for ten years, and then give him forehead ridges. That's Worf.

❏ Worf is the first Klingon to serve in Starfleet and is an important figure in Klingon politics. He has struggled to strike a balance between his Klingon nature and his relationships with humans. Finding a mate is a challenge because Worf likes his women sturdy.

❏ Worf started out on the *Enterprise*-D and then became second in command on *Deep Space Nine.* At the station, Worf likes to stay near the U.S.S. *Defiant,* a tough warship prototype. He's been known to sleep onboard.

❏ Worf likes prune juice and likes to sing Klingon opera, which is really bad opera. He is an expert in combat with the bat'telh (pronounced BAT-leth), a Klingon sword. (He'd be happy drinking prune juice, singing opera, and slicing someone with a bat'telh all at the same time.)

❑ For Worf, honor is everything. If honor required him to bake little finger cakes, he would do it. But he'd do it *honorably*.

What can we say about Worf that wouldn't make him want to beat the living daylights out of us? He has become one the most popular and complex characters in the entire franchise. He began as the flight control officer on the *Enterprise,* then took over as security chief when Tasha Yar was killed. He continued in this position until the *Enterprise* was destroyed. Worf is easily recognized by his forehead ridges, long, flowing hair (in later years), and Klingon bandolier, which he wears over his uniform to proclaim himself a Klingon warrior and honor his heritage.

The episodes featuring his development are among the best ever made. They are also among the most complex, and if you can understand them, you could be a trusts and estates lawyer.

ABOUT WORF

Worf, son of Mogh, was born on the Klingon homeworld Qo'noS, around 2340. As a child, Worf accompanied his parents to the Khitomer Outpost in 2346. The Romulans conducted a sneak attack on Khitomer, and Worf's parents were killed. A Federation starship responded to the massacre, and a human crewman, Sergey Rozhenko, rescued Worf. He and his wife, Helena, adopted Worf and raised him as their own.

Worf grew up on the farm world of Gault, and then moved to Earth. Needless to say, Worf found it difficult to fit in with Terrans (*Star Trek* lingo for "Earthlings"), considering that Klingons are far stronger and more aggressive than humans. When Worf was a child, he was uncontrollable.

At the age of thirteen, Worf accidentally killed a boy during a soccer match. He realized that if he was going to live among humans he would have to learn restraint. This restraint defines him as a character. Since then he has been frightened about losing control and hurting his friends. Worf loves his adoptive parents very much, although their humanity sometimes embarrasses him.

KEY WORF EPISODES

"The Icarus Factor" To help Worf celebrate the ten-year anniversary of his Age of Ascension, the crew sets up a reenactment of the ritual on the holodeck for him. This ritual involves the supplicant being hit with painstiks, which are basically cattle prods. We learn here that being a Klingon is like continually pledging a fraternity.

"The Emissary" K'Ehleyr (Kay-lar), an old flame of Worf's, surprises Worf on the *Enterprise*. They make love and Worf proposes marriage. (He does this in typical Klingon fashion, by screaming.) She turns him down cold.

"Sins of the Father" Worf meets his brother Kurn for the first time and Kurn informs him that the Klingon High Council (the ruling body of the empire) is planning to brand their dead father, Mogh, a traitor. This means that, under Klingon law, Worf and his children will be considered traitors. With Picard as an advocate, Worf returns to the homeworld to confront the council. They learn that it was actually Duras's father who was the traitor and civil war would result if it were found that such a powerful member of the council was a turncoat. Worf drops his challenge in order to protect the Klingon Empire and is cast out from Klingon society.

"Reunion" K'Ehleyr returns, and guess what? Worf's a daddy. His son, Alexander, had been conceived last time K'Ehleyr visited. K'Ehleyr helps expose Duras as the true traitor, and Duras kills her. Worf challenges Duras and kills him. Worf sends Alexander home to be raised by Worf's adoptive parents.

"Redemption" The Klingon Empire is in civil war. Worf resigns from Starfleet to fight on the side of Gowron, the Klingon Emperor. Working with Picard, Worf is able to help Gowron consolidate power.

"New Ground" Worf's son Alexander returns to the *Enterprise* and Worf decides to take a more prominent role in his son's life. Worf wants his son to be a Klingon warrior, but Alexander resists the idea.

"Firstborn" Alexander returns from the future with a terrifying message: he must become a Klingon warrior because in the future, Worf will be killed unless Alexander can prevent it. Worf decides to allow Alexander to develop in his own way and to worry about the future when it comes.

"The Way of the Warrior" (*DS9*)   Worf joins the crew of *Deep Space Nine*. After helping the station fend off the Klingon fleet, Worf is promoted and his career is put on the command track.

"Looking for Par'mach in All the Wrong Places" (*DS9*)   Worf falls for a Klingon woman named Grilka, who rejects him in favor of Quark. Then Worf and Science Officer Jadzia Dax start dating the Klingon way—by beating the hell out of each other.

THE MOVIES

Although Worf was prominent in the battle against the Borg in *Star Trek: First Contact*, he has not grown as a character in the movies. In *Star Trek: Generations*, Worf was promoted to commander. The crew of the *Enterprise* celebrated this on the holodeck by making Worf walk the plank of an old-style sailing vessel. After the *Enterprise*-D was destroyed, Worf considered leaving Starfleet but was talked into joining the crew on *Deep Space Nine*.

WORF ON *DEEP SPACE NINE*: "NOW WILL SOMEONE WATCH THE SHOW?"

Worf climbed aboard *Deep Space Nine* in the double episode "The Way of the Warrior." (*Deep Space Nine*'s ratings needed a lift, and since Worf is so popular, he transferred.) A major shift in the balance of power of the Alpha Quadrant was occurring when the Klingon Empire attacked the Cardassians and it looked as though the Federation was next. They began threatening the station, and Captain Sisko asked for Worf to be transferred to the station as a resource.

Gowron, the Klingon Chancellor, closely tied to Worf from *Next Generation*, invited Worf to join him in his war against the Cardassians. Worf decided to stay with Starfleet and help the station, enraging Gowron. Their friendship ended. In a memorable pitched battle, *Deep Space Nine* fought off a fleet of Klingon warships, thanks to Worf, who decided to stay on the station permanently as second in command.

However, Worf's decision to side with the Federation has haunted him. Gowron took revenge by stripping Worf's family of their lands and titles. Worf's brother Kurn, who still lived in the empire, was disgraced. Kurn came to *Deep Space Nine* because he had nowhere else to go. He wanted to commit suicide over his disgrace, and he asked Worf to help perform the ritual. (Worf, because he loves his brother, started sharpening the Ginsu knives.) The crew intervened before Worf was able to complete the ceremony. They all tried to incorporate Kurn into life on the station, but Kurn was determined to kill himself. Finally, Worf allowed Dr. Bashir to wipe Kurn's memory clean. With his identity erased, he no longer remembered Worf or his family's disgrace. After changing Kurn's name to Rodek, Worf arranged to have him adopted by another Klingon family. Thus, in an act of love and responsibility, Worf's brother is gone. If you see an episode with a Klingon named Rodek, watch carefully because it will be a family reunion episode.

Worf's greatest challenge remains his relationships with other Klingons. Although Worf helped save the Klingon Empire several times, he is still branded a traitor by Gowron, the Klingon Chancellor. Their passionate feud is always a complication in any Federation-Klingon negotiation. Worf and Gowron recently fought a hand-to-hand battle because Worf and the rest of the *DS9* crew believed Gowron to be a changeling. (Changelings are amorphous creatures that can assume any shape, and they are a grave threat to the Alpha Quadrant.) Worf bested Gowron in combat and was about to kill him when Odo interfered, revealing General Martok to be the impostor. Gowron told Worf that he should have killed him when he had the chance. The real General Martok, however, has great respect for Worf, and has embraced him, which means that Worf, son of Mogh, is now a member of Martok's family.

While on *Deep Space Nine,* Worf fell in love with Science Officer Jadzia Dax, and their relationship has only grown stronger. In fact, Jadzia has promised to marry Worf if he returns safely from the latest battles against the Dominion. She created this incentive because Worf, like all Klingons, longs to die honorably in battle.

Like Spock, Worf is torn between two worlds. He wants to be as Klingon as possible, but his human upbringing has conditioned him to human values. So Worf goes on and on about honor and the

Klingon way, but in the end sides with the humans and values his relationships with them. He is a rare, valuable, and endlessly entertaining Federation resource.

DEANNA TROI (MARINA SIRTIS)

In a Nutshell

- ❏ Deanna Troi is half human and half Betazoid. Since Betazoids are telepaths, this means that she has empathic abilities. She is able to feel what others are feeling.
- ❏ Deanna is the ship's counselor, the ship's psychologist.
- ❏ She had a long, intense relationship with Riker before her duty on the *Enterprise*.
- ❏ Trekkers cannot decide who is the more annoying character on the ship: Troi or Wesley Crusher.

Deanna Troi is a nightmarish version of a social worker: she knows what you're feeling before you do. She also has a talent for stating the painfully obvious in virtually every episode she's appeared in. For example: If Picard is negotiating with some alien, she'll often say "I feel he's hiding something, Captain." However, she is a valued crew member and follows the long Starfleet tradition of good-looking officers wearing revealing outfits.

You can find everything you'd want to know about this woman on the Internet because there are plenty of Marina Sirtis–Counselor Troi fan clubs. Primarily a counseling resource, she gives the crew a chance to explain their feelings and motivations. Deanna never fights Klingons or the Borg or carries a phaser or anything. (Actually it would be cool if she did, because then she could blast someone against the wall and ask "How does that make you feel?")

ABOUT TROI

Troi is the product of a marriage between Lwaxana Troi, a Betazoid woman, and Ian Andrew Troi, a human Starfleet officer. Her father died when she was seven years old. As Betazoid culture demands, Deanna was genetically bonded to a Betazoid male named Wyatt Miller when she was a child. She ended up not going through with the marriage because he went off to cure some plague victims.

Troi had an older sister, who died when Troi was a baby. The little girl's death was so traumatic to Lwaxana that she never mentioned the sibling to Deanna. Lwaxana buried the memory so deep that Deanna had to save her mother by mind-melding with her and retrieving it. Yes, Betazoids share the mind-meld ability with Vulcans and God knows how many other races.

Troi has a complicated relationship with her mother. Lwaxana constantly embarrasses Deanna in front of the crew, particularly Picard. See, her mother is a pure Betazoid, and they can read minds. Since her mother has no sense of decorum, hilarity ensues. Lwaxana lusts after Picard deeply, and continually reads his mind and blabs about it to the rest of the crew. You can imagine how much Jean-Luc likes her for this.

Long ago, on Betazed, Deanna fell in love with Riker. He left her for his career, and then paid the price for it by being assigned to the same ship she was. Sometimes they call each other *imzadi*, which is Betazoid talk for "beloved." She loves chocolate. That's about it.

KEY TROI EPISODES

"**Disaster**" Troi loses her empathic powers and feels useless. However, through hard work she is able to remain the ship's counselor. Thus she learns that she doesn't really need her powers to be useful to the crew. She only needs them to be annoying.

"**Dark Page**" Deanna's mother, Lwaxana, falls into a coma. By mind-melding with her, Deanna learns that a section of her mother's memories are being blocked from her conscious mind. Deanna discovers that her mother is racked with guilt over the drowning death of Kestra, Deanna's older sister.

HER RELATIONSHIPS WITH MEN: RIKER VS. WORF

Deanna's stay on the *Enterprise* has been heavily colored by her relationships with Riker and Worf. In the past, Riker chose Starfleet over Deanna, and ending up on the same ship has complicated their duties. However, in true *Star Trek* form, they have refused to allow their feelings to interrupt their responsibilities. They have a friendship of sorts, but they really don't do a lot together. Mostly, they are intensely connected to one another; their past intimacies bind them the way simple friendship could not. It's unclear whether their feelings were ever consummated onboard, but it is very likely that they have experienced some warp core breaches together.

Much weirder is the relationship between Worf and Deanna. Deanna isn't the type of woman you imagine would appeal to a Klingon. She talks about feelings all the time, she doesn't wrestle huge furry creatures to the ground, she doesn't play with knives, and she likes to eat her food *after* it's dead. Yet Worf and Deanna have developed a close and possibly romantic relationship.

Worf's troubles as a single parent brought them together. When Alexander, Worf's son, developed problems adjusting to life on the *Enterprise,* Deanna helped Worf deal with him. Worf asked Deanna to help him raise Alexander, and Deanna became a sort of Klingon Godmother. As the *Next Generation* series wore on, Deanna and Worf became closer and closer. It never really got physical, however, until the very last episode of the series. In an alternate future, Worf and Riker, who are generally friends, began a long feud over Deanna. Worf, honorable as always, asked Riker for permission to date Deanna, and Riker said no. Keep in mind that this alternate future may never occur. In the movie features that have followed the series, the Worf-Deanna story hasn't come up. Since Worf is busy with Dax on *Deep Space Nine,* we must assume they are no longer seeing each other.

Deanna's had other lovers from time to time, but generally they are other telepaths just passing through.

THE MOVIES

Star Trek: First Contact augured a tremendous development in Deanna's life. In terms of relative importance, it rivals the destruction of Starfleet by the Borg. The ramifications of what happened to Deanna may reverberate through the next few movies. It's difficult to know how something this big will play out.

Deanna got drunk on tequila.

Not just drunk, but blitzed, blotto, blind. Falling down, laughing, stupid drunk. Of course, we've never seen her drunk, and Trekkers loved it. Let's just hope that Deanna doesn't become a blowsy old empathic drunk. How annoying would that be? "Oh, leave me alone. I can handle it. I can quit anytime I want. Besides, you're just over-compensating because you haven't come to terms with your mother."

DR. BEVERLY CRUSHER (GATES MCFADDEN)

In a Nutshell

- ❏ Dr. Crusher is the *Enterprise*-D's chief medical officer. She is a humanist; a warm, compassionate presence on the ship. She cares for friend and foe alike and takes her oath as a physician very seriously.
- ❏ She is Wesley Crusher's mother and spent most of her time on the ship worrying about him.
- ❏ Picard and Beverly have a close relationship. They are friends but have much deeper feelings for one another.

Unlike her predecessor, Dr. McCoy, Beverly Crusher is a doctor who actually spends some time in sickbay. You will most often find her there, and if she appears on the bridge it's because something is wrong. Played by Gates McFadden,* with her long, flowing red hair, she is a more easily recognized character. Because of her obvious intelligence and dedication to her patients, Crusher is a favorite of Trekkers. Only problem is, nothing much seems to happen to her.

Oh, sure, she gets chosen for away-team missions, but that's because they need a doctor along. And yes, she gets invited to the senior staff meetings, but that's so she can nag the captain: "But are we doing the right thing?" In terms of dramatic story development, though, Crusher doesn't get the nod. However, she is a more commanding presence than Deanna, so perhaps we will see more of her in films to come.

ABOUT BEVERLY CRUSHER

Dr. Crusher comes from a long line of healers. Her grandmother, although not a physician, taught Crusher about the medicinal uses of

---

*A graduate of Brandeis University, McFadden is among the best educated of the *Enterprise*-D's crew.

roots and herbs. Beverly incorporates that "healer" mentality in dealing with her patients. You often get the feeling that she would be at home running an on-campus college health center.

Crusher's maiden name was Howard, and her female ancestors had some very strange qualities. For generations the Howard women had been romanced by a ghost named Ronin. Ronin entered the women's spirits and made them feel special and loved. It turns out that Ronin was an alien, an "anaphasic" life-form that fed off the life energies of the women. Beverly resisted the alien and destroyed it.

You might notice a wistful, pained quality about the good doctor. This is probably because her husband, Jack Crusher, died years ago, shortly after they were married, leaving her to raise Wesley on her own. Jack served on the *Stargazer* under the command of Jean-Luc Picard, and died while on an away mission. Wesley was five years old at the time.

Beverly is known to her colleagues as the "Dancing Doctor." She is a trained dancer, and she hates her nickname. Yet she ran the *Enterprise*-D's theatrical company, putting on plays like *The Pirates of Penzance*. (Since McFadden was a theater professor at Brandeis, this is a natural role for her.)

Beverly took a leave from the *Enterprise*-D during the second season to become the head of Starfleet Medical on Earth. She was replaced by Dr. Katherine Pulaski. She returned in the third season, but they didn't spend a lot of time explaining why she left Starfleet Medical.

KEY CRUSHER EPISODES

"The Host" Beverly falls in love with Odan, a member of the race known as the Trill. (Worf later is involved with Dax, another Trill, on *DS9*.) However, Odan changes bodies as often as Worf changes his socks, and she is unable to continue a relationship with him (her, it, whatever) when Odan's next host body turns out to be female.

"Attached" Captured by a hostile alien race, Jean-Luc and Beverly have alien devices planted at the bases of their skulls that allow them to share one another's thoughts. It also makes them inseparable, as it causes them to become ill if they walk too far away from one another (also known as "Honeymoonism"). Of course, this leads to the inevitable "I never knew you felt that way about me" conversation.

"Suspicions" Beverly takes a stab at solving a mystery: while a new technology for metaphasic shields is being tested, a scientist dies on the project. Beverly tests the technology herself in a shuttlecraft, and in the process discovers a murder has been committed. This episode gave Beverly a chance to break out of her caregiver role.

"Remember Me" Beverly seems to be the only person left aboard the *Enterprise* after an experiment by Wesley goes awry. Instead of running down the hallways in her underwear singing "Old Time Rock and Roll," Beverly attempts to find out what happened to the crew. It turns out that Beverly is stuck in a static warp bubble that is closing, becoming smaller and smaller. Wesley finally saves his mom from the collapsing miniuniverse, and Beverly grounds her son to this universe until the end of the millennium.

THE MOVIES

It's tough being a single mom on a Federation starship. Wesley was constantly in danger due to his duties as wunderkind on the bridge. After Wesley joined the Traveler on his gallops around the universe, Beverly has more free time on her hands. We have yet to see her use it. She's been present with the crew as they fought the Borg, but the bridge crew has seen much more action. Like Deanna, she's in the background during a fight. She has command experience, however, and we shouldn't count her out for important developments in the future.

GEORDI LA FORGE (LEVAR BURTON)

In a Nutshell

❑ Geordi La Forge is the chief engineer aboard the *Enterprise*-E and held the same position aboard its predecessor, the *Enterprise*-D. Blind from birth, he can be recognized by the visor that he wears, which provides him with superhuman eyesight across the electromagnetic spectrum. (In reality, the visor is a

girl's hair band that LeVar Burton found in a dime store.) In
the movies, his visor has been replaced by ocular implants,
mechanical eyes that provide the same sight.

❑ Geordi is the stereotypical Trekker. He is fascinated by
technology, totally committed to being a goody-goody Starfleet
officer, and can't get a date to save his life.*

❑ Geordi is Data's closet friend.

ABOUT LA FORGE

Born blind, Geordi spent the first five years of his life in darkness.
At age five, he received the VISOR, a remarkable device that
connected to implants in the sides of his head and enabled him to
see. His mother, Silva, was a Starfleet officer, and his father was an
exobiologist. Geordi, like the other members of the *Enterprise's*
crew, graduated from Starfleet Academy.

As his first assignment Geordi ran a shuttle between Jupiter and
Saturn (maybe this is the job you get if you don't graduate near the
top of your class at the Academy). While on an inspection run,
Geordi met Captain Picard. Picard made an offhand remark about
the shuttle's engines being out of whack, and Geordi stayed up all
night fixing the problem. Picard was so impressed that he asked for
Geordi to be assigned to the *Enterprise*-D.

Before joining Picard, La Forge served as an ensign on the U.S.S.
Victory. While on a mission to a strange world, he picked up a virus
which later caused him to transform into an alien and, like a salmon,
to return to the planet.

When he first came on board the *Enterprise*-D, La Forge was the
flight control officer, and steered the ship from his post on the
bridge. Soon he was promoted to lieutenant and became the ship's
chief engineer. He manned that post until the destruction of the
Enterprise-D, and evidently continues as the chief engineer of the
Enterprise-E.

Geordi is close to Data, and whenever Data has a question about
what it's like to be human, he asks Geordi. Data and Geordi are the

---

*Remember, I said "stereotypical" Trekker. As we all know, these stereotypes
have no basis in reality whatsoever.

ship's technogeeks, and they love trying to coax the ship into doing more or figuring out new ways of saving it. Perhaps they are close because whenever Data needs repair work, Geordi opens him up and looks under his hood (so to speak). Geordi talked Data into keeping the emotion chip he recovered from Lore, his evil brother. Later, when Data wanted to experience emotion, Geordi implanted the chip.

KEY LA FORGE EPISODES

"Booby Trap" With the *Enterprise*-D in trouble, La Forge seeks help from the person who created the ship: Dr. Leah Brahms. La Forge activates a holodeck program re-creating Dr. Brahms, and together they find a way to save the *Enterprise*. Of course, Geordi develops a crush on the program's version of Dr. Brahms, and wonders what she would be like in person. Geordi learns how much fun one can have with holodeck programs.

"Galaxy's Child" Geordi finally meets the girl of his dreams, Dr. Leah Brahms. Dr. Brahms turns out to be cold and disdainful of his modifications to "her" *Enterprise*-D. Just as they begin to work well together, she finds the holodeck program of herself that Geordi has been using as a fantasy and goes berserk. Leah tells Geordi that they can never be lovers, but they can be friends. Geordi loses her phone number.

"Aquiel" La Forge falls for Aquiel Uhnari, a Starfleet officer suspected of deserting her post at a deep space relay station and murdering another officer. Aquiel's got a vicious temper, and she was caught tampering with records. The crew fears La Forge is being duped by Aquiel. Although a shape-shifting alien is found to be responsible for the disappearance of the other officer, Aquiel's career is damaged by the allegations. Aquiel leaves the *Enterprise* but returns Geordi's affections. They promise each other to meet again.

"Interface" In this episode, we meet Geordi's father (played by Ben Vereen). The U.S.S. *Hera*, with Geordi's mother in command, is reported lost. While engaged in another rescue mission, Geordi believes that he has seen his mother, but it turns out merely to be pesky aliens impersonating her. (There isn't a person alive who doesn't know what this feels like.)

THE MOVIES

Geordi's visor causes him problems because hostile aliens like to tap into it and gain control of him in one way or another. For example, he was once brainwashed into becoming a Romulan assassin. In the movies it's been no different. In *Generations*, Geordi's visor was indirectly responsible for the destruction of the *Enterprise*. Lursa and B'Etor, the Klingon sisters, kidnapped Geordi and figured out a way to see through his visor. Once they saw the secret frequency of the *Enterprise*-D's shields, they set their photon torpedoes to penetrate them. Without shields, the *Enterprise* was a sitting duck.

The troublesome visor was eliminated in *First Contact*, and Geordi now sports mechanical eyes, which are blue and give him an intense appearance.

WESLEY CRUSHER (WIL WHEATON)

In a Nutshell

☐ Wesley is Dr. Crusher's son. Even though he is a teenager, he has been an acting ensign aboard the *Enterprise*-D and a technological wunderkind. He is much too smart for his own good.

☐ Trekkers cannot decide who is more annoying, Deanna or Wesley.

☐ Wesley eventually transcends simple humanity when he teams up with the Traveler, a godlike being who can manipulate time and space. Wesley learns to activate his own similar powers, and goes off exploring the universe with the Traveler. Since he left, he doesn't write, he doesn't call.…oy!

Wesley Crusher's first appearance on the *Enterprise* worried long-time *Trek* fans. A teenager on the bridge? What could they be thinking? As time went on, Wesley continued to be a controversial figure. Some fans loved him, while some devised ingenious ways of killing him off.

Why such a negative reaction to Wesley? Well, having a genius teenager at the helm can be very annoying. Watching intelligent, accomplished Starfleet officers being outreasoned by a kid whose voice is still cracking from the burdens of adolescence tears Trekkers' hearts out.

It didn't matter that Roddenberry felt that Wesley was the character most like himself. What mattered was that a fifteen-year-old was piloting a *Galaxy*-class starship. Trekkers never got to pilot starships when they were in high school. They wanted to, they prayed for it every night, but all they did was run the Science Fiction Club's slide show.

About Wesley

Being raised without a father is difficult for anyone, but on a starship it is at least doubly so. You're constantly facing danger, your mom's treating wounded in sickbay, and if you break a window you'll get sucked into the vacuum of space and explode. Wesley's father died when Wesley was five years old, but that didn't keep him from becoming the most intelligent, resourceful, mature little doctor's son in Starfleet.

Although Picard now seems a bit more cuddly, at the beginning of *Next Generation* he was not fond of children. He didn't agree with Starfleet's decision to put families onboard, and he really didn't want Wesley on the bridge. But to a technogeek like Wesley, the bridge was like fetish porn. He couldn't stay away. Which meant that every week Wesley had to save the *Enterprise*.

Wesley tried to get accepted into Starfleet Academy when he was fifteen, a relatively early age for a human applicant. Even though he was a child prodigy, way too smart for any kid his age, he didn't make the cut. He stayed onboard, and (get this) he got academic credit for his time spent on the *Enterprise* (another reason for college-age Trekkers to hate him). The following year, Wesley was granted admission to the Academy. Although it looked as though we would finally be rid of him, he missed his transport to the Academy and had to wait another year to enroll.

Picard, in one of his softer moments, had promoted Wesley to acting ensign and made him helmsman. He piloted the ship for a few episodes until a midterm spot opened up at the Academy. Then off he went. You'd think that he'd make a model cadet, a brilliant student-officer. But tragedy marred his first year at the Academy, when he and an elite group of cadets called Nova Squadron tried a complicated space stunt, resulting in the death of a classmate. Although Wesley testified to the truth, he received a reprimand and was forced to repeat his freshman year. (Overachieving Trekkers all over the world smiled.)

Not surprisingly, Wesley soon lost his fascination with Starfleet. He dropped out and visited Mom Crusher on the *Enterprise*. Wesley decided to go off on his own, to seek his own destiny. Picard was very disappointed, especially when Wesley interfered with Picard's mission to resettle a colony. The Traveler then appeared to Wesley, informing him that he was more than just a smart kid; he had the ability to bend space and time. The Traveler offered to help Wesley develop his abilities, and the two of them wandered off into the distance. What could Beverly say— "I want you back in this dimension by dinnertime"?

KEY WESLEY EPISODES

"Final Mission"   Picard and Wesley are stuck on a desert planet, with Picard near death. Does Wesley save him and earn his admiration and gratitude? What do you think?

"The Game"   The entire *Enterprise*-D crew is brainwashed by a video game. Wesley is the last to resist, and it is great fun watching the now-evil crew trying to track him down. Of course he saves the ship.

"Journey's End"   Wesley quits Starfleet. He has a vision of his dead father, Jack Crusher, who tells him to go his own way. Later, the Traveler appears and offers to tutor Wesley in the use of his dormant powers.

SECONDARY CHARACTERS

Here are some people who appeared repeatedly and have important roles.

GUINAN (WHOOPI GOLDBERG)

Guinan is perhaps the most enigmatic member of the *Enterprise*'s crew. She's the bartender of the Ten-Forward lounge. A member of a race called the El-Aurians, known as a "race of listeners," Guinan counsels the crew on subjects ranging from love to liquor. Guinan introduced Worf to prune juice, his favorite drink. She is extremely close to Picard: Their bond, according to her, goes beyond friendship, beyond family. (It is unknown whether she ever lent him money.)

Guinan is hundreds of years old; El-Aurians live much longer than we do. Guinan's people were nearly wiped out by the Borg, but they survived by spreading out across the galaxy. Somehow she found herself on Earth in the year 1893, where she knew Mark Twain, and met the crew of the *Enterprise* when they went back in time to stop a group of aliens from killing people in that time period.

Guinan has been married several times, and has many children. We have never met any of them, but we have heard that one child didn't turn out well because he didn't listen.

She has superhuman abilities. For example, Guinan and Q are bitter enemies. She seems to be the only creature that Q fears. In addition, she has an unusual sense that enables her to tell when a time line is wrong. This is handy in the event an "alternate universe" appears.

Captain Kirk ended up rescuing Guinan from the Nexus, that energy vortex where all your dreams come true. (In Guinan's perfect world, she lives in a round little apartment like the inside of Jeannie's bottle.) On a separate historical note, Whoopi Goldberg says she was inspired to become an actress by Nichelle Nichols, who played Liutenant Uhura in the original series.

NATASHA "TASHA" YAR (DENISE CROSBY)

The first security officer onboard the *Enterprise,* Tasha Yar died during season one. She contributed to the *Star Trek* universe in two ways: she's slept with Data, and she was integral to an alternate universe screwup in the great episode "Yesterday's *Enterprise*" (see chapter 3). Tasha, a tall, athletic blond human, grew up on a wartorn planet, and her parents were killed when she was five. Evading marauding gangs, Tasha cared for her younger sister, Ishara Yar, and eventually escaped as a teenager, finding her way to Starfleet Academy.

LWAXANA TROI (MAJEL BARRETT)

Deanna's mother has appeared on several episodes. A pure Betazoid, she is a telepath. Irresistibly attracted to Picard, she chased him around the *Enterprise* through several episodes, reading his mind and telling everyone about it. She later popped up on *Deep Space 9*, and became romantically involved with Odo, the shape-shifter. She actually married Odo in a ceremony designed to free her from another, less desirable marriage. (It seems they still need divorce lawyers in the twenty-fourth century.)

RO LAREN (MICHELLE FORBES)

A wild card. Born on the planet Bajor, she spent her childhood in prison camps run by the Cardassians, who occupied the planet. Strong-willed and independent, she was disciplined many times as a Starfleet ensign. Although suspicious of her, Picard took her under his wing because he felt she had great promise as an officer. Riker never trusted her, fearing that she would betray Starfleet.

Riker was right. Ro's hatred for the Cardassians who plundered her world was so great that she violated Picard's trust and joined the Maquis, a resistance group within the Federation bitterly opposed to the peace treaty between the Federation and the Cardassians. She quit Starfleet for good, and will be arrested if she is found.

Q (JOHN DELANCIE)

A godlike being, he is a member of the race known as Q. Q lives in the Q Continuum, and is a major troublemaker for the *Enterprise* crew. Q is obnoxious, and uses his powers to play with people's lives for his own amusement. He ushered in the *Next Generation* by putting the crew of the *Enterprise* on trial for being savages. During the last episode Q decided to destroy humanity, but Picard solved a key riddle and proved humanity was worth saving. Q continues to be a factor in the *Star Trek* universe, having appeared on several episodes of *Star Trek: Voyager*.

Without a doubt, Q has had a devastating impact on the Federation. In a fit of pique, he transported the *Enterprise* to a distant part of the galaxy to meet the Borg. This is like introducing your good-looking friend to Don Juan or Sadie Hawkins. Although Q saved the ship just before the Borg could destroy them, it was too late. The Borg had learned of the Federation's existence and came after them, and were barely defeated.

THOMAS RIKER (JONATHAN FRAKES)

As mentioned earlier, Thomas Riker is the duplicate of William Riker. Thomas quit Starfleet and joined the Maquis, and succeeded in stealing the advanced warship *Defiant* from *Deep Space Nine*. He proceeded to kick Cardassian butt with it until he was convinced to give up. Currently he is a prisoner of the Cardassians, and is serving a life sentence.

REGINALD BARCLAY (DWIGHT SHULTZ)

Barclay is a nervous engineer who serves under La Forge. He has an overactive imagination and is one of the only officers we've seen who hasn't come off like some perfect, hyperefficient genius. He lacks confidence, is a hypochondriac, and works with Deanna to try to improve his social skills. Generally a source of unusual events, Barclay has had his IQ temporarily boosted to 1200 by an alien probe, and has also been turned into a man-size spider. Needless to say, he's not a lot of fun at parties.

TNG CHARACTERS QUIZ

1. What was Picard's greatest tragedy?
    a. His abduction by the Borg
    b. His British accent
    c. Being named Jean-Luc
    d. Wesley Crusher

2. What happened to Worf when he reached the Age of Ascension?

   a. His voice changed
   b. He received a Cross pen set from his Tante Ruthie
   c. He walked through a line of Klingons who stuck him with painstiks
   d. He was forced to listen to music by John Tesh

3. What does Worf want his son, Alexander, to become?

   a. A dentist
   b. A doctor
   c. A warrior
   d. A diplomat

4. Why is Data now able to feel overwhelming emotions?

   a. Years and years of therapy
   b. He's just that kind of guy
   c. He majored in English at Brandeis
   d. He implanted the emotion chip designed by his creator

ANSWERS

   1, a; 2, c; 3, c; 4, d.

6

THE CHARACTERS—
STAR TREK: DEEP SPACE NINE

When talking about this series, Trekkers refer to it as *"DS9."*

A show based on a space station is necessarily different from a show set on a starship. Instead of going boldly where no one has gone before, lots of people show up, do some shopping, and leave. *Deep Space Nine* has more of a "neighborhood" feel to it; we get to know the area around the station more than any one area in *Next Generation*. *Deep Space Nine* is composed mostly of non-Federation characters, some of whom are merchants on the station. As such, the story "arcs" are more detailed and less diverse than in previous *Star Treks*. Perhaps this is why the show has not been as popular as *Next Generation*. *Deep Space Nine*'s crew is very different from the two previous shows. Although the ship's commander, Benjamin Sisko, is a man of action like the first two captains, his role onboard the station is more diplomatic and "cultural exchange-y." Sisko walks a tightrope every week and, like a true alpha male, he wins most every time.

BENJAMIN SISKO (AVERY BROOKS)

In a Nutshell

- ❏ Sisko is the commander of Federation Station *Deep Space Nine*, a space station in orbit around Bajor, a planet recently freed from captivity. A widower, he is raising his son, Jake Sisko, alone, and the two are very close. Ben Sisko is *muy macho*.
- ❏ Sisko is a religious figure to the people on Bajor, the planet around which *Deep Space Nine* orbits. They call him "the Emissary."

❑ Sisko is an avid baseball fan. Although baseball is dead in the twenty-fourth century, Sisko likes to attend re-created baseball games on the holodeck.

❑ Sisko...likes...to...pause...before...each...word,...much... like . . . Kirk.

ABOUT SISKO

We know that Sisko's father is a chef who owns a Cajun restaurant in New Orleans. We also know that Sisko, like all good Starfleet captains, graduated from Starfleet Academy. During his youth, Sisko developed a friendship with a Trill named Curzon Dax, a friendship that will last a good part of his life, since that Trill became *Jadzia* Dax, who serves aboard the station as science officer. While at the Academy, he was captain of the wrestling team, which comes in handy for diplomatic dealings with Klingons. After graduation, he met his future wife, Jennifer, at Gilgo Beach on Earth. They had one child together: Jake.

Sisko and his family were assigned to the U.S.S. *Saratoga* when tragedy struck in the form of the Borg. The *Saratoga* was part of the fleet trying to stop the Borg at the Battle of Wolf 359. Led by the altered Picard (Locutus), the Borg destroyed the *Saratoga*. Benjamin was able to get his son into a lifeboat, but he could not reach Jennifer, who was killed. To this day, Sisko harbors a barely restrained hatred for the *Enterprise* captain.

After the *Saratoga* disaster, Sisko was assigned to the Utopia Planitia Fleet Yards on Mars. This design facility was where the *Enterprise*-D was built, along with other types of starships. Sisko worked hard for three years designing a ship that could defeat the immense Borg threat. The result was the *Defiant,* a tough little starship with awesome firepower and maneuverability. Later this ship would be stationed at *Deep Space Nine* to combat the threat posed by the Dominion, yet another awesome threat to the Federation. (If you've noticed, there are a lot of awesome threats to the Federation. This is why we never hear of anyone getting insurance in Federation space.)

After Mars, Sisko was promoted to commander and sent to *Deep Space Nine*. At the time, this was considered a backwater post, almost an insult to Sisko. However, Sisko discovered a stable wormhole, the only one known in the galaxy, nearby, turning *Deep Space Nine* into a key strategic foothold for the Federation.

Sisko was the first to make contact with aliens living in the wormhole (creatively referred to by the crew as the "wormhole aliens"). These formless beings exist in several dimensions simultaneously, and have no concept of linear time: They live in all time periods, and are not aware of chronological time passing. (Some of these aliens work for the Department of Motor Vehicles, and should be referred to as the "Department of Motor Vehicle Aliens.") Sisko taught the aliens about time by imagining a baseball game (without George Steinbrenner). The unpredictability of baseball allowed the wormhole aliens to understand a human's perception of time. Having bonded with Sisko, they agreed to keep the wormhole open for travelers, enabling the Federation to visit the distant Gamma Quadrant.

Sisko, through his contact with the aliens, became a full-fledged religious icon to the Bajorans. The Bajorans believe that the wormhole aliens are actually deities known as the "Prophets," who watch over the planet. It was prophesied that an "Emissary" would discover the "Celestial Temple" (read, "the wormhole") and bring the Prophets back to Bajor. Bajorans believe Sisko is the Emissary and granted him this exalted title. As Emissary he is asked to bless marriages (and once in a while he opens a new shopping mall).

Since the Gamma Quadrant on the other side of the wormhole is filled with nasty aliens, Sisko is the Federation's point man in a number of skirmishes. His importance to Federation security cannot be overestimated.

Although Sisko hasn't been kidnapped by the Borg or held hostage by the Cardassians, he has faced danger repeatedly. A recurring threat to him are the denizens of the mirror universe, a dimension where the same characters exist, except their fundamental natures are opposite. This "parallel universe" was first established in the original *Star Trek*, in the episode "Mirror, Mirror" (see chapter 3).

Sisko is a big baseball fan; his hero is the legendary twenty-first-century player Buck Bokai. He also loves ancient spacecraft and especially admires old Bajoran space-sailing ships.

KEY SISKO EPISODES

"Emissary" Sisko is assigned to *Deep Space Nine,* discovers the wormhole, and becomes the Emissary. This means that Sisko gets instant credit in all Bajoran department stores.

"The Jem'Hadar" Sisko, his son, Jake, and Quark and his nephew Nog are held prisoner by a new alien threat: the Jem'Hadar. (These lizardlike aliens are the shock troops of the Dominion, an evil collection of alien races in the Gamma Quadrant.) Sisko and crew are saved, but at the loss of several ships, including a *Galaxy*-class starship. Trekkers everywhere taped the program to watch a ship that looks just like the *Enterprise* get its butt kicked over and over again.

"Through the Looking Glass" Seized by the Miles O'Brien from the mirror universe, Sisko meets the mirror of his dead wife, Jennifer. Sisko is able to convince Jennifer to cease work that would enable the mirror Bajorans to further enslave humanity. In this episode, Ben must say goodbye to his wife again, and return to his own universe.

"Crossover" This time the evil Jennifer kidnaps Jake Sisko, in order to blackmail Benjamin into coming back to the mirror universe to help build the *Defiant.* Jennifer is killed by the mirror Kira, and Sisko loses his wife for the second time. (Trekkers everywhere wonder if they have a mirror twin and whether the twin is having more fun than they are.)

"The Way of the Warrior" Sisko shaves his head and grows a goatee. Testosterone flies around the station hitting people in the back of the head.

"For the Cause" Sisko begins an affair with Kassidy Yates, captain of a merchant vessel. Odo suspects that Kassidy is a spy for the Maquis and it is discovered that she has a minor role in shipping supplies to the rebel organization. A security officer Sisko implicitly trusted, Michael Eddington, turns out to be the real traitor. He steals valuable equipment from under Sisko's nose, and Sisko vows to track him down.

"For the Uniform" Maquis agent Eddington reappears, threatening the Federation with sabotage. Sisko takes off after him in the

Defiant. It seems Eddington has fooled him completely, and succeeds in luring Sisko away from the real target. Starfleet pulls Sisko off the case, telling him that he's become too emotionally involved. Sisko defies orders and Eddington beats him again. They have a macho faceoff via holographic communication, and it's clear this feud is just beginning.

"Rapture" On the cusp of Bajor's admittance to the Federation, Sisko begins to have religious visions of the future, our proof that Sisko's status as the Emissary is more than just a pipe dream. Sisko's visions convince him that Bajor should delay joining the Federation. By speaking out against this union, Sisko influences the Bajoran population to reject the proposal. Sisko wants the visions to continue, but Dr. Bashir finds that they are causing brain damage. After Sisko slips into a coma, Jake disobeys his father and gives Bashir permission to treat Sisko, thereby eliminating his ability to see into the future. Sisko is devastated when he awakens.

KIRA NERYS (NANA VISITOR)

In a Nutshell

❏ Kira is the first officer of the station, and its liaison to the Bajoran government. As a former member of the Bajoran resistance group Shakaar, she is one tough liaison officer. She deeply resents the Cardassians, and Gul Dukat, the former prefect of the station, in particular. She is proud of her former terrorist status, and her loyalties lie with Bajor first, Starfleet second.

❏ Major Kira is a religious woman who believes deeply that the wormhole aliens are the Prophets of Bajoran legend. She also seems to feel that she has to become romantically involved with every Bajoran priest or Bajoran resistance leader she meets.

❏ Major Kira carried a baby for the O'Briens, when the pregnant Keiko O'Brien suffered an injury and the baby had to be transferred to Kira's uterus. This child was born healthy, and so has two mothers. He has his work cut out for him. (As Woody Allen once said, "I find that very few people survive *one* mother.")

ABOUT KIRA

Born on Bajor while it was occupied by the evil Cardassians, Kira is forever emotionally scarred. At the age of twelve she joined the resistance and was eager to please the older members of the Shakaar resistance cell. As part of this cell, she freed the prisoners of the Gallitep labor camp, a brutal gulag. She fought the Cardassians for years, but the Cardassians thought of her as a minor terrorist, mostly an errand runner.

When the Cardassians gave up Bajor, Kira rose to some prominence. She opposed inviting the Federation in to take over Terok Nor, the mining station in orbit around the planet. Nevertheless, she was assigned to *Deep Space Nine* as first officer and Bajoran liaison. Her terrorist past has caught up with her: Once in a while someone appears who has a big grudge against her and the Bajoran resistance movement. Most of her growth as a character has revolved around whom she's dating and being a surrogate mother to the O'Briens' baby. Kira feels pangs of loss at having a child who belongs to someone else. She will probably have to stay near the child, or have one of her own.

Kira is deeply involved in the fledgling solidarity efforts of the Bajoran government. Bajor's religious clerics are very politically powerful, and the position of Kai is the height of religious power. The current Kai is Vedek Winn, played by Louise Fletcher, and she isn't much nicer than she was as Nurse Ratched in *One Flew Over the Cuckoo's Nest*. Kira distrusts her and would prefer a different Kai, but she still respects her position.

Kira may be having romantic feelings for Odo, the station's security officer. Their working relationship has always been complicated by Odo's crush on her. (*See* Odo.)

KEY KIRA EPISODES

"**Shadowlands**"   Kira becomes romantically involved with Vedek Bareil, a Bajoran priest of some import.

"**Life Support**"   Vedek Bareil, Kira's love, is the key negotiator in treaty discussions with the Cardassians, but is injured in an explosion. Dr. Bashir replaces parts of Bareil's brain with positronic circuits (you know, the ones Data has), and slowly but surely, Bareil's identity slips away. He survives long enough to complete the negotiations but dies afterward. Because of this, Kira finds more reason to hate Vedek Winn, a conservative priest who was a competitor of Bareil's. (Don't worry about getting this stuff straight. It's very political.)

"**Crossfire**" Kira begins dating Shakaar, the resistance leader she fought alongside for years. Odo, who secretly loves Kira, feels deep pain watching them fall for each other.

"**Looking for Par'mach in All the Wrong Places**" A weird family episode. Kira, pregnant with the O'Briens' child, moves in with them. Miles gives her massages and dotes on her. An overpowering attraction seizes them. Barely able to restrain themselves, they agree to avoid one another.

"**The Darkness and the Light**" A mysterious assassin begins killing off members of Kira's old resistance cell. Kira loses most of her old friends. The assassin turns out to be a Cardassian permanently scarred by one of Kira's terrorist attacks. (It's going to be a lot harder to find people from Kira's past now.)

ODO (RENE AUBERJONOIS)

In a Nutshell

❏ Odo is the chief security officer on *Deep Space Nine*. He is a changeling, a gelatinous being who can assume virtually any shape or form. You'd think that he'd be surrounded by women because of this ability, but he's a sourpuss. He adopts a humanoid form and has a strange-looking face because he can't mimic certain features correctly. Every sixteen hours or so, Odo has to rest by reverting to his gelatinous state and sleeping in a little bucket.

❏ Odo is in love with Kira Nerys, and this was revealed to her by a future version of himself. Now he is even more uncomfortable in her presence.

❏ Odo is considered an outlaw among his people, the Founders, because he is the only changeling to have killed another changeling. They punished him for this crime by making him a "solid" (human) for a short time.

❑ Odo is a real law-and-order type. Inflexible and moralistic, he intensely dislikes Quark, the Ferengi bar proprietor.

ABOUT ODO

Odo was a mystery for a long time. There are no creatures like Odo in the Federation, and Odo believed that he was the only existing shape-shifter. He was found as an infant, and a Bajoran researcher named Dr. Mora studied Odo for months. He subjected the young changeling to a painful series of tests, and Odo grew up resenting his "father." Reaching adulthood, Odo became the security chief on the station under the Cardassians. His rigid, law-abiding nature enabled him to work both for the Federation and for a much harsher Cardassian system of justice. However, he is haunted by the execution of several innocent Bajorans he prosecuted.

Odo was one of hundreds of changelings sent into the Alpha Quadrant by the Dominion, all of them programmed with the strong desire to return home. The Founders did this in order to explore the galaxy and find out more about the societies they want to conquer. He is now a major factor in a serious battle between the Founders and the Federation. Because he is the only changeling on our side, he is both valued and suspect. We know how good he is, but others wonder where his true loyalties lie.

Odo aches to be with his people but cannot accept their fascistic tendencies. The Founders are hell-bent on dominating the universe and will not allow Odo to interfere. Odo wants more than anything else to rejoin his people in the Great Link (where all the shape-shifters pool together into a giant, oozing, disgusting ocean of slime). In his spare time Odo practices his shape-shifting abilities by mimicking the furniture on the station.

KEY ODO EPISODES

"The Search"   Odo discovers that he is a Founder, shape-shifters who rule an empire known as the Dominion. (This is like finding out Darth Vader is your father.)

Heart of Stone"   Kira is trapped within a rocklike creature, which is slowly strangling her. Unable to save her, Odo tearfully confesses his love for her. Surprise! "Kira" is actually a changeling, attempting to discover how close Odo is to his human friends.

"Broken Link"   Odo finds that he has been infected with a deadly virus by his people, the Founders. They force him to return to the Founders' homeworld to stand trial for the crime of killing another changeling. The verdict? Guilty. The sentence? Odo is transformed into a solid, since he has chosen to live among the humans. Strangely enough, now that he's just a weird-looking human, women like him. Go figure.

"The Begotten"   An infant changeling is found and Odo tries to raise it. He clashes with Dr. Mora, the man who raised him, because Odo wants to be more gentle with the creature. Alas, the infant changeling is fatally ill, but before it dies it merges with Odo. Odo finds that he can shape-shift again, and looks forward to turning himself into an Ethan Allan bedroom set.

JADZIA DAX (TERRY FARRELL)

In a Nutshell

- ❏ Jadzia Dax is a Trill, an alien race that is a joined species. Jadzia is the pretty humanoid female with the dots on her face, and Dax is the larvalike symbiont implanted in her abdominal pouch. (You think that's gross; you should see them swimming in their little pools.) The symbionts live hundreds of years; Jadzia is Dax's eighth host, so Jadzia is wise beyond her years.
- ❏ Jadzia is the science officer on *Deep Space Nine*. She has a deep friendship with Sisko, who calls her "old man." (Sisko and the symbiont's previous host, Curzon Dax, were best friends.)
- ❏ Jadzia Dax knows a great deal about Klingon society and is Worf's lover. In fact, she has promised to marry him if he survives the war with the Dominion.

ABOUT DAX

Any way you look at it, Dax is the weirdest character on the station. She is an attractive young woman who has been a man several times and is hundreds of years old. How do you talk about someone like that? To discuss Jadzia Dax, we have to break her down into her separate parts.

Jadzia (the humanoid) wanted to be joined with a symbiont since she was a child. Trills have internal pouches designed to house symbionts, and on her planet, having an old, slimy, larvalike creature implanted in your abdomen is a great honor. She studied hard and, after being rejected once, was chosen to be a host. (She's one of the few Trills to have been given a second shot at it.) Jadzia has a strong science background, which suits her well on the station.

Dax (the symbiont) has gone through seven bodies now, meaning it is several hundred years old. The symbiont was close friends with Sisko while in the body of Curzon, and has done many interesting things in past lives. The nature of Trill existence raises compelling questions. Once, while in a previous body, the symbiont was accused of murder. Should the current host still be liable? Well, it turns out Dax was innocent, but having two people in one raises some fascinating legal questions. For example, who gets to use the remote control?

KEY DAX EPISODES

"Dax"   Dax is accused of a murder committed while in a previous body. Will Jadzia be prosecuted? Of course. Will she be convicted? What, are you joking?

"Blood Oath"   Dax risks her life helping three old Klingon friends exact revenge on an enemy. (Note for advanced *Trek* students: these Klingons, Kor, Koloth, and Kang, were *Star Trek* villains in the original series. They are played here by the same actors who played them thirty years ago. All of them clashed with Kirk. How cool is that?)

"Equilibrium"   Dax falls ill, and the crew takes her to the Trill homeworld. They discover that the authorities have been restricting applicants for the "joining" because there is a shortage of symbionts. (We get to see the slimy Trills slipping in and out of their electrically charged ponds.)

"Facets"   It's time for Dax to meet the former hosts of her symbiont in a Trill ceremony. Their personalities take over the bodies of her friends, and one of them turns out to be a psychopath, whose existence had been repressed because Trills aren't supposed to make mistakes like letting some nut become a host.

"**Rejoined**" The episode that had to happen. Dax confronts a woman her symbiont was married to while in a male host. That old magic is still there, but the equipment isn't.

"**Looking for Par'mach in All the Wrong Places**" Dax makes her move on Worf. Love hurts, especially with a Klingon, because they like to choke each other as foreplay. A relationship for the nineties: she's a joined creature hundreds of years old and he's a violent, honor-driven warrior. What do you get the couple that has everything?

MILES EDWARD O'BRIEN (COLM MEANEY)

In a Nutshell

- ❏ O'Brien is the chief of operations aboard the station. He is a noncommissioned officer, meaning that he didn't graduate from Starfleet Academy.
- ❏ O'Brien is married and has two children. He is very proud of his marriage to Keiko. He is a tinkerer, and he can fix just about anything.

ABOUT MILES O'BRIEN

Miles O'Brien is a transfer from *Star Trek: The Next Generation,* where he served on the *Enterprise*-D under Picard. In fact, he met his wife, Keiko Ishikawa, on the *Enterprise,* and Captain Picard performed their marriage ceremony. What's great about O'Brien is that he has a stable family with him on the station, eliminating the need to have him fall in love with an alien every season. He is a loyal, noble character, a favorite with Trekkers. He's also been through a lot.

O'Brien fought in the war between the Federation and the Cardassians. During this war, he served on the U.S.S. *Rutledge,* under Capt. Ben Maxwell (a very intense guy who later went a little loco and started destroying Cardassian ships until Picard stopped him). O'Brien is known as the hero of Cestus III because he

distinguished himself in battle on that planet. He was forced to kill a
Cardassian during this battle, and forever resents the Cardassians for
what they "made" him become: a killer.

KEY O'BRIEN EPISODES

"**Tribunal**" The Cardassians arrest Miles and put him on trial
for a crime he did not commit. Under Cardassian law, you're
assumed guilty *before* a trial, so he's in a heap of trouble. The crew is
able to determine that he is innocent and convince the court to let
him go.

"**Visionary**" O'Brien accidentally jumps a few hours into the
future and witnesses the station's destruction by the Romulans.
Before he dies from the radiation that caused the time shift, he
convinces the older version of himself to go back in time and warn
the station. The older version (three hours older) remains in our
time and picks up his life where he left off. (Does this mean he can
never be late again?)

"**Hard Time**" Miles is arrested on an alien world for a crime he
did not commit. (Again? This is getting suspicious.) The crew can't
save him in time, and he is sentenced. The aliens implant the
memories of twenty years of a prison sentence in his mind, and for
O'Brien, those years were *real*. Through counseling, he comes to
grips with the programming, and with the memory of his cellmate,
whom he "killed" during his final years of captivity. As with Picard,
Trekkers everywhere wonder how much this man can take.

"**The Begotten**" O'Brien begins to feel desire for Kira, who is
carrying his and Keiko's child, Kirayoshi. It's okay because they
catch themselves before any damage is done. Keiko doesn't suspect a
thing.

O'BRIEN AND HIS FAMILY

Miles has two children, Molly and Kirayoshi. Occasionally they
are threatened, like when a wraith possessed his wife's body and
threatened to kill her and the kids unless he helped the wraith
destroy its enemies, the wormhole aliens. (O'Brien killed the wraith
instead.) Most of the time, however, they are safe on *Deep Space*

Nine. O'Brien is a dedicated father, except when he and Dr. Bashir are on the holodeck reenacting famous battles. O'Brien is the definition of the weekend warrior: during the week he's repairing the replicators and come Saturday he's dressed up like the Red Baron.

DR. JULIAN BASHIR (ALEXANDER SIDDIG)

In a Nutshell

❑ Dr. Bashir is the chief medical officer on *Deep Space Nine.* A handsome young man, he's like some of the doctors on *ER,* except *he's* a doctor because he had his intelligence genetically enhanced as a youngster.
❑ Like the doctors on *ER,* he fools around with anybody he can.
❑ He saves people and performs spontaneous acts of kindness. He is friends with the mysterious Cardassian tailor, Garak.
❑ Bashir loves to play on the holodeck. In his favorite program he becomes a sixties secret agent similar to James Bond.

ABOUT BASHIR

After graduating second in his class in medical school, Bashir signed up for *Deep Space Nine* because he thought himself an adventurer. We have learned that he feels he sabotages himself in academic pursuits, and perhaps the reason he went so far into space is that he feels inadequate.

Bashir's world has recently been rocked by his parents' disclosure that he was born "slow." His parents wanted him to be brilliant more than anything, so they illegally tampered with his genetic code and made him smart. This crime is so serious in the Federation that Bashir's career was at risk. Bashir remained at his post, but only because his father willingly went to prison to pay for the offense.

KEY BASHIR EPISODES

"Melora" Bashir falls in love with a female alien known as an Elaysian. It's difficult for Elaysians to move in our gravity, which is too strong for them. Bashir designs a technology that allows her to walk among the humans, and they begin dating. (Of course, this means he has the power to make her swoon at any time, which must be attractive to our man Bashir.)

"Our Man Bashir" Our good doctor is on the holodeck, playing James Bond. When the simulation goes awry, the crew's lives depend upon him staying alive to the end of the holodeck's program.

"In Purgatory's Shadow" and **"By Inferno's Light"** In this two-parter, Worf and Garak are taken prisoner by the Dominion and find Bashir in prison as well. This means that the Bashir on the station is a changeling assuming the doctor's form, and therefore means trouble for the station. The impostor, in a runabout, tries to destroy the Bajoran sun, but Kira, piloting the *Defiant*, blows him out of the sky.

"Doctor Bashir, I Presume" Oh, a big revelation. Bashir's parents visit the station just when Bashir is being considered as the model for a new holographic medical program, which means that Bashir's image would be in use in every sickbay in Starfleet. It is revealed that Bashir's parents genetically altered him to be brilliant. His father was imprisoned for this crime, and Starfleet declines to use Bashir as a model for the holographic program.

QUARK (ARMIN SHIMERMAN)

In a Nutshell

- ❑ Quark is a member of a race called the Ferengi, whose culture is based upon pure mercantilism. He is the owner and bartender of Quark's bar on the Promenade section of the station.
- ❑ Quark constantly schemes to make profits illegally, often through smuggling. For this reason he has an antagonistic relationship with Odo, the station's security chief.
- ❑ Quark's relationship with his brother, Rom, is strained. Quark dominated his brother for years before Rom quit working at Quark's and joined the station's engineering team. Quark's relationship with his nephew, Nog, is also strained because Nog joined Starfleet Academy. Quark's relationship with *everybody* is strained.

❏ In one of the strangest couplings ever witnessed on television, Quark married a Klingon named Grilka. Even though they are now divorced, they still manage to wrestle on the holodeck every once in a while.

ABOUT QUARK

Quark is comedy relief for *Deep Space Nine*, always getting himself into some ridiculous trouble only a Ferengi could get into. We know very little about his life before he came onto the station. We do know that he reached the "Age of Ascension" (the Ferengi bar mitzvah) and left home to seek his fortune. Quark is deeply disappointed with himself. Ferengi measure their worth by their wealth, and Quark feels he cannot compete with his cousin Gaila. Gaila is an arms merchant who owns his *own moon!* We also know that his mother, Ishka, is a fiercely independent woman who has caused him much embarrassment and grief. His father, Kelgar, remains a mystery.

KEY QUARK EPISODES

"The Nagus" The Ferengi leader, the Grand Nagus, visits Quark, and annoints Quark leader of the Ferengi business world. However, because he immediately becomes the target of assassination attempts, he loses enthusiasm for this position and quits.

"Profit and Loss" Here we meet the great love of Quark's life, Natima Lang. She is a Cardassian political dissident, dedicated to altering the Cardassians' warlike ways. In our first glimpse at the warm and fuzzy side of Quark, he helps her escape from the station when the Cardassians demand her arrest.

"The House of Quark" After Quark accidentally kills a Klingon, Grilka, the Klingon's widow, kidnaps him and forces him to marry her. She does this so she can control the family's wealth through him (Klingons don't let women own property). Although they get divorced, Quark develops feelings for Grilka, a strong, sexy Klingon woman.

"Family Business" Quark's mother, Ishka, is in big trouble.

She's conducting business, earning profit, and wearing clothes—everything a female Ferengi is forbidden to do. Quark is able to save his mother, but she will continue to be an annoyance to him.

"Little Green Men" An accident sends Quark, Rom, and his nephew Nog back in time to New Mexico in 1947, where their ship becomes the famous UFO that crashes near Roswell. Although Quark wants to do business with the twentieth-century humans, he realizes that he is in danger and must return home.

ELIM GARAK (ANDREW ROBINSON)

In a Nutshell

- ☐ Garak is a Cardassian, a militaristic, inscrutable race. He owns a tailor shop on the Promenade of the station. So what if twenty-fourth-century technology renders tailors obsolete?
- ☐ Garak's past is shrouded in mystery, but it is now clear that he was once a major operative of the Obsidian Order, a top-secret espionage agency within the Cardassian military. Garak was dismissed from the order for unknown political reasons. Garak's dream is to return to Cardassia in a position of power and deal some payback to his enemies. Garak is an expert in torture.
- ☐ Garak is a lonely man. Although he is friends with Dr. Bashir, others on the station shy away from him. Hey, maybe it has something to do with his being an expert in torture!
- ☐ He has been romantically involved with a very young Cardassian woman named Ziyal. Ziyal is half Bajoran and half Cardassian and is the daughter of Garak's worst enemy, Gul Dukat. (If you really want to get back at your enemy, start sleeping with his half-Bajoran daughter.)

ABOUT GARAK

Originally slated as a destabilizing influence on the station, Garak has grown to become a friendly face, if not a trusted one. He has even gained some grudging respect from Worf. Everything that Garak says must be taken with a grain of salt, because he lies frequently, and well. This is what we know.

He worked for the Obsidian Order, serving under Enabran Tain. At some point while working for the intelligence service, Garak was responsible for the death of Gul Dukat's father, which goes a long way toward explaining their bad blood. Garak was forced out of the order, and Tain sent him into relative exile on the station. Only recently have we discovered why: Tain is Garak's father. Tain wouldn't tell Garak that they were related, but Garak suspected it, and was always faithful to him. Before Tain died he finally admitted to Garak that he was his father.

It's easy to recognize Garak: He has gray skin and reptilian scales along his neck. He's also very polite for a guy with scales on his neck.

KEY GARAK EPISODES

"The Wire"   Garak has a brain implant that creates addictive chemicals to prevent the wearer from experiencing pain, a gift from the Obsidian Order. When it malfunctions, his withdrawal symptoms devastate him. While treating him, Dr. Bashir learns about Garak's involvement with the order.

"Improbable Cause" and "The Die Is Cast"   In this two-part episode, the Obsidian Order and the Tal Shiar (the Romulan intelligence agency) plan to conduct a sneak attack on Odo's people, the Founders. During the operation, Garak is ordered to torture Odo for information. Odo suffers greatly, and confesses to Garak about his great desire to return to the Great Link of the Founders. The sneak attack fails, and the Romulans and the Cardassians are demolished by the Dominion. Tain (Garak's father) is presumed dead.

"In Purgatory's Shadow" and "By Inferno's Light"   Garak and Worf are taken prisoner by the Dominion. In prison, they find Tain, who survived the disastrous attack on the Founders. Tain finally admits to Garak that he is his father. Garak, who suffers from claustrophobia, confronts his fear by slipping into a darkened wall section to repair a communication device. Even Worf acknowledges Garak's bravery.

SECONDARY CHARACTERS

GUL DUKAT (MARC ALAIMO)

The former prefect overseeing the domination of Bajor, Gul Dukat turned the station over to the Federation after the Cardassian-Federation treaty. A military man, he and Kira have an antagonistic relationship. Although Dukat grudgingly respects Kira, she despises him. Dukat is also a political chameleon. He became leader of the civilian Cardassian government, and Sisko saved him from destruction when the Klingons attacked Cardassia. Sisko probably regrets that decision, because now Gul Dukat is a dangerous man. His negotiations with the Dominion have resulted in the Cardassian Union's alliance with this most deadly enemy of the Federation. Together they attacked *Deep Space Nine* and, for a time, regained control of the station.

Dukat has a family on Cardassia, but also had a Bajoran mistress, with whom he had a child, Ziyal. Dukat attempted to kill Ziyal because Cardassian custom demands that the children of mistresses be killed. Kira saved Ziyal from Dukat's agenda by moving her onto the space station. Dukat and Ziyal reconciled, but when Ziyal started diddling Garak it enraged Dukat. He asked her to leave the station, and when she didn't, he declared that she was dead to him. Dukat meant business: He tried to destroy the entire Bajoran star system. Get used to seeing Dukat. He's not going away.

JAKE SISKO (CIRROC LOFTON)

Benjamin Sisko's son has grown up on *Deep Space Nine*. A promising writer, he often gets inspiration from events on the station. He's a likable teenager and a complete coward. He once accompanied Dr. Bashir to a wartorn planet to write about the experience and when the Klingons attacked he hid under a chair. Yes, dived under a chair and fired a phaser in the air like a nut. Jake was ashamed of his behavior, and he wrote a story about being a coward. It's okay, though, because we all know how sensitive writers are. (But if Hemingway were alive he'd slap Jake's face.)

Like some other *Star Trek* characters, Jake had the opportunity to live an entire alternate life in the episode "The Visitor." Ben Sisko disappeared into another dimension, reappearing every few years to visit Jake. Jake, now old and near death (and a famous writer), sacrificed himself to bring his father back to our reality. Fortunately, Sisko and Jake returned to the place and time from which he disappeared, present-day *Deep Space Nine*. The entire life that Jake lived may or may not come true. (That's the benefit of alternate realities: they give scriptwriters lots of breathing room.)

ROM (MAX GRODENCHIK)

Quark's brother Rom is a Ferengi nerd, a phrase we once thought to be redundant. Dominated completely by Quark, Rom unionized the workers at the bar and eventually left his brother's employ. He is now an engineer working for Miles O'Brien on *Deep Space Nine*. He is very attached to his *moogie* (mother), Ishka, and stands up for her against Quark. Rom is very proud of his son, Nog. Rom has surprised all Trekkers by marrying Leeta, the gorgeous Dabo girl, who was formerly Dr. Bashir's girlfriend.

NOG (ARON EISENBERG)

Quark's nephew. Rom's son is the first Ferengi in Starfleet Academy. He is very close friends with Jake Sisko. They actually roomed together on the station for a short time, and they fought often because Nog is into physical fitness and cadet cleanliness, and Jake is a cowardly, sloppy writer.

GENERAL MARTOK (J. G. HERTZLER)

Currently the Klingon representative on the station, General Martok was once second in command of the Klingon Empire and Gowron's right-hand man. Martok was kidnapped by the Dominion and replaced with a shape-shifter. The fake Martok convinced Gowron to break the treaty with the Federation which pushed the entire Alpha Quadrant to the brink of war. The crew of *Deep Space Nine* was able to expose Martok's double, and the original Martok was freed. You can recognize Martok now because he only has one eye, having lost the other while fighting numerous Jem'Hadar warriors in prison. General Martok admires Worf, so much so that he made Worf an honorary member of his family.

GOWRON (ROBERT O'REILLY)

The big Klingon kahuna, Chancellor Gowron is the leader of the Klingon Empire. He has stripped Worf's family of land and title because Worf refused to join him in his war against the Cardassians. Despite his aggressive nature, he is as obsessed with honor as any Klingon. You can recognize Gowron by his long cape, forehead ridges, and scary Marty Feldman eyes.

DS9 CHARACTERS QUIZ

1. Whom does Odo hate more than anyone else on *Deep Space Nine?*
   a. Kai Winn
   b. Quark
   c. Bill Gates
   d. Kathie Lee Gifford

2. Garak was a member of which evil intelligence service?
   a. The Obsidian Order
   b. The McLaughlin Group
   c. The Yale Club
   d. *Consumer Reports*

3. What kind of food does Sisko's father cook?
   a. Creole
   b. Polish
   c. African
   d. Centaurian

4. Why is Bashir such a good doctor?
   a. His Park Avenue practice
   b. He makes house calls
   c. He's been genetically altered to be smarter and more skilled with his hands
   d. He watches *ER*

ANSWERS

   1, b; 2, a; 3, a; 4, c.

7

The Characters—
Star Trek: Voyager

The newest *Star Trek* series has an all-new crew, and all-new space to explore: the Delta Quadrant. Because the series is young, these characters are still evolving. (I mean that literally, as we will see.) *Star Trek: Voyager* is *Star Trek* in its purest form: one ship, deep space, no friends.

What It's About

On a mission to track down a missing Maquis ship with a Federation spy onboard, the U.S.S. *Voyager,* under the command of Capt. Kathryn Janeway, was hurled across the galaxy by an advanced alien known only as the Caretaker. *Voyager* sustained heavy damage, and key personnel, such as the first officer and the ship's doctor, were killed. The crew found the missing Maquis ship and some Maquis crew members; they, too, had been transported.

The Caretaker's technology was far beyond that of the Federation, and he resided in a huge facility known as the Array. The Caretaker had been sustaining a race called the Ocampa, providing them with energy for centuries. Now dying, the Caretaker brought alien races from all over the galaxy to the Array, hoping to find one suitable to continue his job caring for the Ocampa. The Caretaker revealed to Captain Janeway that there was another Caretaker, but she had become bored years before and left for deep space.

The Caretaker died before he could find someone to mate with him and take his place. A hostile race, known as the Kazon, attempted to seize the Array in order to destroy the Ocampa. Even though it was the only way for the ship to get home, Janeway destroyed the Array to protect the Ocampa. The Maquis ship was destroyed fighting the Kazon, so *Voyager's* crew is now half Starfleet, half rebel Maquis. At high warp, it would take them seventy years to get home. They are in deep, deep doo-doo.

KATHRYN JANEWAY (KATE MULGREW)

In a Nutshell

- ❑ Janeway is the captain of *Voyager*. She's a tough, by-the-numbers commander who sometimes goes with her gut instincts. More like Captain Kirk than Captain Picard, she is *muy macho*.
- ❑ She has a very strong attachment to Tuvok, her Vulcan security chief. She trusts him and seeks his counsel more often than any other member of the crew. He was the Federation spy she was trying to find when the Maquis ship disappeared.
- ❑ Janeway wants to obey the Prime Directive, but when one of her crew members is threatened, watch out! All bets are off.
- ❑ When she goes onto the holodeck, she likes to re-create—how can I put this—"Harlequin-type" romances. In real life, Janeway may have a growing attraction for her first officer, Chakotay.

ABOUT KATHRYN JANEWAY

Captain Janeway graduated from Starfleet Academy, and while there was the undisputed expert at pulling all-nighters. She served for a time on the Starship *Al-Batani* under Tom Paris's father. She has a "significant other" named Mark and a dog named Molly back at home in the Alpha Quadrant. She was assigned command of the *Voyager* for a specific mission: to bring home Tuvok, a Federation spy in the midst of the Maquis rebels.

Janeway's biggest concern is how to get her crew back home from the Delta Quadrant. Her original strategy was to avoid taking sides in conflicts between alien races and to follow the Prime Directive not to interfere with other cultures. However, this strategy has been altered slightly. Janeway is now more willing to shoot from the hip, to risk the Directive to rescue crew members. She realized that the Prime Directive is easier to follow when you have an entire

Federation backing you up. Out here, *Voyager* needs friends, and quickly.

Kathryn likes to play on the holodeck much like anyone else. In Kathryn's holofantasy, she's a beautiful headmistress in Elizabethan England, hired to care for the children of a mysterious, handsome widower. Oy vey. Using the ship's computer, Janeway re-created Leonardo da Vinci on the holodeck. Now she seeks his counsel, paints in his studio, and calls him "Maestro."

KEY JANEWAY EPISODES

"Cathexis" Janeway starts using the holodeck to role-play a trashy holonovel. Trekkers fear a guest appearance by Fabio.

"Threshold" Lieutenant Paris takes a warp shuttle past the warp-10 barrier and, as a result, experiences an accelerated evolutionary process. He goes mad, kidnaps the captain, and takes her past the warp-10 barrier. They both mutate into giant salamanders. They mate on a planet and produce a bunch of little salamanders. *Leaving the babies on the planet, they return to* Voyager. The Doctor cures them. Janeway loses his phone number.

"Deathwish" *Voyager* finds a member of the Q Continuum locked in a comet. The prisoner-Q requests asylum on *Voyager* and is hotly pursued by the original Q (John DeLancie). The prisoner-Q's crime? He wants to die. Since no member of the Q has ever died, no one knows what to do. The Q conduct a hearing with Janeway as judge to determine whether the prisoner-Q should be allowed to kill himself. Janeway rules that the Q have a right to end their interminable boredom.

"Macrocosm" Giant viruses invade *Voyager*, flying around the ship and stabbing the crew with huge proboscises. Janeway does a passable Sigourney Weaver, armed with grenades and a phaser rifle, and takes her ship back.

"Resolutions" Janeway and Chakotay contract a fatal illness while on an away mission. The planet has some healing factor that keeps them alive, but they will die if they return to the ship. Janeway orders the crew to continue on their way home. Janeway and Chakotay build a little nest and prepare to live out the rest of their lives on the planet. The *Voyager* crew finds a cure and returns for them. No sex took place between the captain and Chakotay, but you can tell they were thinking about it.

"**The Q and the Grey**" The original Q appears, and wants Janeway to have his love child. Even though it's not every day you get to make love to a god, Janeway says no and encourages Q to find a nice Q-ish girl and settle down.

CHAKOTAY (ROBERT BELTRAN)

In a Nutshell

- ❏ Chakotay comes from a tribe of Native Americans who settled on a planet near the Cardassian border. You can recognize Chakotay by the tattoo on his face. No one has any idea what this tattoo represents.
- ❏ Chakotay was a member of the Maquis and in command of the ship *Voyager* was looking for when they disappeared. He is now the first officer aboard *Voyager*.
- ❏ He often talks to his "spirit guides," spiritual presences that give him advice when he needs it. He contacts them through a Medicine Wheel or through deep meditation.
- ❏ Chakotay had his neural system linked to a group of Borg survivors. These survivors mentally forced him to activate a Borg ship, and the possibility exists that he may be susceptible to further Borg manipulation.

ABOUT CHAKOTAY

Chakotay grew to manhood on a planet settled by Native Americans who journeyed there from Earth. Comfortable on their new planet, they thrived in harmony with nature. But this planet was disputed territory. A treaty ending the Cardassian war ceded the planet to the Cardassians, and the tribe had to be relocated.

An enraged Chakotay, by then an Academy graduate, resigned Starfleet and joined the Maquis resistance group. In his resistance cell were B'Elanna Torres and Tuvok (who was spying on him for the Federation), among others.

Chakotay and his crew, fleeing the Cardassians through the Badlands, were transported to the Delta Quadrant by the Caretaker. He teamed up with Captain Janeway and destroyed his own ship, saving *Voyager*. Janeway, in a power-sharing move, made Chakotay her first officer because he was the leader of the Maquis contingent aboard *Voyager*. Once appointed first officer, Chakotay swore his loyalty to Janeway, and to *Voyager*.

When he was younger, he disappointed his father by not embracing his cultural traditions. In time, his Native American heritage became essential to his character, and he seems to have seen *Dances With Wolves* about twenty times.

One thing you can say about Chakotay is that he hasn't been lucky in love. Chakotay's demon lover from hell was Seska, a Cardassian agent surgically altered to look human. Seska was spying on the Maquis for Cardassia, but certainly didn't plan on living out her life in the Delta Quadrant. Resentful of Janeway for stranding them there, Seska teamed up with the Kazon to try to seize control of *Voyager*. Although she was defeated, Chakotay got the real scare of his life when Seska told him he was the father of her child.

KEY CHAKOTAY EPISODES

"Cathexis"   Chakotay meets evil energy aliens, who drain his brain of consciousness. How to warn *Voyager* of the evil energy aliens? What? Did you say he should use his Native American Medicine Wheel and signal the crew from the spirit plane? And have the Doctor reintegrate his consciousness into his empty body? Sounds nuts, doesn't it? Well, it works.

"Tattoo"   On a distant planet, Chakotay finds the aliens whom his people once called the "sky spirits." They aren't too happy to find *Voyager* prospecting the planet for minerals. Trying to save Chakotay from the spirits, Janeway irresponsibly loses two shuttlecraft and then sends *Voyager* into the planet's atmosphere. (Now we know that Janeway will risk the entire ship for one person, especially if he's good-looking.)

"Maneuvers"   Seska, now allied with the Kazon, steals Federation technology from *Voyager*. Chakotay goes after her and is captured. Seska steals some of Chakotay's DNA and impregnates herself with it.

"**Basics, Parts I and II**" Seska, that flirt, sends a message to Chakotay that she has delivered their son and that the baby's now in danger. Chakotay consults his spirit guides, and they tell him to go to them. Wrong move. It is a trap. Seska seizes control of *Voyager* and strands the crew on a planet, leaving the holodoctor to regain control of the ship. Chakotay wins the "Home Shopping Network Gullibility Award."

"**Unity**" Chakotay finds a group of people who have escaped from the Borg, and he falls for their pretty female leader. (Well, she's not that pretty without her wig covering her Borg skull implants.) Since they are all near death, Chakotay allows them to connect him with their neural network in order to help them heal faster. (This connection has some aftereffects. When they make love he's able to feel what it's like to be his own lover.) The group seizes mental control of him and forces him to reactivate a dead Borg ship. Chakotay may be vulnerable to further Borg manipulation in the future. He loses his own phone number.

TUVOK (TIM RUSS)

In a Nutshell

☐ Tuvok is a full-fledged Vulcan and is *Voyager*'s security chief.
☐ Tuvok is 120 years old, in his prime for a Vulcan.
☐ He's a stick-in-the-mud, just now learning how to live with humans. His relationship with Neelix is particularly strained, but Neelix is particularly annoying. He does have a close relationship with Kes, and they frequently mind-meld. He is loyal to Janeway, having served as her tactical officer in the past.

ABOUT TUVOK

We know more about Tuvok than about any other character on the ship, which is interesting, because Tuvok is the first full-blooded Vulcan we've come to know well. (Remember, Spock was half human.) Tuvok has had two separate Starfleet careers spanning both halves of the *Star Trek* universe. Almost eighty years earlier, Tuvok was an ensign on the U.S.S. *Excelsior,* serving under Captain Sulu. In fact, he was present for the mission on which Sulu helped Captain Kirk expose the conspiracy to stop the first Klingon-Federation peace treaty.*

Tuvok found it difficult to be surrounded by illogical humans, so he quit. Like Spock, he returned to Vulcan to undergo *Kolinahr* to purge himself of emotion. And like Spock, he failed to complete the training. Tuvok also experienced *Pon farr,* the mating urge, and married a Vulcan woman named T'Pel. They raised a family.

At some point, five decades after he quit, Tuvok rejoined Starfleet. He met Janeway and became her tactical officer. As a special assignment, he became a spy for the Federation and infiltrated the Maquis. He was serving on Chakotay's Maquis raider when it was transported to the Delta Quadrant.

Still visibly impatient with human foibles, he has resigned himself to learning how to live with other species. He is especially interested in mind-melds, and it seems like he's made one with almost every crew member. (He's a mind-meld floozy.)

KEY TUVOK EPISODES

"Learning Curve"   Tuvok trains the rebellious Maquis crew members in the Starfleet way. He pushes them too hard at first, but eventually earns their respect. He also learns how to interact with them.

"Meld"   Murder on *Voyager.* Ensign Suder, a Betazoid member of the Maquis, kills a crew member. Tuvok mind-melds with Suder to give him Vulcan-like control of his violent tendencies. Because Suder is a Betazoid, it backfires, and Tuvok cannot control the violent impulses he inherits from Suder. Tuvok becomes scary, locking himself in his room and wrecking the place. Eventually, Tuvok regains control, and the captain gives him a new dinette set.

"Tuvix"   In a strange transporter accident, Tuvok and Neelix

---

*As seen in *Star Trek VI: The Undiscovered Country.*

merge into one being, who calls himself Tuvix. An interesting creature, he seems to embody the best of both men. He even tries to continue Neelix's relationship with Kes. Janeway orders him, at gunpoint, to go back in the transporter to be separated into Tuvok and Neelix.

"Flashback" Tuvok starts having strange hallucinations. An examination reveals that a repressed memory is surfacing and if it isn't dealt with, Tuvok will die. Janeway and Tuvok mind-meld, going back in time to Tuvok's duty aboard the *Excelsior*. In the end, an alien life-form in Tuvok's mind is responsible for his illness, and they kill it.

"Alter Ego" Tuvok and Ensign Kim fall for the same holodeck character, who is really a lonely alien woman looking for companionship. This alien understands Tuvok, bringing him out of his shell for a short time. She threatens to destroy *Voyager* unless Tuvok stays with her. Tuvok confesses that he finds her compelling but cannot love her.

THOMAS EUGENE PARIS
(ROBERT DUNCAN MCNEILL)

In a Nutshell

- ❏ A devil-may-care ladies' man, Lieutenant Paris is the helmsman and pilot of *Voyager*. He is dedicated to Janeway, who believed in him enough to pull him out of a Federation prison to serve onboard *Voyager*.
- ❏ He is close friends with Harry Kim.
- ❏ He and B'Elanna Torres are destined to have an affair. He's been pursuing her in his spare time.
- ❏ He is the first pilot to break the warp-10 barrier, which puts him in a category with Chuck Yaeger, Neil Armstrong, and Zefram Cochrane. It also turned him into a giant salamander, which puts him in a category with *Monty Python's Flying Circus*. (He got better.)

ABOUT PARIS

Tom Paris is the ship's bad boy. The son of a respected Starfleet admiral, Paris is a brilliant pilot who gave up a Starfleet career to join the Maquis. (Evidently he felt trapped in the shadow of his great father.) On his first Maquis raid, he was captured by the Federation and sentenced to a penal institute in New Zealand. Janeway, with orders to find a missing Maquis ship, asked Paris to come along as an observer in exchange for a pardon. Paris agreed.

His bad luck was complete when *Voyager* was transported to the Delta Quadrant. With some of the crew dead, Paris was tapped to become helmsman. Finally able to shine without his father looking down at him, Paris has become an excellent officer, earning a field promotion to lieutenant.

Deeply involved in the ship's leisure activities, Paris designed a holodeck program of a bar in France where the crew can go to play pool, relax, and act French. Thankfully, none of the crew actually *becomes* French.

KEY PARIS EPISODES

"**Ex Post Facto**" While on an alien planet, Paris is convicted of a crime he didn't commit. (What *is* it with these guys?) Sentenced to re-live the murder in his memories every fourteen hours for the rest of his life, Tuvok mind-melds with him to prove his innocence. (Is it possible that Tuvok, you know, gets a kick out of these melds?)

"**Threshold**" Paris breaks the warp-10 barrier, and becomes genetically unstable. At the peak of his madness, he kidnaps Janeway and takes her past the barrier. They both evolve into giant amphibians, mate, and have lots of little amphibians. The Doctor restores the pair to normal, but the question remains: What should they do for a second date?

"**Investigations**" Paris, who has seemed more and more irritable, leaves *Voyager* and enlists as a pilot for an alien merchant vessel. It turns out his erratic behavior is part of a ruse to infiltrate the Kazon and discover the traitor on *Voyager*. The saboteur is found and killed, and Paris gets to act normal again.

"**The Chute**" Paris and Harry Kim are in prison, and Paris loses his sanity. Kim keeps Paris alive long enough for a daring *Voyager* rescue. Kim and Paris become best friends.

"**Blood Fever**" A Vulcan crew member with a crush on Torres tries to mate with her during his *Pon farr*. Somehow, he tele-pathically transfers his mating frenzy to Torres. She goes berserk, trying to force herself on Tom Paris. Paris plays the good guy, fending off sexy B'Elanna's advances. However, here their mating dance begins in earnest.

B'ELANNA TORRES (ROXANN BIGGS-DAWSON)

In a Nutshell

- ❑ B'Elanna is half human, half Klingon. She is *Voyager's* chief engineer. B'Elanna is embarrassed by her aggressive Klingon nature, but it is responsible for much of her strength of character.
- ❑ You can recognize B'Elanna by the soft forehead ridges she has, which make her look like she's frowning all the time.
- ❑ B'Elanna was a member of the Maquis and served under Chakotay on his ship.
- ❑ B'Elanna is now dedicated to Janeway, who has shown great faith in her by making her chief engineer.

ABOUT B'ELANNA

We're learning more about B'Elanna all the time. Another in a series of *Star Trek* half-breeds, B'Elanna's mother was a Klingon, and her human father must have been a brave man. Well, not that brave. Her father abandoned them, and her mother moved them to the Klingon homeworld. B'Elanna was admitted to Starfleet Academy (no easy feat, as we know), but couldn't handle the discipline. She quit the Academy after her second year.

Joining the Maquis gave B'Elanna an outlet for her natural Klingon aggression. B'Elanna served on a Maquis raider under Chakotay, and her feelings for him were more than just friendly. Coming aboard *Voyager* was traumatic for B'Elanna. She didn't like Starfleet's rigid hierarchy and resented goody-goody Starfleet officers like Harry Kim. However, an opportunity to become *Voyager's* chief engineer presented itself, and Janeway allowed B'Elanna to prove herself. Since she's an inveterate tinkerer, she fought for the job and got it.

KEY B'ELANNA EPISODES

"Faces"   The Vidiians, a hostile alien species, kidnap B'Elanna, and somehow separate her into two beings, her Klingon half and her human half. The human half has difficulty facing fear, and the Klingon half has difficulty thinking strategically. They put their heads together and develop a plan. The Klingon B'Elanna sacrifices her life so that human B'Elanna can escape. Back on *Voyager*, the Doctor restores B'Elanna to her normal self.

"Prototype"   B'Elanna finds a damaged robot and fixes it. A mistake. More robots come and it turns out that they are killers. They kidnap B'Elanna and force her to make more of them. When they start fighting each other, B'Elanna and *Voyager* slip away.

"Dreadnought"   An old creation of Torres's returns to haunt her. An intelligent Cardassian bomb, which Torres reprogrammed in her own voice, is targeted on an innocent world. In order to save them, B'Elanna has to argue with herself for a whole hour.

"Blood Fever"   Vorek, a Vulcan crew member, goes through *Pon farr* and wants B'Elanna, but B'Elanna just wants to be friends. Somehow, B'Elanna experiences *Pon farr* as well. She tries to seduce Tom Paris, who resists her because she's not in her right mind. Yeah, whatever. Vorek and B'Elanna fight, she knocks him out, and the *Pon farr* is over. Trekkers everywhere say, "That's all?" Everyone loses everyone else's phone number.

HARRY KIM (GARRETT WANG)

In a Nutshell

- ❏ Harry Kim is the operations officer of *Voyager*, responsible for all the parts of the ship working together. He's a smart, resourceful young man, and he's boring as hell.
- ❏ Like Miles O'Brien, Kim has inherited the mantle of "Most Likely to Have Weird Alternate Universe Stuff Happen to Him." The real Harry Kim is dead, and he's been replaced by a counterpart from another dimension.
- ❏ He left a girlfriend named Libby in San Francisco. He remains true to her despite the fact that he's legitimately out of town.

ABOUT HARRY KIM

Ensign Harry Kim is from a very tight-knit Asian family. Since *Voyager* is his first assignment out of Starfleet Academy, he has had precious few experiences to draw from as he journeys through the Delta Quadrant. He was very successful academically, and he has a love for mathematics. He is also interested in some Vulcan mental disciplines. A very enthusiastic young man, he has a strong character and is eager to please. Because of this, the writers love to watch him get trashed. Although we don't know much about his past, we do know that his worst fear is to be operated on without anesthesia. (Like that isn't everybody's worst fear.)

KEY KIM EPISODES

"Emanations" Kim is accidentally transported to a world in another dimension. In order to get back, he has to die. He dies, and the Doctor brings him back to life. Unlike Spock, who also came back from the dead, Kim remembers everything.

"Non Sequitur" Kim wakes up at home in twenty-fourth-century San Francisco with his girlfriend. Aware that he is in an alternate universe, Kim finds Paris, who is a bum hanging out in a bar in France, the very same bar that exists on the holodeck. Paris helps Kim get back to his universe while the "bum" Paris gets a newfound enthusiasm for life.

"Deadlock" *Voyager* is split into two ships, one in a separate dimension. Harry travels to the other *Voyager* and is killed. The Harry from the other *Voyager* comes to our ship and lives on. How do we know if this is the same Harry Kim? We don't.

"Alter Ego" Harry Kim is in agony because he's fallen in love with a holodeck character named Marayna. He goes to Tuvok to learn how to repress his emotions. Tuvok investigates, falls for the holodeck character, and Harry is furious. Of course, the holodeck creature is an alien, so Tuvok and Kim work out their troubles over a nice game of Kal-To. (Kal-To is to chess what chess is to tic-tac-toe.)

"Favorite Son" Harry Kim discovers that he's really part alien, and a planet of female aliens want him to mate with them.

(However, they really just want to suck the life out of him.) What is this, Castle Anthrax?

KES (JENNIFER LIEN)

In a Nutshell

❑ Kes is a member of an alien race known as the Ocampa. She has a life span of only nine years. Very intelligent and able to absorb huge quantities of information, she's studying with the Doctor and has become his medical assistant. She's the crew member closest to the Doctor and most convinced of the Doctor's humanity.

❑ She joined the crew with Neelix, whom she was seeing at the time. Now she's a free woman.

❑ Kes has strong latent telepathic abilities. Tuvok is working with her to help develop them, but we are still waiting for Kes to start the Psychic Friends Network on *Voyager*.

❑ She can mate only once in her entire life to produce children.

ABOUT KES

Remember the Caretaker, the alien who caused the entire show by hijacking *Voyager* to the Delta Quadrant? Well, the Ocampa are the alien race the Caretaker felt responsible for. Kes joined the *Voyager* crew when *Voyager* saved her people by destroying the Array before the evil Kazon took it over. Since the Ocampa have a nine-year life span, this actress knows to keep her resumé handy.

When she came onboard, Kes was only one year old, so how much history could she have? We don't know much about her prior life except that her father was named Benaren and (surprise, surprise) he's dead.

Kes and Neelix were inseparable when they first came aboard. Although Kes's attraction to Tom Paris caused some friction, nothing, it seemed, could come between them. They broke up anyway, but no one has told us when or why.

Unfortunately, Kes has left *Voyager*. She began to resonate at a different quantum frequency and had to "die" to save *Voyager*.

KEY KES EPISODES

"**Elogium**"   Space aliens accidentally trigger sexual maturity in Kes. Kes is concerned that if she doesn't mate immediately, she'll never be able to have a child. Neelix or Paris, which daddy should she choose? Luckily, it's a false alarm.

"**Cold Fire**"   In deep space, Kes meets other Ocampans who have lived beyond their years and have developed scary mental powers. Although they invite her to stay, Kes declines. Since it *is* possible for the Ocampa to live beyond nine years after all, Kes can sit on that resumé for a while.

"**Warlord**"   Kes is possessed by an alien warlord, who turns her into a leather-suited seductress from hell. Soon thereafter, she and Neelix break up. Connection?

"**The Gift**"   Kes's "death," a sacrifice to save *Voyager*. But does anybody actually stay dead in *Star Trek?*

NEELIX (ETHAN PHILLIPS)

In a Nutshell

❑ Easily the most annoying character on the ship, Neelix, the Talaxian, is a former junk trader who got onto *Voyager* promising to be an adviser and guide through the Delta Quadrant. Effusive and gregarious, Neelix also likes to call himself the ship's morale officer. Yes, he's Julie from *The Love Boat*, except with spots, bad teeth, and red whiskers. He organizes luaus on the holodeck and broadcasts a morning news show on the ship.

❑ Neelix was once involved with Kes, but they've broken up. Take a good look at Neelix. Who's going to date him now?

❑ Neelix really wants Tuvok to like him, but Tuvok secretly would like to open an airlock and ask Neelix to check the weather outside.

ABOUT NEELIX

Neelix is from Talax, a planet in the Delta Quadrant. He fought in that planet's war against the Haakonians, and he is guilt-ridden about his self-perceived cowardice in that conflict. His family was killed by a terrible weapon called a metreon cascade, which was unleashed by the Haakonians on Rinax, a moon of Talax.

Neelix became a junk trader and fell in love with Kes. Both volunteered to stay with *Voyager* and help it through the Delta Quadrant. He became the ship's cook when *Voyager* had to turn off the food replicators to conserve energy.

KEY NEELIX EPISODES

"**Phage**" Neelix is attacked by the evil Vidiians, who steal his lungs right out of his body. Kes saves his life by donating one of hers. Good thing this happened before they broke up.

"**Jetrel**" A Haakonian scientist named Jetrel comes onboard. His goal: to recreate all the Talaxians destroyed by the weapon he designed. This episode reveals Neelix's feelings of self-loathing for not being with his family when they were killed by the Haakonians. (Tuvok probably wishes Neelix was with his family, too.)

"**Fair Trade**" Neelix begins to doubt his value to *Voyager* as the ship moves beyond the region he is familiar with. He goes undercover to procure maps from dangerous criminals. Janeway gives him the "You're a member of this crew, dammit" speech.

THE DOCTOR (ROBERT PICARDO)

In a Nutshell

❑ The Doctor onboard *Voyager* isn't an organic life-form. He is a holographic representation of a doctor: the Emergency Medical Holographic (EMH) Program. He has been functioning since the beginning of the series when the ship's real doctor was killed.

❑ The Doctor was originally supposed to be named Zimmerman, after the doctor who created the program, but for reasons not explained to us, he has yet to pick a name.

❑ The Doctor has grown into a full-fledged life-form, with emotions and goals. He is training Kes to be his assistant, and he likes to sing opera.

ABOUT THE DOCTOR

The Emergency Medical Holographic Program is in use on many Federation starships. For example, in *Star Trek: First Contact*, Dr. Crusher activated the program to distract the Borg while sickbay personnel evacuated. This means that Robert Picardo should be able to keep his *Star Trek* career going for quite a while.

The Doctor is a very complex program, but was only designed as a temporary replacement. He is programmed with the experience of forty-seven individual medical officers and the knowledge of two thousand medical reference sources. He wasn't designed to function over a long period of time, and this has led to problems with the stability of his program. The Doctor works on the same basis the holodecks do: he is a program, with a body created by holographic projectors. The Doctor can make his body solid or ephemeral. He doesn't need to breathe or eat. He cannot be injured physically.

Originally the Doctor could only exist in sickbay or on the holodeck. Now, however, the Doctor has a portable holographic projector he can wear on his sleeve, allowing him to travel anywhere. If he loses the projector while outside of sickbay or a holodeck, he will be destroyed.

Strangely enough, the Doctor is probably the most popular character on the show, and he's a computer program. What do you think that says about us?

KEY DOCTOR EPISODES

"Projections" The Doctor's program suffers malfunctions. He begins to hallucinate and question the nature of his existence.

"Lifesigns" A Vidiian hematologist, Danara Pel, is found near death. The Doctor does an amazing thing: he places her consciousness in a holographic body that shows us her true appearance before she became ill. They fall in love. She gives him a really stupid name: Schmulis. They have a date on the holodeck, parked on Mars in a '57 Chevy (what do you want, it was Paris's idea). She leaves the ship to rejoin her people in her deformed body.

"The Swarm" The Doctor's medical program is getting too big and becomes unstable. He's also getting stupid. Although the Doctor could be rebooted (turned off and back on), that would erase all the memories he's accumulated, as well as his personality. Kes and B'Elanna work to save the Doctor by summoning the original Dr. Zimmerman in a separate repair holoprogram. They merge the Doctor with the repair program and save the Doctor's personality. But now the repair program is gone—so let's hope the Doctor doesn't get sick again.

"Future's End" The Doctor gets his portable holographic projector from five hundred years in the future. He also experiences pain for the first time, which devastates him and makes him empathize with his patients.

"The Darkling" Doc tries to make himself more interesting by adding the programs of famous people like Ghandi and Lord Byron. Instead, he creates a second personality, a dark side that doesn't comb his hair as well as the good Doctor does. B'Elanna gets rid of all the pesky programs and restores the Doctor.

SEVEN OF NINE (JERI RYAN)

As *Star Trek: Voyager* entered its fourth season, a new character joined the *Voyager* crew, and she's one of their most lethal foes—a Borg. Named "Seven of Nine" (Borg refer to themselves by their number in a small unit), she is a human who was assimilated by the Borg as a young girl. During the incident with Species 8472 ("Scorpion, Parts I and II"), Janeway severed Seven of Nine's connection to the Borg collective, and she was forced to stay on *Voyager* and adapt to human society.

Because she was stolen from human society as a young girl, she is something of a "wild child." As her Borg implants were removed, it became clear that she was half Borg, half human. The Borg destroy all individuality during the process of assimilation, so helping her rediscover her humanity will not be easy. However, with her knowledge of the Borg collective and their technology, she is a valuable resource as Voyager carefully makes its way through Borg space. An unpredictable and unforgettable character, she is a daily challenge to Janeway and her crew.

VOYAGER CHARACTERS QUIZ

1. The Doctor was given a name by Danara Pel, a woman he loves. What did she call him?

   a. Snookums
   b. Schmulis
   c. Schmukins
   d. The Worm

2. How long did Kes and Neelix date?

   a. Too long
   b. Not long enough for Neelix
   c. We don't know
   d. All of the above

3. What does Paris do in his spare time?

   a. Dates half the ship
   b. Dates the other half of the ship
   c. Gets convicted for crimes he didn't commit
   d. Pretends he's in France
   e. All of the above.

4. What species of alien is "Seven of Nine"?

   a. Romulan
   b. Vulcan
   c. Someone who liked *The Mirror Has Two Faces*
   d. Borg

5. What does Chakotay do when he's troubled?

   a. Eats chocolate
   b. Plays video games
   c. Calls starbases and asks if they have Prince Albert in a can
   d. Communes with his spirit guides

ANSWERS

   1, b; 2, d; 3, e; 4, d; 5, d.

-8-

The Aliens;
Or,
"Why Do They All Have
Weird Foreheads?"

Even a new *Star Trek* viewer will notice that all the aliens seem to be just like humans except for some strange forehead or ears. There is an official *Star Trek* explanation for this, and here it is:

Millions of years ago, an intelligent race traveled the galaxy and discovered that they were terribly alone. So before dying out, they "seeded" countless worlds with their DNA. Each "seeded" race developed differently on each world based upon the environment. These humanoid aliens looked like us except they were strangely featureless and bald. This original race even left a secret message in the DNA of various races which we eventually deciphered. They hoped that discovering our common heritage would cause all the races to live together peaceably. Yeah, right.

But there is an unofficial explanation for why they all look alike, and here it is: it's cheaper to do it that way.

Star Trek has more aliens than they know what to do with. Here are the ones you should know about.

THE GOOD GUYS
The United Federation of Planets

The ultimate good guys, the Federation is an alliance of approximately 150 planets with its headquarters on Earth. (The writers picked that number because that's about as big as the United Nations.) These cultures united for mutual trade, defense, and diplomatic reasons. The Federation stretches between the Alpha and Beta Quadrants, bordered by the Alpha Quadrant by the Cardassian Union, and by the Beta Quadrant by the Romulans and the Klingons.

Starfleet is the military and exploratory arm of the Federation. Comprised of crew members from many planets, Starfleet is a cross between NASA and the U.S. Navy. Although their main duties involve exploration and research, Starfleet has a strong military background and outlook. Starfleet Headquarters is located in San Francisco.

Federation science is among the most advanced in the galaxy and is considered to be slightly ahead of that of the Romulans and the Klingons. Federation starships are powerful, fast, and varied in size and shape, depending upon their function. They are also well appointed, with comfortable quarters and facilities.

HISTORY

Founded in the year 2161, the Federation is governed by the Federation Council, which is made up of representatives from each planet. The council is led by the Federation Council President, who is often a member of some weird alien species with a bad haircut. This may be explained by the fact that the Office of the Federation President in located in Paris.

As new species are encountered, they are considered for admission to the Federation. The process is a thorough one that takes years to complete.

VULCANS

These are the first aliens who made contact with humanity, as we saw in *Star Trek: First Contact*. They are among mankind's closest allies and a founding planet of the United Federation of Planets. The planet Vulcan is a hot, dry world, with strong gravity. Because of this, Vulcans are physically stronger than humans, and live for about two hundred years. They have all sorts of physical adaptations, such as inner eyelids, that make them tough characters. Their blood is green due to its high concentration of copper, and their internal organs are in different positions. For example, their hearts are where our kidneys are. I don't even want to think about where their uvulas are.

How to Spot Them

Vulcans have pointed ears, and eyebrows that lend them a demonic appearance. Calm and composed, they have a regal bearing and an elegant appearance. Most often they have dark, straight hair.

History

Thousands of years ago the Vulcans were a warlike race. Ruled by their passions, they almost destroyed themselves. A Vulcan named Surak helped lead his people out of this dark age by teaching logic as a discipline. When the Vulcans removed emotion from their lives, Vulcan society flourished. At this point in history, a portion of the population that did not want to acccept the rule of logic left the planet to settle elsewhere. These people became the evil Romulans.

Society

Vulcans live by the rule of logic. It guides their personal lives and their planetary decisions. Suppressing emotion has had ramifications, of course. Every seven years of their adult lives, Vulcans experience *Pon farr*, the time of mating. Their logic is stripped from them, and they must return home to mate, or die trying. (On Earth this is called *spring break*.)

During *Pon farr*, all bets are off. Vulcans frequently fight for their mates. To avoid this problem, Vulcans are betrothed to their husbands and wives when they are seven years old. However, when the time comes to do the deed they can challenge the entire process, choose champions, and fight to the death. Kirk and Spock fought such a battle on Vulcan once. Only Kirk's apparent death brought Spock out of his blood fever.

Vulcans by definition cannot show emotion. To do so is indicative of a major illness or syndrome. In case of such illness, Vulcans can use meditative methods to heal themselves.

They are also telepaths. They can communicate with each other and other races using only the power of their minds. However, this experience is draining and requires discipline. Touching the face facilitates this type of communication. (In addition, really spooky music on the soundtrack helps *a lot.*)

Vulcans are essentially nonviolent, but will use force when it is necessary, and logical, to do so. The Vulcan nerve pinch is a famous technique by which a humanoid can be rendered unconscious. It is applied by the fingers to the base of the neck, and the victim is out cold in seconds. Although Kirk was never able to learn it, Data picked it up pretty quickly.

Vulcans often undergo *Kolinahr,* a long, intense ritual designed to remove all emotion. Both our favorite Vulcans, Spock and Tuvok, have failed to complete it.

Vulcans are famous for their greeting: "Live long and prosper."

FAMOUS VULCANS

Spock   Science officer of the U.S.S. *Enterprise*
Sarek   Spock's father and famous ambassador
Surak   Father of Vulcan logic
Tuvok   Tactical and security officer of the U.S.S. *Voyager*
Vorek   Engineering ensign on U.S.S. *Voyager*
T'Pau   High-ranking official and a relative of Spock's. She presided at his almost-wedding.
Valeris   Prodigy of Spock's and member of conspiracy to sabotage Klingon-Federation peace talks
Saavik   Starfleet officer who helped retrieve Spock's body from the Genesis Planet

BETAZOIDS

Betazoids are a race of telepaths and come from the planet Betazed. They are capable of reading minds and also of sensing emotion. Their special abilities usually manifest in adolescence, but once in a while a Betazoid child is *born* with telepathy. These unfortunate few have a difficult time learning how to screen out others' thoughts.

The planet Betazed is very beautiful and is a popular tourist destination. Largely because of the inhabitants' telepathic abilities,

Betazed culture is based on openness and truth. You can't get away with anything there.

How to Spot Them

Betazoids are identical to humans except for their black irises, which give them an eerie appearance.

Society

Betazoid children are often telepathically linked to their future spouses. Later they are able to find one another through this link. Betazoids celebrate marriage in a weird way: they attend the wedding completely naked. Their eating habits are unusual. While they eat, someone bangs a huge gong methodically during the meal.

Famous Betazoids

Deanna Troi   Counselor aboard U.S.S. *Enterprise*-D
Lwaxana Troi   Mother of Deanna Troi
Lon Suder   Deceased, murderous ensign aboard U.S.S. *Voyager*

BAJORANS

Bajorans inhabit Bajor, of course, a planet located near the Cardassian border. They are the main alien species on *Star Trek: Deep Space Nine,* because the station is in orbit around that world. Very similar to humans, they are not yet members of the Federation, but they have been under investigation for membership. Bajor recently discovered it is at the entrance of a stable wormhole, called the Bajoran or Idran Wormhole. This hole in space is a shortcut to the Gamma Quadrant and is the home of an alien race.

How to Spot Them

Bajorans differ anatomically from humans, but appear very similar. They also have different biological processes: for example, during pregnancy, Bajoran females sneeze uncontrollably. They have several raised ridges on the bridge of the nose. In addition, all

Bajorans wear customary ear jewelry on the right ear, two studs with a chain connecting them.

HISTORY

Bajoran civilization stretches back twenty-five thousand years. A deeply spiritual people, Bajorans have a proud history of producing great architects, sculptors, and artists. Tragedy struck Bajor in the twenty-fourth century when the Cardassians invaded and occupied Bajor for almost fifty years. During this time, Bajoran resistance groups fought the Cardassians through terrorist campaigns. These fighters eventually drove the Cardassians away, and Bajor was returned to its people, albeit with its buildings destroyed and its fields poisoned. A long period of rebuilding took place while several governments wrestled for dominance.

SOCIETY

Bajoran society is wrapped around the Bajoran religion. Most Bajorans look to their religious leader, the Kai, for guidance. Bajorans believe that the wormhole is actually a celestial temple, and that the aliens living there are the Prophets written about centuries ago. Conservative Bajoran religious figures oppose the teaching of the scientific basis of the wormhole (sound familiar?).

Bajorans believe that the Prophets provided them with eight religious objects, orbs known as "Tears of the Prophets." Each one of these orbs provides a different extrasensory perception. Most of these orbs are still in the possession of the Cardassians, and are keenly sought by the Bajorans.

FAMOUS BAJORANS

Major Kira Nerys   First officer and Bajoran liaison on *Deep Space Nine*

Kai Winn   A conservative religious figure and Bajoran spiritual leader

Shakaar   Former terrorist and public figure

Vedek Bareil   Deceased popular Bajoran religious cleric

Leeta the Dabo Girl   Good-looking employee of Quark's Bar

OCAMPA

An alien race in the Delta Quadrant, the Ocampa live in a subterranean paradise, and until recently all their needs were provided for by an alien known the Caretaker. The Ocampa have a life span of nine years, and as compensation can process information and learn very quickly. (Me, I'd take the longer life span.) However, some groups of Ocampa have been found that live up to twenty years or more.

The Ocampa have powerful telepathic abilities, enabling them to communicate mentally, and possible clairvoyant abilities as well, allowing them to foresee possible futures. They reach sexual maturity in a process called Elogium, at which point they are able to bear one child. This event occurs only once in their life. When their biological alarm clock goes off, it *goes off.*

HOW TO SPOT THEM

The Ocampa are very similar to humans, except they have pointy ears and pixielike features.

HISTORY

The Ocampa once lived on the surface of their world, but the Caretaker, conducting what he thought were harmless scientific tests, accidentally destroyed their ecosystem. Guilt-ridden, the Caretaker set up the Array and provided the Ocampa with energy until he died.

FAMOUS OCAMPA

Kes   Medical assistant on the U.S.S. *Voyager*

TALAXIANS

The Talaxians are an alien race that resides in the Delta Quadrant. Not much is known about them except that they were in a prolonged conflict with the Haakonians, who destroyed the Talaxian moon Rinax, resulting in hundreds of thousands of deaths.

HOW TO SPOT THEM

Talaxians have spotted, elongated heads, with a red mane running along the middle of the skull. They sport red whiskers. They look a lot like the cowardly lion from *The Wizard of Oz*.

FAMOUS TALAXIANS

Neelix   Guide and cook aboard U.S.S. *Voyager*

THE SOMETIMES GOOD, SOMETIMES BAD GUYS

KLINGONS

Once a most dangerous enemy, the Klingons are now allies of the Federation. This alliance is extremely unstable, due to the hostile nature of Klingon psychology and changing political loyalties. The planet Qo'noS (pronounced *kronos*) is the Klingon homeworld, a forbidding place, located in the Beta Quadrant near the Romulan Empire. Klingons are a warrior race: they are much stronger and tougher physically than humans. Their bodies contain extra organs for almost every major function, making them extremely difficult to kill. If you are lucky enough to wound one, you will find that they have lavender-colored blood. Technologically advanced, they can pose a major threat when provoked.

HOW TO SPOT THEM

They are not hard to recognize. Bigger physically than most humans, Klingons have dark skin and large forehead ridges. They wear black and silver uniforms with silver bandoliers. They look a little like members of the rock group KISS except any Klingon can sing better than Paul Stanley. They are fond of wearing beards and mustaches, which are signs of honor.

During the original *Star Trek*, Klingons seemed quite human. It was only when the movies came along that money could be spent to make them look more fearsome. So how do they explain the two distinct forms of Klingons we have seen over the years? They don't. Worf tells us that "it is not discussed with outsiders." *Star Trek* theory holds that the Klingons surgically altered their appearance along the borders with the Federation to facilitate infiltration. I don't know about that. Even with the surgery, they didn't fit in all that well.

HISTORY

Klingon civilization first arose fifteen hundred years ago, when they were united by Kahless the Unforgettable. Kahless is a legendary figure to the Klingons, the archetype of the Klingon warrior. Klingons like to sing songs about Kahless, boasting of the monthlong battles he fought. For centuries after his rule, the Klingons spread aggressively outward, conquering star systems and taking what they needed.

Their first encounter with the Federation was a diplomatic disaster and resulted in a century of hostility. However, after the explosion on the Klingon moon Praxis, which toppled the Klingon economy, the empire was forced to open a dialogue with the Federation. These peace talks led to the signing of a treaty, which was broken for a short time by Gowron, the Klingon Chancellor. The treaty, known as the Khitomer Accords, currently remains in effect.

Kahless the Unforgettable returned in the twenty-fourth century in the form of a genetically designed duplicate, programmed with Kahless's memories. Gowron reluctantly agreed to allow this doppelgänger to assume the figurehead position of Emperor.

SOCIETY

Klingons value honor above all else. The status of Klingon warrior is the most exalted in their society. Death on the battlefield is the most meaningful death for a Klingon and is celebrated, not mourned. As you can imagine, Klingon medical science isn't very advanced, because they are not particularly interested in saving people. Klingons fight until they, or their enemies, are dead.

Upon the death of a Klingon warrior, his comrades howl at the sky, to warn the spirits that a warrior is coming to join them. Klingons believe that if you die an honorable death you will cross over into *Sto-Vo-Kor* (the Klingon equivalent of Valhalla), and take your place in the ranks of the honored dead. For this reason, Klingons value hand-to-hand combat and like to play with knives.

The bat'telh, a Klingon sword, is a favorite weapon. For honor to be satisfied, fighting must take place face-to-face. A Klingon's greatest wish is to be praised in song. Klingons rise in rank by physically challenging their superiors; only the strong survive.

Klingons like their food good and fresh, and only occasionally dead. Gagh, a favorite dish, is best served alive.

Klingon mating rituals are long, involved, and violent. Choking is an accepted form of foreplay. (Of course, for real pain, you can't beat the good old Earth custom, the *blind date*.)

Klingon society is feudal. Klingon families are huge and powerful, often owning tracts of land and starships. The largest, most highly regarded families possess seats on the High Council, the ruling body of the Klingon Empire. The High Council appoints a Chancellor, through whom the Klingon Empire speaks. Succession to positions of power is determined through combat, and ancient rules and tradition govern these battles to the death.

Klingon society is sexist, with Klingon women getting the worst of it. Klingon men are usually the providers, and women the bearers of children. Klingon women are generally barred from owning property or troops. For example, if a Klingon woman remarries, her new husband will lay claim to that which she possesses. In rare instances, a Klingon woman will be able to retain control of property. For example, Lursa and B'Etor, the Duras sisters, controlled the Duras family when Worf killed Duras in battle.

KLINGON TECHNOLOGY

Klingon weapons are very powerful, but not varied. Disruptors and photon torpedoes are the weapons of choice. Klingon warships follow a standard design, with a slender neck protruding from the main hull and two warp nacelles below the ship. (Most often you can tell the good guys' ships from the bad guys' ships by following this simple rule: if the nacelles are above, they're good. If they're below, they're bad.) Some Klingon ships possess a huge forward-mounted disruptor, which we have yet to see fired in combat. One Klingon warship is the Bird-of-Prey, often painted to resemble giant, warlike birds. Klingon ships all carry cloaking devices which shield them from detection. However, to fire their weapons, Klingon ships must de-cloak. (Klingons like all the face-to-face combat stuff, remember).

Klingon ships are often just are large as Federation starships, but their interior appointments are far more stark. Klingon weapon systems are a little stronger than ours, but our shields and engines are better, so we can fend them off adequately, and run. Technologically they lag a bit behind the Federation.

KLINGON LANGUAGE

Klingons are probably the most popular alien race among Trekkers. It's not hard to figure out why. With their painstiks, mating rituals, and rites of succession, being a Klingon is like being a New York Rangers fan. But it wasn't until *Star Trek* really gained strength as a movement that Trekkers invented the Klingon language. That's right. Some linguistics professors who are Trekkers got together and designed the Klingon language, and now there are people out there who understand the guttural exchanges among these aliens. It's even possible to sit in your car and learn conversational Klingon while driving to work. Why learn a language that almost nobody understands? Ask a Latin major. The Klingon language is rich, strong, and just perfect for establishing a little authority over your *Trek* addict. (For examples, please turn to chapter 11, "The *Star Trek* Convention.")*

KEY KLINGON PHRASES

"Today is a good day to die."
Translation: I have nothing to lose, so I would be happy to fight you to the death. Usually uttered in the face of an overwhelming adversary.
"The Klingon who kills without showing his face has no honor."

---

*For more Klingon information, refer to Marc Okrand's great books *The Klingon Way* and *The Klingon Dictionary*, published by Pocket Books.

Translation: Don't be a Romulan.

"Better to die on our feet than live on our knees."

Translation: Klingons serve no one.

"Four thousand throats may be cut in one night by a running man."

Translation: Even if the odds are against you, you will succeed if you strike at the right time.

"Destroying an empire to win a war is no victory, and ending a battle to save an empire is no defeat."

Translation: We like to fight, but we're not stupid.

FAMOUS KLINGONS

Worf, son of Mogh   Second in command on *Deep Space Nine*

Kurn (Rodek)   Worf's brother

Alexander   Worf's son

Gowron   Klingon Chancellor

General Martok   Gowron's aide and Klingon representative on *Deep Space Nine*

Grilka   Klingon woman who was married to Quark

Duras   Candidate for Chancellor and Klingon traitor. Killed by Worf

Lursa and B'Etor   Duras's sisters. Killed by *Enterprise*-D

K'mpec   Former Chancellor who had been in office longer than any other chancellor. Killed by Duras

Gorkon   Deceased Klingon Chancellor who began the peace process

Q

Generic name for a race of godlike creatures with the power to control space, time, and matter. With a snap of their fingers, they can erase your existence or give you unlimited power. These entities are playful, petulant, and obnoxious. Though it seems nothing is beyond their power, the Q do fear certain races, such as the El-Aurians. The Q are often bored and seek contact with other races for amusement. They will not hesitate to torture or tease a group of beings if it suits them.

How to Spot Them

Although they have no physical shape, they will take human form to communicate with us. They can be recognized by the speed and suddenness of their appearance, and the breadth of their power.

History

The origin of the Q is unknown. They reside in a dimension known as the Q Continuum. This Continuum is composed of many Q, and they have organized a society of sorts. Rules for the behavior of individual Q exist and are enforced by other Q. On rare occasions, a Q may be punished by being stripped of its powers or being imprisoned.

The Q Continuum's most serious crisis occurred when Quinn, a Q, decided to commit suicide out of boredom. No Q had ever died, and the Continuum feared anarchy would result. A hearing was held aboard the U.S.S. *Voyager,* and Captain Janeway ruled that Quinn could end its existence.

After the death of Quinn, civil war broke out in the Q Continuum. The Q decided to begin reproducing again in an attempt to reinvigorate the Continuum.

Famous Qs

Q   Original Q, who harassed *Enterprise*-D
Q2   Second Q, who supervised original Q
Quinn   Third Q, who committed suicide

EL-AURIANS

Known as a race of listeners, the human-looking El-Aurians are great to talk to, but they don't reveal much of themselves or their society. They have lifespans measured in centuries and a number of unusual powers and senses. For example, they can sense changes in the space-time continuum, something humans cannot do without massive amounts of tequila. And the all-powerful Q seem to fear them for some reason.

How to Spot Them

Whoopi Goldberg played an El-Aurian. So did Malcolm

McDowell. If you can find something to distinguish them from other humans, let me know.

HISTORY

The El-Aurians' planet was destroyed by the Borg, and they scattered across the universe in panic. They are still homeless as of this writing.

FAMOUS EL-AURIANS

Guinan   The bartender in the Ten-Forward lounge aboard the *Enterprise*-D

Dr. Tolian Soren   Scientist who attempted to destroy a solar system to return to the Nexus, as seen in *Star Trek: Generations*

FERENGI

The Ferengi are a race of merchants organized by a strict adherence to the laws of capitalism (not to be confused with Republicans). Originally from the planet Ferenginar, the Ferengi have spread throughout the galaxy. A strictly independent people, they seek only to do business and acquire great personal wealth. They have been known to double deal in a conflict, selling arms to both sides. The Ferengi have a strict code of behavior, but it is a kind of behavior foreign to most species. Klingons, for example, despise the Ferengi and consider them to be without honor.

HOW TO SPOT THEM

Ferengi are not particularly attractive to us humans. They are short, with bulbous foreheads, huge ears, and pointy teeth. (Ferengi prefer their teeth that way, often using a tooth sharpener.) They usually cover the base of their skulls with a skirtlike headdress.

SOCIETY

Ferengi society is organized around a series of commandments known as the Rules of Acquisition. These rules, numbering in the hundreds, are the best indication of what lies in the Ferengi soul. A few examples:

Rule 1: Once you have their money...you never give it back.

Rule 6: Never allow family to stand in the way of opportunity.

Rule 18: A Ferengi without profit is no Ferengi at all.

Rule 60: Treat people in your debt like family...exploit them.

Rule 284: Deep down, everyone is a Ferengi.*

The main Ferengi administrative agency is the FCA (Ferengi Commerce Authority), a cross between the IRS and the CIA. It is all-powerful and deeply feared by Ferengi citizens. It can strip a Ferengi of his property, instantly ruining him. Agents of the FCA are paid by those they are investigating. (Hey, it really is like the IRS!)

The leader of the Ferengi is a figurehead known as the Grand Nagus, who wields vast power over other Ferengi by doling out trade territories and commercial opportunities.

The Ferengi are deeply sexist, probably even more so than the Klingons (or the French). Ferengi women are forbidden to do almost anything, such as conduct business or wear clothes. That's right, Ferengi women must walk around naked at all times. The Ferengi male is a chauvinistic creature that seeks to mate with every woman he sees. In Ferengi culture, rules of courtship are a bit strange. The male will not speak to the female except to command her and the female is expected to perform all the little niceties such as prechew the man's food so it's easier for him to eat. (All right, so it's not *exactly* like France.)

The capitalistic Ferengi culture extends to death. At the end of a Ferengi's life he will sell his organs on the common market to the highest bidder. Once such a sale takes place, the Ferengi must die to complete the transaction.

FERENGI TECHNOLOGY

Supposedly, Ferengi technology rivals that of the Federation. We haven't seen much of their equipment, other than a few ships and a whiplike energy weapon that looks really stupid. The principal Ferengi battleship is called a Ferengi Marauder, and it looks a little

---

*For the entire list, see Ira Steven Behr's *The Ferengi Rules of Acquisition*, published by Pocket Books.

like a giant croissant. (Again, the similarity to the French.) These vessels come equipped with a "plasma weapon" that can disable a Federation starship.

THE BAD GUYS

BREEN

Little is known about the Breen except they are very hostile and live on a very cold planet. You can recognize them from the environmental suits they wear which conceal their faces with a dark band of glass. The Romulans have a saying: "Never turn your back on a Breen."

They use organic spaceships, which means that the vessel itself is a life form.

ROMULANS

The Romulans are an enigmatic race and a dangerous foe of the Federation. Not only are they powerful and technologically advanced, but they are also deceitful and cunning. Usually *Star Trek* villains have some code that constrains their behavior to known limits, but not the Romulans. They seem to be capable of anything.

The Romulan Star Empire was formed millennia ago when their ancestors left the planet Vulcan because they did not want to accept logic as a guiding principle. Romulans, therefore, are Vulcans from hell: what the Vulcans would have become if they had not become the clear-thinking, logical pussycats we know and love. The Romulan Star Empire is located in the Beta Quadrant near their bitter enemies, the Klingons.

HOW TO SPOT THEM

During the early *Star Trek* years, Romulans and Vulcans were identical in appearance. (In fact, Mark Leonard, who played Spock's father, also played the first Romulan ever encountered.) As with the Klingons, bigger budgets have allowed some change. You can now recognize Romulans by the small forehead ridges over their eyebrows. They wear silver and black uniforms, with huge *1980s-look-at-the-*

new-blouse-I-got-at-Marshall's-and-it-was-50-percent-off-type shoulder pads. I mean, they are big shoulder pads. Think of it this way: *shoulder pads = Romulans.*

ROMULAN TECHNOLOGY

The Romulans possess advanced, unique technology, some of which is not completely understood. For example, instead of using antimatter to generate power for the warp engines, Romulans use a type of black hole, an artificially generated quantum singularity. They also have powerful disruptors which can obliterate a Federation starship.

The main Romulan ship is called a Warbird. These huge vessels are twice as big as the *Enterprise*-D and just as powerful. It seems they're a little slower than our ships, so, again, we can outrun them if we have to. You can recognize a Warbird instantly. Big, green, and eerie-looking, these ships almost seem to have a "face" looking at you, with the chin jutting out defiantly. Romulan vessels use a cloaking device very similar to that of the Klingons.

SOCIETY

Not much is known of Romulan society, but it seems analogous to ancient Rome. The leader of the Romulans is called the praetor. Members of the council are called proconsuls. Women and men serve together in politics and in battle. Romulans are capable of some tenderness but have an extreme violent streak.

A neutral zone separates the Federation and the Romulan Star Empire. This region, about a light-year across, was the result of negotiations after the last interstellar war. It is considered an offense to travel into the neutral zone, and to do so violates the treaty.

Romulan society is shrouded in mystery, but the Federation is aware that a resistance movement is growing. Dissidents exist who oppose the aggressive military nature of the government. However, they are being systematically rooted out and destroyed by the government. The goal of the dissidents is unification, the rejoining of Vulcan and Romulan societies. The famous Spock, now an ambassador, is hiding out on Romulus, one of the empire's homeworlds (the other is Remus, or Romii, depending on whom you ask), trying to achieve this goal.

On a lighter note, Romulan Ale is a potent alcoholic beverage that is popular across the galaxy, but is illegal within the Federation.

FAMOUS ROMULANS

Sela   Half-Romulan, half-human daughter of Tasha Yar. High-ranking military officer and major pain in the neck

Tomalak   Romulan officer who often turns up in *Star Trek* episodes

Selok   Romulan subcommander who was a spy in the Federation, posing as a Vulcan ambassador

THE BORG

Probably the most feared enemy in the galaxy, the Borg are a technologically superior group of cybernetic humanoids. Half organic and half machine, they have been the primary threat to both the Alpha and Beta Quadrants for the last few years. The Borg exist in a collective consciousness without individual differentiation. They assimilate other races and incorporate them into their collective by adding Borg implants and turning them into the Borg. They are the ultimate cult.

Individual Borg are very strong, and each one has different hardware attached to his or her limbs based upon his or her duties, much like a vacuum cleaner. They do not think as individuals, preferring to communicate with other races in the voice of one hivelike mind. Although they are born human-looking, they receive cybernetic implants at an early age. These implants rewrite DNA and can make you very ugly very quickly.

When an individual Borg is killed, another one instantly takes its place. This new Borg is now immune to what killed the one before it. Dead Borg are removed from the collective consciousness by the removal of small devices. The bodies of the dead Borg then disappear, avoiding those hard-to-remove Borg stains on nice, clean Federation carpets.

How to Spot Them

The Borg are humanoids that have black, mechanical devices attached to their bodies. They wear black rubber suits and have tubes sticking out of their skin. The process of becoming a Borg robs the skin of its original color and turns them all into a uniform shade of gray. (Basically, it's like working at the Gap.)

The Borg speak in one collective voice. They like to interrupt, and are fond of saying things like, "Resistance is futile," "You will be assimilated," and "Death is irrelevant." (The Gap Borg like to say "It's preshrunk!")

History

The Borg originate from the Delta Quadrant, but little is known about how they developed. They control hundreds of star systems and huge areas of space.

The Borg first encountered the Federation when the *Enterprise*-D was transported into Borg space by Q, the godlike pain in the ass. The Borg almost destroyed the *Enterprise*-D, which was sent back home by Q in the nick of time.

In the twenty-fourth century, a Borg known as Third of Five was found by the crew of *Enterprise*-D, who named him Hugh. Separated from the collective, this Borg began to develop an individual personality. When he was returned to the Borg collective, his experiences were downloaded by the rest of the Borg. The promise of individuality was attractive to some of the Borg, and a splinter group formed, led by Hugh. This splinter group had its own type of ship, a weird, asymmetrical vessel capable of opening wormholes to travel large distances. Directionless, Hugh's splinter group fell under the spell of Lore, Data's brother. They were defeated by the crew of the *Enterprise*-D.

The Borg invaded the Federation twice, each time with only one ship. The first time they succeeded in reaching Earth and destroyed much of Starfleet. That Borg ship was destroyed by the *Enterprise*-D. The second time they also reached Earth and sent a small ship back in time to prevent Earth from using warp engines and to stop First Contact with the Vulcans, allowing the Borg to assimilate

Earth. They were defeated by the crew of the *Enterprise*-E, and the Borg Queen was destroyed. We do not know what the effect the Queen's death had on the collective.

BORG TECHNOLOGY

Since the Borg have absorbed the technology from hundreds of civilizations, they have reached a powerful level of technical sophistication. Every aspect of their technology seems to be more advanced than that of the Federation. Their weapons are extremely dangerous and difficult to defend against.

The Borg have the ability to drain defensive shields of their power. They have extremely powerful tractor beams capable of seizing a ship until its defenses are destroyed. Then the Borg use a cutting beam to chop ships into little bits and absorb them.

Once struck by a weapon, the Borg use their collective mind to find a way to neutralize it. Starfleet has found a way to confuse them for a limited time by constantly changing the frequencies of their phasers.

Borg ships are generally huge and cube-shaped. Recently we have seen a new spherical ship used by the Borg. These ships are extremely decentralized, without any bridge, engineering, or living areas. Because of this, the vessel can continue to operate even if 78 percent of it were destroyed. Individual Borg "plug into" the vessel to help her regenerate at amazing speed. Borg ships travel much faster than any other known ship, able to move at warp 9.99 for extended periods of time. It's unknown what method of propulsion they use, but it ain't rubber bands.

The Borg destroy civilizations by scooping up whole cities from planets and absorbing them. While they are primarily interested in technology, they will grapple with individual creatures if threatened.

SOCIETY

The Borg collective is organized around the Borg Queen, who embodies the whole of the Borg hive-mind. We don't know how many Borg Queens there are. Apart from that, the term "Borg society" is an oxymoron, like "student life" or "jumbo shrimp."

FAMOUS BORG

Hugh   Borg individual befriended by crew of *Enterprise*-D
Borg Queen   Leader of the Borg; killed by Data

THE DOMINION

In the Gamma Quadrant, an evil empire yearns to destroy the Federation, the Klingons, and the Romulans. They are the Dominion, and they are a frightening bunch. Composed of many races, they are, in a way, an anti-Federation. The following comprises what we know of this dangerous foe.

THE FOUNDERS

The Founders are the rulers of the Dominion. These shape-shifters can adopt any form, impersonate any being. They virulently hate other species, which they call "solids." Lovers of order, they see the universe as a chaotic place that needs to be subdued. The Founders distrust all races, even the ones they dominate.

Founders do not eat, drink, or make love. They must rest once every sixteen hours by returning to a gelatinous state. (In this way, they most resemble first-year law students.)

HOW TO SPOT THEM

You can't. They assume other identities. In their pure form, they appears as golden, gelatinous beings able to form tentacles. Although impersonating humans is difficult for them, certain Founders have become skilled at it.

The Federation has developed a blood screening test: they take a sample of blood, and if it turns into the gelatinous material of the Founders' natural state, then the donor is a changeling. It is feared that one day the Founders will develop a method of fooling the test or Princeton Review will develop a coaching course.

HISTORY

The Founders were not always so warlike. However, after years of living in fear and being discriminated against by countless civilizations who tried to destroy them, the Founders became xenophobic. Retreating to their hidden world, they eventually began a campaign to subdue other races before they could attack.

FOUNDER TECHNOLOGY

The Founders do not have technology per se: they steal it from the other races they come into contact with. Nonetheless, the technology they do control is very advanced, in some cases beyond that of the Federation.

SOCIETY

Founder society is unique: these shape-shifters like to pool together into a vast ocean of slime. They call this joining the Great Link. In the Great Link, Founders share their thoughts and deepest secrets, and plan strategies.

Founders may be brutal toward other societies, but toward each other they are loving and respectful. Crime is nonexistent. In fact, until recently, no changeling has ever harmed another.

The Founders have sent hundreds of changeling infants into the universe with instructions to return. They did this to gather information on other species in order to decide whom to conquer.

FAMOUS FOUNDERS

Odo   Security chief on *Deep Space Nine*. He's the only changeling to have killed another, and he was punished by the Great Link by having his shape-shifting powers removed.

VORTA

We know virtually nothing of the Vorta except that they are basically the lawyers for the Founders. They interact with other species for the Founders and maintain order. As the leash-holders for the Jem'Hadar, they are responsible for feeding them and maintaining order. They are cunning and deceitful.

The Vorta reproduce through cloning; each is a carbon copy of his great-grandfather. They consider this to be the most efficient method of reproduction.

How to Spot Them

Human-looking except for their ears, the Vorta look like giant vampire bats. Other than that they are pretty cute.

Jem'Hadar

A most dangerous adversary, these warrior aliens are the shock troops of the Dominion. Bred for combat, they are extremely strong and fast. They have a short life span, and reach maturity faster than Macaulay Culkin. They don't eat, drink, or make love.

How to Spot Them

The Jem'Hadar have a fearsome appearance. Bluish-gray in color, they are tall and powerfully built. They have tiny spikes surrounding their faces, and the backs of their heads curve to touch their necks, forming a carrying handle of sorts. All Jem'Hadar have a tube in their necks connected to their uniforms. The tube pulses with a white-colored liquid.

Society

Jem'Hadar are genetically engineered warriors. The Founders designed them to be interchangeable and ruthless. To maintain control of them, the Founders handicapped their ability to produce a key enzyme called the White. Without this enzyme, the Jem'Hadar cannot survive. A Vorta accompanies them on every mission, and is entrusted with the White that they need to survive. The White is injected into the Jem'Hadar necks by a tube delivery system in their uniform. In addition, Jem'Hadar are programmed from conception to revere the Founders. It is beyond their ability to harm a changeling, so when they see Odo, they freeze up.

The Jem'Hadar live to fight; they feel useless unless they are pounding someone on the head. They do have an honor code: it is considered bad form to kill a foe who can no longer defend himself. The Jem'Hadar are fond of saying, "Victory is life!" and "Today we are dead, we fight to regain our lives." They take themselves *way* too seriously.

JEM'HADAR TECHNOLOGY

These guys are tough. They wear cloaking devices that can shield individual warriors from detection. Jem'Hadar fighting ships are beetle-shaped and very, very fast. The ships also carry cloaking devices. Although smaller than most Federation starships, these fighters are capable of taking out a *Galaxy*-class starship like the *Enterprise*-D. The Federation doesn't understand how their technology operates, but they have recently captured a Jem'Hadar ship, so expect some progress in this area.

CARDASSIANS

The Cardassians are an aggressive militaristic race in the Alpha Quadrant that has recently allied with the Dominion. The Cardassians were once a peaceful, powerless people, and widespread famine killed millions. When they adopted violent military tactics, they conquered worlds and formed the Cardassian Union.

HOW TO SPOT THEM

Cardassians have gray skin and reptilian scales on their necks. They wear silver and black uniforms with large chestplates. They have dark hair and raised bumps on their faces. Bajorans call them "spoonheads."

SOCIETY

We know very little of Cardassian society; we do know that you don't want to live there. The Cardassian system of justice is particularly screwy. A suspect is convicted before trial, and the sentence has already been determined before the defendant even sees the inside of a courtroom.

Cardassians are ruled by a High Council whose members are

appointed somehow. The Cardassian military is all-powerful in society. The intelligence service of the military, the Obsidian Order, was much feared until they were defeated by the Founders in the Gamma Quadrant.

Affairs outside of marriage can occur, but if children are produced, the father may choose to kill them.

Cardassians are enigmatic and revel in skulduggery. Their lives are often comprised of many layers of secrecy and obfuscation. When a Cardassian faces death, it is customary for him to reveal his secrets to a family member as a final confession.

CARDASSIAN TECHNOLOGY

Cardassians have advanced technology, but they are no match for the Federation or the Klingons. In fact, they were recently at war with the Klingons and were getting pasted until they joined the Dominion. Their ships have a dusky yellowish color and look a little like giant fish. In fact, when you first see their ships, you'll probably think, "Oh, these guys aren't so tough." You're right.

FAMOUS CARDASSIANS

Elim Garak   Tailor and spy aboard *Deep Space Nine*

Gul Dukat   Leader of Cardassia. Former prefect of *Deep Space Nine*

Ziyal   Daughter of Gul Dukat and Garak's main squeeze

Enabran Tain   Deceased father of Garak and head of Obsidian Order

Seska   Deceased Maquis member who spied for the Cardassians. Surgically altered to appear human.

THE KAZON

Never a credible adversary, these rock-headed aliens live in the Delta Quadrant and regularly harassed *Voyager* until the ship left their space. They are divided into large sects that frequently combat one another for resources. Violent and backward, they are no fun at a party.

How to Spot Them

The Kazon are dark-skinned and have big, rocklike heads. They wear fur-lined outfits and look absolutely ridiculous.

Kazon History

Suffering for years in slavery to a race called the Trabe, the Kazon finally overthrew their masters and took over the planet and the Trabes' technology. They immediately separated into sects and fought among themselves. Although they tried several times to organize, the Maj (leaders) of each sect were power-hungry and deceitful.

Kazon Technology

The Kazon have warp travel and that's about it. They do not have replicators, transporters, or photon torpedoes. Yet for some reason they were always a threat to *Voyager.* Each sect longed to get ahold of *Voyager*'s advanced technology to take over the other sects. They did take over the ship, but were defeated by the Doctor and Ensign Suder, the murderer imprisoned on *Voyager.* Considering that they were repelled by one psychopath and a hologram, the Kazon are pretty pathetic.

THE VIDIIANS

Residing in the Delta Quadrant, the Vidiians are the winners of the "Ugliest *Star Trek* Villain of All Time Award." As technologically advanced as the Federation, they are truly a scary people. The Vidiians suffer from a disease they call the Phage; apparently, it's a more intense form of leprosy. The disease eats away at the body, causing a slow and painful death. Much of the population has been infected and the Vidiians have no cure. Trying to stay ahead of the disease, the Vidiians find healthy alien species and harvest their organs, transplanting them into their bodies to prolong their lives.

How to Spot Them

If you see a bunch of aliens that have scarred, multicolored faces that look as though the flesh is rotting off, that's the Vidiians. You'll find them chasing *Voyager* through the Delta Quadrant.

HISTORY

Originally the Vidiians were a prosperous, beautiful people. When they were stricken by the Phage, their society dedicated its combined efforts to developing a cure. Now, obsessed with their declining health, the Vidiians are organ pirates, brutally attacking any species in an attempt to save themselves. It appears that some Vidiians are not yet infected by the virus, suggesting that their society may be quarantine-based.

VIDIIAN TECHNOLOGY

Although Vidiian technology is roughly equal to that of the Federation, their medical technology far surpasses ours. Vidiians are literally able to beam your heart out of your body while you watch. Their ships look like large forklifts, and while *Voyager* can fight them off and outrun them, if the ship is not at full strength they are in big trouble. The Vidiians are physically weakened by the Phage, but they are also desperate, so they fight with a particular urgency.

FAMOUS VIDIIANS

Danara Pel   The Holodoctor's main squeeze, one of the decent Vidiians. She'll help *Voyager* when she can

SPECIES 8472

These beings are the most terrifying enemy any Federation ship has encountered. Powerful enough to destroy the Borg, we know very little about them. There is no known name for this mysterious life-form, and the Borg refer to them only by number. Species 8472 are able to absorb any life-form through infection: their cells have extraordinary immune responses that enable them to destroy anything that penetrates them—chemical, biological, or technological. A typical Species 8472 cell possesses one hundred times the amount of DNA that human cells do; their biological functions are incredibly complex. The Borg are unable to assimilate them, but they have the ability to absorb the Borg. Once someone is infected by the cells of Species 8472, tendrils emerge from his body to surround and take over the helpless victim. No medicine known to Federation science can stop the inexorable spread of their disease. In addition, Species 8472 can communicate telepathically.

Species 8472 emerged recently in the Delta Quadrant, in the middle of Borg space. They come through an artificially created quantum singularity (a black hole) from another continuum where they alone exist. They have punched a hole from their universe to ours, and they plan to take over our galaxy.

How to Spot Them

Species 8472 stand about two meters tall, have three legs, two arms, and long, nightmarish faces. They are yellowish-gray in color and terribly hostile. They don't appear to wear uniforms.

Species 8472 Technology

Not much is known about these fearsome aliens' technology. Their ships are composed of organic living tissue, which means that their vessels can regenerate themselves when damaged. Their weapons are very destructive; they fire a type of energy bolt that can destroy Borg vessels. Several ships linked together can fire a beam powerful enough to destroy a planet!

THE POWER TABLE

Here is your quick guide to who can beat up whom, from most powerful to pussycat:

Q
Species 8472
The Borg
The Dominion
The Vidiians
The Federation (us)
The Klingons (tie)

The Romulans (tie)
The Cardassians
The Ferengi
(and way down on the list)
Tribbles
The Kazon

THE ALIEN QUIZ

1. Which Klingon is called the "Unforgettable?"

   a. I forget
   b. Kahless
   c. Kor
   d. Natalie Cole

2. Which race is known as "the race of listeners"?

   a. Larry King
   b. The terrible Oprahs
   c. The El-Aurians
   d. Klingons

3. How can you tell the Bajorans from humans?

   a. They have forehead ridges
   b. They have ridges on the bridge of their noses
   c. They have pointy ears
   d. They actually like elevator music

4. What is a Romulan spaceship called?

   a. The funky chicken
   b. A Warbird
   c. My Yiddishe Mama
   d. A planetscraper

5. Who are the "lawyers of the Founders"?

   a. The firm of Dewey, Cheatem and Howe
   b. The Vorta
   c. The Bar Association
   d. Jacoby and Meyers

6. What do the Jem'Hadar need to survive?

   a. Chocolate
   b. Any album by the Gypsy Kings
   c. *Mystery Science Theater 3000*
   d. The White

7. Why did the writers give the Federation 150 members?

   a. That's the number in the United Nations
   b. That's all the chairs they have
   c. The hall is only rented till midnight
   d. The caterer is very expensive

8. How can you spot a Betazoid?

   a. They are talking to you but their lips aren't moving
   b. They have black eyes
   c. They have really fun, naked weddings
   d. All of the above

9. How do you piss off an Ocampa?

   a. Take away her bat'telh
   b. Serve her dead meat
   c. Tell her you'll call her back in ten years
   d. Hold your finger near her face and say, "I'm not touching
      you. Does this bother you?"

10. Which alien could defeat the Borg?

   a. The Cardassians
   b. Species 8472
   c. The Dominion
   d. The Bajorans

ANSWERS

   1, b; 2, c; 3, b; 4, b; 5, b; 6, d; 7, a; 8, d; 9, c; 10, b.

-9-

TECHNOBABBLE;

OR,

"WHAT THE HELL IS WARP, ANYWAY?"

If you want to get a handle on what's going on in *Star Trek*, you'll have to learn a little about the fantastic twenty-fourth-century technology that Trekkers love. Not only are they familiar with these gizmos, they can probably tell you in minute detail the specific function of every device.

But for the non-Trekker, there isn't anything as intimidating as the technical language that pours casually from crew member's mouths...(for translations of the following phrases, see "Translations" at the end of this chapter):

"Perhaps it's a particle of preanimate matter, caught in the matrix."

"Its hull is pure neutronium; our phasers have no effect."

"Data, fluctuate phaser resonance frequencies, random settings. Keep them changing, don't give them a chance to adapt."

And my favorite:

"The phase inducers are connected to the emitter array, the override is completely gone, and the pattern buffer has been locked into a continuous diagnostic cycle." (Personally, I've felt this way some Sunday mornings.)

There is a word for this type of talk: *technobabble*. With a cadence all its own, technobabble flows gracefully from someone who seemingly understands it. Actually, this language that Trekkers speak isn't as complicated as you think.

Why? Because *Star Trek* is one of the few sci-fi programs that actually tries to keep its inventions in the realm of the scientifically possible. Almost every device mentioned is a possibility and operates according to the laws of physics as we understand them. Sometimes the machines are a little too convenient and the technical solutions that save the day seem a bit far-fetched, but the writers have really thought this stuff out. And they're careful because there is an army of Trekkers out there ready to correct them, and some of them are the guys who didn't have to study for their AP physics exam.

THE BASICS: "WARP ONE, ENGAGE!"

In order for the crew of the *Enterprise* to go where no one has gone before, the ship has to be fast. I mean really fast, because the gulfs between habitable worlds are bigger than casino lobbies in Las Vegas. In fact, the ship has to travel far faster than scientists today believe is possible.

You see, Einstein proved that no object could travel faster than light,* which is a snail's pace compared to the the speed of *Enterprise*. For example, at the speed of light (which we can't even dream of attaining yet) it would take four *years* to reach the nearest star. In addition, there's the little problem of time dilation. It's not enough that Einstein proved we can't go faster than light; oh, no, he also proved that the closer you come to the speed of light, the slower time passes. If you took a speed-of-light trip to Alpha Centauri (the nearest star), it would take four years to get there, but for you it would only seem like a few hours. Only when you returned and realized that *Rocky X* is already out on video would you become aware that eight years had passed.

Needless to say, this provides a problem for scriptwriters. You can't have all this time passing during a one-hour show. Somehow, faster-than-light travel had to be achieved. Thus, the concept of *warp speed* was "invented." In *Star Trek*, spaceships travel beyond the speed of light by "warping" the space around the ship. By creating a warp "bubble," the ship is able to circumvent the ordinary rules of the universe. Isn't that convenient? Hmmm?

Well, there's a catch. It takes a tremendous amount of energy to

---

*About 186,000 miles per second, or the speed at which you run from a *Star Trek* convention.

warp space around a big ship like the *Enterprise*. Roddenberry realized that no present-day power source could do the job. He decided that the ship would be powered by antimatter. Antimatter is exactly what is sounds like: the opposite of matter. Antimatter particles are exactly like normal matter except that they have the opposite spin and electrical charge. Antimatter is not found in the natural world, because when matter and antimatter meet, they completely destroy one another. This destruction yields tremendous energy, which is used to power the warp engines.

Consequently, a matter-antimatter reaction is not to be taken lightly. Magnetic bottles (not glass, but force-fields) contain the dangerous antimatter, and they must be monitored constantly. Occasionally antimatter containment is lost and then you are on your way to a warp core breach. This makes everyone on the ship run around screaming their heads off. Then the antimatter and matter make contact in an uncontrolled way, and the ship is blown to bits, along with everything else in the neighborhood. Although the warp core is designed to be ejected in an emergency, it never seems to work properly. Keep in mind, though, that when you see a warp core breach you are watching a really cool episode. Trekkers love warp core breaches.

"FIRE PHASERS AND PHOTON TORPEDOES!"

Needless to say, there are lots of bad guys out there, so the vessel needs to defend itself. Phasers and photon torpedoes are the primary weapons of Starfleet. Phasers look like laser beams, but they actually change the energy states of matter. By "disrupting" normal matter, they can have subtle and devastating effects. Phasers can be set on "stun" to knock someone out for a few minutes or they can be set on higher settings to vaporize rock and destroy structures. The settings for a phaser are as follows:

1. Light stun
2. Medium stun
3. Heavy stun
4. Heat
5. Burn
6. Vaporize
7. Mix
8. Blend
9. Purée

Phaser beams travel at the speed of light. It's possible for warp-driven craft to outrun them, so photon torpedoes are used for combat at warp speed. Photon torpedoes are warp-powered containers of matter and antimatter. They travel very fast and explode with tremendous power. Sometimes you can put things inside them; for example, Spock's body was ejected into space in a torpedo. The *Enterprise*-D carried 275 of these babies.

"BEAM ME UP, SCOTTY"

Because starships are so big, they generally can't make planetary landings. While this is convenient in terms of saving money on special effects, it's extremely inconvenient in terms of plot development. How can the *Enterprise* pick up guest stars and investigate strange new worlds when they have to spend thousands of dollars to lift off and land this huge spaceship? Easy: Guests get beamed aboard, and crew members get beamed down to check out unexplored turf.

Transporters ferry crew members and material from one place to another. They do this by breaking a person or object down into molecules, converting the matter to energy, and beaming it to another location, where the person or object rematerializes. Practically speaking, modern science isn't even close to providing something as wonderful as a transporter. But the transporter illustrates the lengths the writers will go to make the show credible in the eyes of Trekkers. As evidence, I have two words for you: *Heisenberg Compensators.*

A large barrier to the feasibility of a transporter is Heisenberg's "uncertainty principle." Heisenberg (a well-respected scientist) suggested that at any time it is possible to know the motion or the position of a subatomic particle, but not both. (Pesky things, these subatomic particles.) If that's true, a computer couldn't keep track of all the molecules that make you, and once "you" were "beamed" to a planet you couldn't rematerialize. So, to cover their bases, (and to stave off the letters from Cal Tech), each transporter device comes complete with a Heisenberg Compensator to counteract the principle. Ta da!

A final note on the technology of *Trek:* it follows certain rules. If you know the rules, you can keep up with the program.

Rule 1: Everything leaves a trace of something else. There is always a way to track something, or reconstruct an event because of evidence left behind, such as resonance patterns, ion particles, eddy currents. That way, the crew can always figure out a mystery by the end of the episode.

Rule 2: Machines are interdependent. A crew member can often solve a problem with one device by substituting another. That way, the crew can show how resourceful they are.

Rule 3: Technology is our friend. Although our machines tend to run away from time to time, there is always another machine that can help stop it.

Rule 4: Keep your wits about you. Be skeptical. One of the great pleasures of watching *Star Trek* with your Trekker will be figuring out the mistakes writers make. If you hear something mentioned that you can't understand and you can't find it in this book or any other, don't worry. Chances are, the writers don't understand it either. That's the fun of it.

Rule 5: The science of *Star Trek* is clean. Some science fiction movies, such as *Star Wars,* show a futuristic world with aged, scarred technology, where well-used space ships are held together with bailing wire. Not *Star Trek*. The Federation has smooth, well-functioning craft, as do most of the alien races. The bridge of the *Enterprise*-D is referred to by some insiders as *Embassy Suites.*

THE *ENTERPRISE*

Whichever version you prefer, the *Enterprise* is a huge ship. The original *Enterprise* was 289 meters long (948 feet, about the length of three football fields). It had twenty-three decks, with all sorts of science labs and crew accommodations. It even had a bowling alley. There were 430 people onboard, and as time went on, each new version of the famous ship got bigger and bigger. The *Next Generation*'s *Enterprise*-D was 641 meters long (2,103 feet), literally a city in space, complete with crew members' families along. There were 1,012 people onboard. Botanical gardens, recreational facilities, bigger, more luxurious staterooms: The *Enterprise* is sort of like the Ford Thunderbird; you recognize the original designs in the later incarnations, but they are really cramming too much stuff into it.

A NEW *ENTERPRISE*, AND MAN, IS IT COOL-LOOKING

The latest version, the *Enterprise*-E, seems a little more pared down. It's not quite as big and families weren't present when they took on the Borg in earnest in *Star Trek: First Contact*. It's also a lot more powerful. They prepared the ship for battle against the Borg (and possibly other enemies the Federation is fighting now). It's a sleeker vessel, and it means business.

The *Enterprise* and *Voyager* are prime examples of Starfleet shipbuilding. Composed of three distinct sections, most Federation ships employ similar designs that fulfill requirements of warp travel: the *primary hull*, which is shaped like a flying saucer; the *secondary hull*, which was originally cigar-shaped but flattened out in later versions; and the *warp nacelles*, the two cylinders that stick out from the secondary hull. The crew lives mostly in the primary hull and it contains everything they need to survive, like the bowling alley. The secondary hull holds the key engineering equipment, like the main warp engines. The warp nacelles take the energy from the warp engines and generate the warp field that allows the ship to travel.

In times of great emergency the primary hull can separate from the secondary hull, but this wreaks havoc on the bowling alley.

DEEP SPACE NINE

The space station known as *Deep Space Nine* is not a Federation construct; it was designed by the Cardassians. Originally known as Terok Nor, it was an old mining station, and it was built by Bajoran slave labor. Subsequently the technology on the station is a blend of clean Federation-style design and alien technology. The station is much bigger than any starship, and is home to many races. Population varies according to how many ships are docked to the station. In fact, ever since the Bajoran wormhole was discovered it has been an interstellar center of commerce. There's a bar, a tailor shop, and a Promenade, which makes the station more like a mall than a military base. Ralph Lauren has no plans that we know of for a store on *Deep Space Nine,* but it would fit in really well.

Guarding *Deep Space Nine* is one of the most powerful warships in the Federation's arsenal. The U.S.S. *Defiant,* a rare prototype, was designed specifically in answer to the Borg threat after they laid waste to much of Starfleet. A small, uncomfortable ship, the *Defiant* looks unlike any other Federation vessel. Flat and oval-shaped with its nacelles built into the sides, it's a pug-nosed dreadnought. Its weapons look and sound like no other in Starfleet, phasers firing like Gatling guns as the ship does barrel rolls in space. The *Defiant* is wrapped in ablative armor, which dissipates heat and makes this, in Commander Riker's opinion, "a tough little ship." (By the way, Riker's copy, Thomas Riker, who stole the ship, used the exact same words to describe it.) Worf commands the *Defiant* often and has been known to set up his quarters on the ship because its Spartan accommodations appeal to his Klingon sensibilities.

U.S.S. *VOYAGER*

Star Trek: Voyager is obviously an attempt to recapture the spirit of the original show. The actual ship, the U.S.S. *Voyager,* is about the size of the ship from the original show, but improved technology has reduced the number of crew members to 150. Since the devastating battle with the Borg at Wolf 359, Starfleet had to build new ships, and quickly. Although *Voyager* is smaller than the *Enterprise*-D, the ship is among the most technologically advanced in Starfleet. You can recognize the U.S.S. *Voyager* by its long, oval-shaped primary hull, and by its "variable geometry" nacelles. When *Voyager* goes to warp, its nacelles rise into the standard position. This may solve the problem warp travel causes to the space-time continuum. Then again, it may just look cool. You can recognize *Voyager* by its unique appearance, which some Trekkers refer to as an FTI ("flying travel iron").

Voyager is also distinguished by its ability to land on, and take off from, planets. *Voyager* can lower itself through an atmosphere, extend huge landing pads, and softly touch down on a planet. When it does this, the whole crew goes to "blue alert."

Voyager is unlike any other class of Federation ship. By using *bio-neural gel-packs, Voyager* combines standard electronics with biological tissue to organize and process data more efficiently than the standard isolinear optical computer chips. There seems to be a *Star Trek* trend of merging technology with biological design. This means that *Voyager* is the only starship we know of that can catch cold.

THE TECHNOBABBLE DICTIONARY

Star Trek is awash with technical jargon, and there is not enough space in these pages to define every term. In fact, some of this stuff is still being coined. However, becoming familiar with the following definitions will enable you to sound a lot like a *Trek* expert when necessary.

antigrav   Devices used to transport heavy or dangerous material by making it float in midair. As in "Man, to get Scotty out of the bathroom we had to use the *antigrav.*"

away team   When a planet requires investigation, it is a commanding officer's duty to assemble an away team to go to the planet's surface and check things out. Generally Commander Riker commands the away teams, because Picard is too important to the ship to enter into hazardous situations. (However, Kirk always went on away-team missions and the more dangerous the better.)

antimatter   Matter's exact opposite in spin or electrical charge. Explodes when it comes into contact with matter. Really, really nasty stuff.

Badlands   A region of space marked by huge, roiling electromagnetic storms. Ships that navigate the Badlands must be extremely maneuverable in order to dodge the filaments of plasma that can destroy an unwary vessel. Savvy members of the Maquis hide out in the Badlands to avoid capture.

bearings   The way to describe direction in space. As in, "Captain, sensors indicate a giant taco at bearing 32.5." A bearing indicates direction in terms of the ship, regardless of what direction the ship is "heading" toward. If straight ahead is bearing 000, then an object straight ahead is at bearing 000, regardless of where in the galaxy it is heading.

black hole   A star that has collapsed upon itself, creating a small, intense gravity well so strong that light itself cannot escape. Several scientists theorize that black holes create wormholes to other sections of the universe or even other dimensions. A very bad thing to come across. *See also* **Quantum singularity.**

biochips   Cybernetic implants used by the Federation's vicious enemy, the Borg. They enhance the abilities of these creatures and produce all the nutrients necessary for their flesh to survive.

biofilter   A mechanism in a transporter that screens out strange viruses and bacteria.

bridge   The main command center for ships. Generally circular, these rooms resemble blisters on the primary hull. The *Enterprise* and some other ships have a secondary bridge, called the *Battle Bridge,* in the secondary hull. This bridge is used in emergencies, or when the ship separates.

cloaking device   A machine that renders a ship invisible to sensors and sight. Because of the power necessary to run a cloaking device, a ship must de-cloak in order to fire its weapons. Federation ships generally do not have cloaking devices because of a treaty that prohibits Starfleet from developing them. Klingons, Romulans, and the Jem'Hadar all use cloaking devices regularly.

com   Short for command. As in "Mrs. Clinton took the *com,* sir, and now she won't get out of the chair."

communicator   Starfleet radios. First they were small handheld boxes with flip-tops that activated them. Then they were on the wrist during some of the movies, then back to hand-held devices. The latest incarnation is in a pin affixed to the tunic. They are touch and voice activated. The communicator pin is keyed to a specific individual and can provide information on the wearer, such as health status and location. They also serve as homing beacons for the transporter. The pins are a lot more convenient than the handheld jobs, but unfortunately, the actors look a lot sillier talking to their jewelry.

computer   You know what this is. Computers on *Star Trek* are incredibly powerful, orders of magnitude beyond those in use today. (However, I understand that they still can't run Windows 95 without a hitch.) Crew members talk to the computer to get information. The computer's voice on the *Enterprise*-D is actually the voice of Majel Barrett, Roddenberry's wife, and the original Number One. The computers are actually capable of running the ship for a short time, but they cannot take independent creative action.

conn   The position on the bridge that controls the ship's flight. On the *Enterprise,* Chekov and Sulu were at the conn, at helm and navigation. On the *Enterprise*-D, Wesley Crusher took that post. On *Voyager,* it's Tom Paris's position.

cortical stimulator   A medical device used to resuscitate patients who would be long dead in our era. Dr. Crusher puts this little doo-hicky on somebody's forehead, and *shazam!* he's up and eating bran cereal.

deflectors   These are force-fields that surround the ship, protecting it from hazards. Shields protect against both energy and matter, say, a disruptor blast and a meteor. There are different types of deflectors, such as navigational deflectors, which move dust and small objects out of the way of the ship. Deflectors operate on a specific "resonance frequency." If you can figure that frequency out, you can penetrate the shields or drain them. The Klingon sisters, Lursa and B'Etor, destroyed the *Enterprise*-D this way. That's also how the Borg attack ships, by locking on to their shield frequency and draining them. Subsequently there is much talk of rotating the shield modulation, which is sort of like changing the channels on the car radio really fast so no one can hear them.

deuterium   The fuel used by Federation ships for the impulse engines. It is a type of hydrogen and is stored in tanks on the ship.

diagnostics   The mechanism by which you can check if equipment is working properly. Diagnostics are defined by level, "level one" being the most thorough, and "level five" being the most cursory. (For your information, everyone in *Star Trek* always asks for a "level-one diagnostic; no one ever asks for a "level-five diagnostic." No one ever says, "Geordi, give me a really quick, careless check of the transporter system.")

dilithium crystals   Very important. These crystals regulate the matter-antimatter reaction. Without them, Federation starships cannot function. On the original show, dilithium crystals were rare and consequently they were very expensive. Since then, *Star Trek* technology has advanced enough to reformulate dilithium crystals, making them reusable, but they are still necessary for the engines to function. They are still rare and expensive. The *Voyager* crew discovered new crystals that hold together under more intense warp fields, thus enabling them to break the warp 10 barrier.

disruptors   The Klingon and Romulan equivalent of phasers. These are energy weapons with vast destructive force, more damaging than the nice, compassionate phasers.

galaxy   A huge group of stars. The galaxy we live in is a spiral-shaped galaxy called the Milky Way galaxy, named because that how it appeared in the night sky to ancient sky-watchers. Distances between galaxies are so vast that even the *Star Trek* crews can't imagine traversing them in their lifetime.

Genesis Project   A scientific project that resulted in the development of the Genesis Device, which can transform a dead world into a life-sustaining one in minutes. Of course, it can also wipe out an inhabited world just as fast. The program was eventually found to be flawed, and the Genesis Device pronounced a failure. Khan Noonien Singh stole this device and used it to try to kill James Kirk.

graviton   A type of subatomic particle that transmits gravitational force. On *Star Trek* they're always fooling around with graviton beams.

hailing frequencies   What Uhura used to say. These are the frequencies of subspace radio one uses when trying to contact somebody.

hangar deck   The place where shuttlecraft take off and land. Usually located at the rear of a starship. *See* **Shuttlebay.**

headings   A way to describe direction in space. A heading is different from a bearing in that a heading has no relationship to the orientation of a spaceship. For example, if Earth is at heading 000, then, no matter where you are in the galaxy, heading 000 would take you toward Earth.

holodeck   The "virtual reality" rooms aboard a starship or space station. Computers there, using transporter technology, can simulate perfectly any environment for which they have been programmed. They can re-create virtually any situation. If one wanted to have French toast during the Renaissance, as the comic Steven Wright wants to, you could do it on the holodeck. The holodeck can create lifelike reproductions of people. Yes, people can have sex with holodeck re-creations, and it's probably better than some of the blind dates you've had. Picard often used the rooms to live out the life of Dixon Hill, a private detective in the forties.

Holodecks are activated through a communications panel just outside the entrance door. They are used for training purposes as well as entertainment. The holodecks are equipped with safety protocols that prevent injury, but those protocols can be deactivated by an officer with rank. For example, if Worf wanted a really deadly situation to hone his fighting skills, he might say, "Computer, activate Filene's Basement annual bridal gown sale program, remove safety protocols." The computer would reply, "Program loaded. Enter when ready." The door would slide open, and the sound of Worf screaming would echo down the corridor.

hypospray A medical injection device that delivers drugs into the body through the skin without piercing it, doing away with hypodermic needles. Something that the AMA should really get behind.

impulse drive Impulse engines are used for travel at speeds below that of light. They are powered by fusion reactions and use the deuterium stored onboard as fuel. Most starships are equipped with impulse engines for travel within star systems. Traveling between stars on impulse would take decades and is practically impossible due to fuel restrictions. For starships, impulse drive is basically the equivalent of the limited-use spare tire in new cars. It's enough to get you to the gas station, but you can't rotate it with the other tires.

inertial dampers When you're driving and floor the gas pedal, what happens? You get thrown back in your seat. Well, what do you think would happen to you in a ship that suddenly goes to warp? You'd be reduced to chunky salsa, that's what. To prevent that, almost all starships have some sort of inertial damper to counteract the acceleration force created by the powerful engines. Again, this is another example of how *Star Trek* writers respond to the observations of the scientific community. Nobody on the *Millennium Falcon* in *Star Wars* worries about the dangerous effects of inertia.

isolinear chips   Computer chips that store information. They are similar to our own computer disks, except one of these could probably hold the entire Library of Congress, or the next David Foster Wallace novel.

Jeffries tubes   Maintenance tubes that crew members crawl through to fix things. They are interspersed throughout starships. They got their name from Matt Jeffries, the man who designed the *Enterprise.**

latinum   A precious metal, used as currency. Although Earth doesn't use money anymore, plenty of aliens do, and latinum is the most valuable currency. It comes in strips, and characters refer to it as one does to gold. How can any metal be valuable if replicators can make anything? Well, I don't think that replicators can make latinum due to its unusual molecular structure, and the need of the writers to have some sort of currency for dramatic dialogue.

lifepods   The same as lifeboats. Every starship's got them. Several people can live in one for an extended period of time. They can be independently targeted and can land on a planet's surface.

light-year   A unit not of time, but of distance. This is the distance it takes light a year to cross. Since light travels at 186,000 miles per second, this is a huge distance. Whatever you do, don't make the mistake of saying "It would take light-years to get there." This will show that you are a science moron and Trekkers will take advantage of you, raising the price of a Klingon knife at a convention.

M-class planets   Planets are classified in terms of their composition and their environments. An M-class planet is a planet that can support life as we know it. Despite global warming, Earth is considered an M-class planet. However, some sections of Brooklyn are not considered to be M-class.

---

*If you read the footnotes in chapter 1, you'd already know this.

metaphasic shields   A type of advanced shield technology that significantly strengthens defensive capabilities. Allows a ship to enter the dangerous corona of a star. First tested by Dr. Beverly Crusher.

nanites   Microscopic robots capable of entering living tissue. Nanites were developed to perform surgery inside the human body. Wesley Crusher conducted experiments on these and produced a sentient race of nanites that could reproduce. Picard gave them their own planet when they were on the verge of destroying the *Enterprise*. Although they can be destructive, they are generally considered to be benevolent.

navigational deflector   If you've ever wondered what the big radar dish is on the front of the secondary hull of the *Enterprise*, now you know: Sweeping the space ahead of the ship, its deflector beam clears debris that could damage the ship at high speeds. Most Federation ships have these deflector dishes in a prominent place at the front of the ship. It's like those little whistles people put on their cars to scare the deer off the road.

neutronium   A nearly impenetrable substance. The atoms of this substance have had their electrons stripped away, and the atomic nuclei are actually touching. It is often ejected from neutron stars that have exploded. It is much easier to get gum out of your hair than it is to get through this material.

nova   A star, at the end of its life, may grow larger and burn brighter, threatening the worlds that surround it. A **supernova** is a star that consumes itself in a huge explosion. A **supernova with cheese** is a really awful event that we won't even discuss.

Ops   This is a station on the bridge that coordinates the different functions on the ship. On *Next Generation*, Data manned the Ops station; on *Voyager*, it's manned by Harry Kim. On *Deep Space Nine*, the entire command center is called Ops, short for Operations.

PADD   Personal Access Display Device. This is the ultimate laptop computer, a video pad that displays information, and it can download information from much bigger computer systems.

pattern buffer   Okay, say you're being beamed up by the *Enterprise*. Where do your molecules go? Into the pattern buffer.

They're stored there while the computers adjust for any motion between where you're coming from and where you're going to. Because it is a key component of the transporter system, and because it sounds cool, lots of things happen to the pattern buffer in *Star Trek* episodes.

pattern enhancers These cylindrical objects are used as antennae. When interference makes it difficult to "lock on to" (find) something to transport, the crew sets these antennae up around the object or person to strengthen the signal.

phase inducers I have no idea what these are. They seem to be related to **phase transition coils**, which are the part of the transporter system that converts your molecules to energy and back again. If you find out what the inducers are, please let me know.

phaser Short for PHASed Energy Rectification, these energy weapons come in different sizes. A type-1 phaser is a small personal weapon about the size of a pack of cigarettes. They don't show these too often because they are too small to look threatening on TV. (Rumor has it that Roddenberry first imagined the phaser to be a device implanted in a person's finger, but it just looked too stupid for crew members to shoot people with their fingers.)

A type-2 phaser is the sidearm most often seen on *Star Trek*. In the original show it resembled a pistol grip, and the type-1 phaser fit into the pistol grip to increase its power. On *Next Generation* and all the other programs, it looks a lot like a TV remote control. (One thing you can say about the show's producers: They know who their audience is. In fact, you can mail-order a remote control for your television that looks like a phaser. This is a Trekker's dream come true.)

Phasers can overload. They are programmed to warn you by emitting a loud wail, and then they explode like a hand grenade. You probably shouldn't be wearing one when this occurs.

photon torpedo Weapon used for faster-than-light combat. Stored in limited numbers, these missiles contain matter and antimatter which are brought together for massive destructive energy.

plasma A form of ionized gas.

positronic brain Data and his brother, Lore, both have this type of android brain. Positrons are the opposite of electrons (they are actually antimatter), and their presence enables a sophisticated neural network to function.

probe A small, self-propelled instrument used to gather information away from the ship. They come in different classes, from one to eight, from simple to sophisticated.

quadrant One quarter of a galaxy, usually referring to our own Milky Way galaxy. Quadrants are indicated by the first four letters of the Greek alphabet: Alpha, Beta, Gamma, and Delta. Earth is located on the borderline between the Alpha and Beta Quadrants, and most of the action on *Star Trek* has occurred in these quadrants. However, the wormhole near Bajor connects with the Gamma Quadrant, and *Voyager* is lost far away in the Delta Quadrant. Quadrants are huge; it would takes many years at maximum warp to cross them, so a wormhole can be a very valuable shortcut. The *Voyager* crew is searching for wormholes that could lead them home.

quantum singularity The impressive scientific way to say a black hole. If you meet a Trekker at a party and you say the words "quantum singularity" in any sentence, he (or she) will follow you home like a lovesick puppy.

   Romulan ships use an artificial quantum singularity to power their warp engines. No one seems to understand how it works, but it sounds cool and weird.

quantum torpedoes A new weapon recently introduced into the *Star Trek* universe. The U.S.S. *Defiant* is equipped with them, as is *Voyager,* and they pack a hell of a wallop. Despite characters using them all the time, no one has taken the time to explain them to us, so Trekkers have no idea what in the world these cool things are.

red alert A maximum state of alert on starships and starbases. The lights on the bridge change, the klaxon goes off, and everyone onboard gets to his or her station. Defense shields tend to go up immediately during red alert. It's ordered during a serious emergency such as an attack, a catastrophic systems failure, or a repeat of *Lost in Space.*

redshirt A Trekker term for an low-ranking crew member. Redshirts wear red uniforms, and it's well known that these low-ranking crew members are the first to die when a hostile alien is encountered. There is a saying: "Never beam down to a planet wearing a red shirt."

replicator Based on the transporter, this amazing device can create perfect reproductions of objects programmed into the computer's memory. A replicator takes stored matter or energy and makes virtually anything out of it; food, tools, raw materials. However, it cannot make complex machinery. You activate the unit by telling it what you want, as when Captain Picard says "Tea. Earl Grey. Hot."

runabout No, this isn't what the crew does during a warp core breach. This is a large shuttlecraft, capable of warp speed and short interstellar travel. It is mostly used on *Deep Space Nine*.

sector A small segment of a quadrant. There are lots and lots of sectors, but each one is still pretty big. It takes about five days to cross a sector at high warp.

sensors These are devices that can detect and analyze anything you'd want them to. They run along the outside and inside of starships. They are extremely sensitive.

shields *See* deflectors.

shuttlebay Otherwise known as the *hangar deck*. A section of the ship where *shuttlecraft* take off and land.

shuttlecraft A small ship, designed for short trips. There are several classes of shuttlecraft, each with different abilities and sizes. All are capable of sublight-speed travel and planetary landings, and some are capable of warp speed. Basically, they are interplanetary minivans, complete with plush carpeting and sound systems.

shuttlepod A small shuttlecraft, capable of carrying two people, or Scotty by himself in the later movies.

sickbay The hospital aboard a starship or space station. There are lots of neat medical devices here: Look for the medical diagnostic bed that monitors your vital signs, such as heart rate and temperature, and displays them on a screen overhead. (This is not the place to have an affair. Then again, it could be fun, or at least illuminate your partner's true feelings.)

starbase   Numbered Federation facilities for starship repair and the administration of Federation business. Starbases can be huge space stations or located on planets.

starship   A special breed of spaceship designed for travel among the stars, with a specially trained crew. The *Enterprise* is a starship, as is *Voyager.* Starships come in classes, much like naval vessels. The classes are named after the first ship in the class. For example, the original *Enterprise* was a *Constitution*-class ship. The *Enterprise*-D was a *Galaxy*-class starship. *Voyager* is an *Intrepid*-class starship, and the newest *Enterprise*-E is a *Sovereign*-class ship. Certain obscure classes of ships have become *Trek* favorites. For example, the *Oberth*-class ships are smaller starships usually used for scientific and rescue missions. They're popular, but whenever a ship gets destroyed to show how ruthless a villain is, an *Oberth* is the first to go. So if you see an *Oberth*-class starship, try not to get emotionally attached to anyone onboard.

structural integrity field   Starships are so big that they could never withstand the stresses of stopping and starting at high speed, so they use a separate force-field to hold the ship together. Without this force-field, the ship would fly apart. (The 1976 Plymouth Volare could have used a structural integrity field so it could withstand being driven over fifty-five miles per hour.)

subspace   A spatial continuum where faster-than-light travel is possible. Starships create a subspace bubble when they are at warp speed.

subspace radio   A method of communicating over vast distances by sending signals through the subspace that allows warp travel.

synthehol   An alcohol substitute used by the Federation. You can drink gallons of synthehol, feel drunk, but shake it off in a minute. But it doesn't seem to taste very good. They should have stuck with the original name for this beverage: Zima.

Ten-forward lounge   This is the *Enterprise*'s bar, a large lounge located on Deck 10 at the forward section of the saucer. Guinan tends bar here and serves up synthehol. A fun place to hang out, it looks a lot like some modern, soulless hotel chains.

tractor beam   A device that allows one ship to tow another.

Tractors beams are used most often in rescue missions, but they have sinister uses as well, such as imprisoning vessels in order to destroy them.

transporter   The machine that converts matter to energy, beams it to another location, and then rematerializes it. This is the primary method of transport on *Star Trek,* and using it is called "beaming." When people say "Beam me up, Scotty" they are referring to the transporter. You cannot beam through deflector shields and beaming between vessels traveling at warp speed is a delicate matter: They must both be traveling at the same warp speed. Great precision must be used in aiming where someone is beamed; it is possible to be beamed inside solid matter, like a wall or a floor. This is not pleasant. In fact, this is probably the most unpleasant experience anyone's ever thought of. (Trekkers would love to beam Janet Maslin inside a bulkhead.)

tricorder   A handheld sensor instrument. You wave it around, it makes a weird sound, and it tells you what you're looking at on tiny display screens. Over the years, tricorders have gotten smaller and smaller, more and more sophisticated. Nobody has ever explained why they are called "tricorders."

turbolift   The elevators on starships and space stations. They are voice-activated; you tell them where to go, and they take you there. (They differ from New York City taxicabs in that you tell the taxi driver where you want to go and he takes you *somewhere else.*) Turbolifts operate horizontally and vertically (strangely enough, *very much* like New York City taxicabs).

universal translator   Ever wonder how all these alien species all speak perfect English? Well, they don't. The universal translator analyzes alien speech patterns and instantly converts them to English (along with the appropriate accents, of course). Although ships are equipped with these translators, they can be inserted in the ear so that the wearer can converse with almost any alien species.

warp core   The center of the warp drive, where the antimatter is kept in a magnetic bottle to keep it from touching any of the matter in the engine. The warp core is designed to be ejected from the ship in an emergency and they keep a backup unit aboard, but wouldn't you know, the damn thing gets stuck sometimes and blows up the ship.

warp factor   A unit of measurement for faster-than-light travel. When Captain Picard says "Warp one, engage" he is ordering the ship to accelerate to warp factor 1, which is the speed of light. (The actual scientific shorthand for the speed of light is c.) As warp factors increase, the speed of the ship increases exponentially. For example, warp factor 2 is not twice the speed of light, it's ten times the speed of light. Warp travel is measured from 1 to 10, with warp factor 10 at the absolute top of this scale. Warp factor 10 is considered an impossibility in Starfleet; a ship that travels at warp 10 would occupy all points in the universe simultaneously (sort of like Scotty in the later movies). The closer an object gets to warp 10, the more energy must be expended. For example, warp 9.99 is almost four times as fast as warp 9.6. The *Enterprise*-D's maximum speed was warp factor 9.9, and it could hold that speed for only about ten minutes. (By the way, the original show used a different warp scale, one that allowed the *Enterprise* to reach a velocity of warp 14.1 on one occasion. At this time, the 1 to 10 warp scale is the official one.) Some New York City taxicabs have been clocked near the warp barrier.

Voyager's crew, aching to get home as fast as possible, experimented with methods enabling them to travel faster than any Federation ship has ever traveled. Lt. Tom Paris piloted a specially augmented shuttlecraft that actually accelerated past warp 10, known as the transwarp barrier. The results were not pretty.

Warp travel has been found to damage the environment as well. Really, there was an episode in which two researchers discovered that the stresses of prolonged high warp travel caused dangerous rifts to form in the space-time continuum. You don't have to know what this means, but it's not good. Thus, warp travel is restricted by the Federation to warp 5 or below, except for emergencies. (However, Republicans are trying to introduce legislation to raise the warp speed limit in Montana.)

wormholes   "Tunnels" in space itself. It is possible to travel or communicate through wormholes to distant parts of the galaxy in a fraction of the time normally required. Most wormholes are very unstable, existing only a short time before collapsing. The only stable wormhole known is the Bajoran wormhole to the Gamma Quadrant.

yellow alert What happens if the captain is worried, but not enough to order red alert. Yellow alert requires the defense shields to be energized but not activated, and the klaxon doesn't sound. I think you have to immediately leave the bathroom during yellow alert and place all trays in the upright and locked position.

THE TECHNOBABBLE QUIZ

Let's see if you got anything out of this chapter, or whether Dr. McCoy should reeducate you in sickbay.

1. A cube-shaped Borg ship is pursuing the *Enterprise*-D at warp factor 9.99. Photon torpedoes have no effect, and you have no quantum torpedoes lying around. What should you do?

   a. Immediately increase speed to warp 10
   b. Immediately increase speed to warp 9.99999
   c. Try to get away on impulse power
   d. Dispatch a subspace message to home bequeathing your stereo system to your brother

2. Your ship is losing antimatter containment. There is a coolant leak in progress. What should you do?

   a. Run around screaming
   b. Try to eject the warp core
   c. Go to red alert
   d. Bequeath your *Mister Spock's Music From Outer Space* album to your sister
   e. All of the above

3. You have met a strange alien species. They do not understand what you are saying and have some sort of weapon pointed at you. What do you do?

   a. Ask them patiently if they could direct you to *Deep Space Nine*

    b. ASK THEM IF THEY COULD DIRECT YOU TO *DEEP SPACE NINE* IN A REALLY LOUD VOICE

    c. Find their voluptuous female leader and "communicate" with her

    d. Replace the batteries in your universal translator

4. The captain wants you to go on a secret mission to a world several light-years away. He offers you a choice of a shuttlepod, a shuttlecraft, a Class 1 probe, or a runabout. Which do you choose?

    a. A shuttlepod

    b. A runabout

    c. A shuttlecraft, but only if it's equipped with cup holders

    d. A cozy Class-1 probe

5. The U.S.S. *Voyager* goes to "blue alert." What should you be prepared for?

    a. Who knows? I've never heard of "blue alert." It's ridiculous

    b. An X-rated video

    c. A planetary landing attempt

    d. A separation of the primary and secondary hulls, and then, ice cream!

6. Your Trekker friend is on the holodeck having a romantic dinner with Sharon Stone. Does he (or she!) want the safety protocols on or off?

    a. off

    b. off

    c. off

    d. off

7. The original name of the *Deep Space Nine* space station was:

    a. Datsun

    b. Prince

    c. Tox Uthat

    d. Terok Nor

8. A ship that has really ticked you off is traveling at warp. Which weapon do you use?

    a. Phasers
    b. Photon torpedoes
    c. Quantum torpedoes
    d. Well, definitely the photons, and maybe the quantums

9. You're under attack by enemy forces, but you have an injured comrade down on the planet surface. What do you need to do before you can beam him up?

    a. Lower the shields
    b. Go to warp
    c. Do the Macarena
    d. Ask his or her permission

10. The Jeffries tubes are named after:

    a. Matt Jeffries, secretary-general of the United Nations
    b. Matt Jeffries, an alien from Alpha Centauri
    c. Matt Jeffries, the man who designed the original *Enterprise*
    d. Dr. Jeffries, the original first officer of the *Enterprise*

ANSWERS

1, d; 2, e; 3, d; 4, b; 5, c; 6, a, b, c, d; 7, d; 8, d; 9, a; 10, c.

TRANSLATIONS

"Perhaps it's a particle of preanimate matter, caught in the matrix."
This means that something might be caught in the machine we're using to conduct our scan. It could be organic matter, something that might become life, but it isn't life yet.

"Its hull is pure neutronium; our phasers have no effect."
Neutronium is incredibly dense matter, atoms without electrons. Phasers work by disturbing the molecular structure of a target. Neutronium is impervious to phaser fire due to its particularly strange atomic structure.

"Fluctuate phase resonance frequencies, random settings. Keep them changing, don't give them a chance to adapt."
Phasers operate on specific frequencies, as do many other types

of *Star Trek* energies. By changing these frequencies, the crew hopes that it will confuse the enemy and they will not be able to protect themselves against the weapon.

"The phase inducers are connected to the emitter array, the override is completely gone, and the pattern buffer has been locked into a continuous diagnostic cycle."

This refers to a transporter system that has been jury-rigged. This means that the part of the transporter that is responsible for converting matter to energy is hooked up to a part that spits out the molecules that will be put together to form whatever it is that's beaming. The "buffer"—the part of the transporter that stores molecular patterns that are beamed—is connected to a diagnostic system that monitors whether the equipment is working correctly. The end result of this sentence is that someone is preserved inside the transporter system indefinitely. This is how Scotty saved himself for seventy-five years in a crashed spaceship.

10

REALLY COOL THINGS TO SAY TO
YOUR TREKKER;
OR,
"WOW, YOU WATCH *STAR TREK* TOO!"

Hanging out with *Star Trek* fans can be endless fun—especially if you speak the language. *Star Trek* phrases and concepts translate very well to daily life, as we saw in *Star Trek IV: The Voyage Home,* when the crew came to San Francisco in 1987. Trekkers want nothing more than to be able to communicate with someone else *on their level.* If you take the time to brush up on just a few phrases you will go a long way toward making the Trekker in your life happy. Keep this in mind, though: Trekkers have a running TV show playing in their heads twenty-four hours a day. Every day, almost every situation they encounter reminds them of some episode or movie. Remember that woman who showed up for jury duty wearing a Starfleet uniform complete with phaser and tricorder? Well, when the media came calling, she knew just what to say. She basically quoted the fundamental principles of Starfleet to the *New York Times.*

But there's another reason to learn the language. If your friend is a deep Trekker, somebody lost on the other side of the galaxy, you can talk him (or her) back home in the language Trekkers feel most comfortable with. Unless, of course, they draw you to their side of the neutral zone. (See how easy it is?)

Here. Try some situations where Trek-speak can be useful.

SITUATION 1

Your Trekker is driving the car, and you are a passenger. You generally like it when he drives, but today it seems that the Trekster is going a little too fast. Turn gently to your Trekker and say, *"Do we really need to go to warp speed? Impulse power would be fine with me."* You've just told him that you'd prefer a more leisurely drive.

Let's say he responds with *"We are well within normal operating parameters."* He's just told you that he feels he can handle this speed.

You reply, *"Well, hasn't Starfleet imposed a warp factor five speed limit to avoid too much stress on the fabric of space?"* You've just told him that he could get a ticket for going this fast.

At this point he's going to wonder how you know about the warp factor 5 speed limit. He'll smile and say, *"Yes, well, that limit can be exceeded under certain circumstances."*

Now you say, *"Did you clear it with Starfleet Command?"*

He'll get defensive and say, *"Yes, I've cleared it with Starfleet."*

You can then push the matter by saying, *"It would take three weeks to get a message to Starfleet by subspace radio."* You've just told him he's full of baloney. He may get real quiet and continue driving at the same speed. Suddenly, a police cruiser appears in the rearview mirror and pulls you over. In that interminable time, that endless eternity when the state trooper is walking from his car to yours, turn to your Trekker and say into the silence, *"Perhaps today is a good day to die."*

SITUATION 2

Your mother-in-law (or future mother-in-law) calls. Now you may even like your mother-in-law but find her to be a little annoying. No problem. Try these tactics.

The phone rings. You pick it up and recognize your mother-in-law's voice. She begins to talk about the redecoration ideas she has for your house. Crumple a paper napkin into the phone and say, *"I'm sorry, Captain, your transmission is breaking up."* She might change channels on her cordless telephone, or speak louder.

Tell her, *"Our species have much to learn from one another."*

She'll say, "What? Our feces?"

Say, *"My universal translator can only interpret language, not thought processes."*

She'll say, "What are you talking about?"

Hand the phone to your Trekker and say, *"Red alert."*

Say she calls back about the redecorating. This time she doesn't even stop to listen to you, she just interrupts you like the Borg interrupt all humanoids. Press the mute button on your phone, turn to your Trekker, and say, *"I thought the Borg weren't supposed to be interested in human life-forms, only our technology."*

Press the mute button again and interrupt your mother-in-law. In your deepest voice say, *"We have developed new defensive capabilities since our last meeting and we are prepared to use them if you do not withdraw from Federation space."*

Listen to the dial tone. Say to your Trekker, *"I've lost them, Captain."*

Suppose your mother-in-law decides to call again. This time she doesn't even want to talk to you, she wants to talk to the Trekker. Hand the phone to him and say, *"Captain, you are being hailed."* This means that there is an incoming message for him. When he asks who it is, say, *"They are using a Romulan subspace frequency."* This means that the source is probably an enemy.

When he says, "C'mon, who is it?" say, *"Do you want the message on audio or on the viewscreen?"*

At this point he'll take the phone from your hand. Try running around the house making a *"whoop! whoop!"* sound, and say *"red alert"* over and over again.

While he is talking keep saying you have a coolant leak in progress and you estimate two minutes to a warp core breach.

SITUATION 3

You and your Trekker are shopping for groceries. This is a lot of fun because you are planning a big dinner just for the two of you. You get to the register, and you watch as the lazy checkout cashier swipes your steaks across the scanner. They are supposed to be on sale, but the register says they cost twice as much as marked. Turn to your Trekker and say, *"Sir, I'm getting anomalous readings from the tricorder.*" This means that your sensors are registering something that doesn't make sense.

Have the cashier confirm the price on the receipt, and show him the price on the package. While he is trying to figure this out, say: *"I want a level-one diagnostic run on that scanning system."* You've just told the cashier to run a complete, thorough check on the register.

When the cashier says, "Huh?" you reply, *"Make it so."* Take your bags and walk out.

SITUATION 4

You and your Trekker are shopping for a used car. You are looking at a 1985 Ford Taurus with 150,000 miles on it. The salesman points out that the car is a real beauty, that it was only driven by a little old lady from Hoboken, and that it's guaranteed. Sitting at his desk, he tells you that the price is $15,000.

Stare at the salesman very intently as if you are a Betazoid. When he finished talking turn to your Trekker and say, *"I feel he's hiding something, Captain."*

The salesman may say: "I can't be hiding something, I'll show you the car's entire repair record, don't worry about that."

You say to your Trekker, *"I sense he doesn't believe what he's saying."*

The salesman may say, "Look, have you got a problem?"

As your Trekker tries to cool the situation, look at the salesman and say, *"I'm feeling a great deal of hostility from you."*

He'll say *"You're* making me hostile."

You say, *"How does that make you feel?"*

Your Trekker begins, "Look, he's been watching some *Star Trek* lately, that's all...."

As the salesman stands up to throw the two of you out, double over in pain, put your hands in your hair, and say, *"Get out of my head!"*

SITUATION 5

Let's say your Trekker is playing in a volleyball league. (It could be basketball, football, or anything else, but let's say volleyball for now.)

You decide to go watch him play. To make sure he knows you're there to cheer for him, try the following suggestions.

When you first see the opposing team, turn to your Trekker and say, *"In this corner, a group of barbarians. With strange customs and strange ways, I'm sure they'll give us a lot of surprises."* (Line used by an announcer on a planet based on Roman society.)

Whenever your Trekker is about to hit the ball, stand up and yell *"Victory is life!"* (This is what Jem'Hadar say as they go into battle.)

Whenever somebody bumps into your Trekker, yell out *"A clear foul, Proconsul. Your ruling?"* (This line was uttered by a gladiator on that Roman-based planet.)

As the game wears on, start barking out encouragement in terms that only your Trekker will understand. It will make him proud to be with you: *"I wager fifteen hundred quatloos on the human with the blue T-shirt!"* (Quatloos are a ridiculous monetary unit gambled with on the planet Triskelion.)

If he scores a point, jump up and yell, *"Dabo!"* (Dabo is a game of chance on *Deep Space Nine*. It works like Bingo.)

If your Trekker gets tired or winded and is trying to catch his breath, yell out to the line judge or umpire: *"He can't breathe, this Vulcan air's too thin!"* (As if he were fighting on the planet Vulcan.) Then pretend to inject him with a hyposhray drug by pointing at his arm and making a hissing noise.

WATCHING TOGETHER

Trekkers like nothing better than getting together with other Trekkers to watch *Star Trek*. That's because Trekkers love to discuss the show and find flaws with it. Here is a list of things you can say to impress your Trekker with your *Trek* knowledge.

If our ship is being attacked, say, *"I wonder if this will cause a warp core breach?"*

If an alien probe comes on the viewscreen, say, *"Hey, isn't that the same probe they used in episode one-oh-six?"*

As the probe approaches, say, *"What the hell are they waiting for? Why don't they raise the shields?"*

If you really want to impress a Trekker, whenever a big, bad, green Romulan ship appears, ask this question: *"Hey, where do you think they put the navigational deflector?"*

When Kes appears on *Voyager*, ask this question: *"If she only lives for nine years, why does she have to sleep? Don't you think there would've been some trade-off for that fast metabolism?"*

When the crew beams over to a Borg vessel, ask everyone in the room: *"Why didn't they just bring a matter-antimatter bomb with them and blow the Borg up to the Happy Hunting Grounds?"*

To start a fun discussion during a commercial, ask the following question: *"Okay, next* Star Trek *film, the credits go up, the screen goes dark. What's the first scene?"*

If Wesley Crusher or his mother appears on-screen, imitate Bugs Bunny's voice and say, *"Why, Crusher, it's good to see you."**

If the ship is trapped, and escape is impossible, say, *"Are you sure this isn't time for a colorful metaphor?"*†

If the Borg do appear in an episode, say the following, word for word, then watch your Trekker's face: *"I wonder if the Borg power their ships by somehow exploiting the difference in energy state potential between different layers of subspace?"* Then make a kissy face at him.

HOW TO ANNOY YOUR TREKKER

There will come a time when you'll want to annoy your *Trek* fan. Perhaps you're just feeling playful, or perhaps it's payback for something that he or she did. Although I'm not actually recommending them, here are some ways to thoroughly annoy a Trekker. (I take no responsibility for the results of using these tactics.)

Whenever an alien spacecraft approaches, ask everyone in the room, *"Is that the Borg?"*

Every time the Borg appear in an episode, say, *"Well, good night, Gracie."*

Accuse every character you see of being a changeling. Just yell it

---

*Trekkers are huge Bugs Bunny fans.
†Watch *Star Trek IV: The Voyage Home* for this one.

at the screen: *"You're a changeling!"* When your guests tell you to be quiet, just keep muttering it every time a character appears. *"Changeling. Changeling. Changeling."*

After the first teaser of any *Star Trek* episode (the opening segment before the credits), say, *"Oh, they got this one from* Babylon Five!"

At the beginning of every *Deep Space Nine* episode, say to your Trekker: *"Let me get this straight, they're guarding a hole in space?"*

If you're watching *Star Trek: Voyager,* every time Captain Janeway and Tuvok are together in a room, say two words: *"Pon farr."*

Little-Known Facts About the World According to *Star Trek*

❑ All life on Earth was "seeded" billions of years ago by an intelligent race of beings who looked like us but had no hair.

❑ The Greek Gods were actually aliens from another planet who frequently mated with our women.

❑ Methuselah, Solomon, Brahms, and Alexander the Great were all the same person.

❑ Writer Samuel Clemens (Mark Twain) was transported onto the starship *Enterprise*-D back in the nineteenth century.

❑ Amelia Earhart disappeared when she was abducted by aliens and is now cryogenically frozen on a distant planet.

❑ An alien spaceship *really did* land in New Mexico in 1947. It was the Ferengi!

❑ In 1968, the U.S. government tried to launch an orbiting nuclear weapons platform, but it was sabotaged by alien agents trying to keep mankind from killing themselves.

❑ The late-twentieth-century advances in personal computing were not supposed to happen. A computer nerd found a spacecraft from the twenty-ninth century and used it to invent advanced computer chips and make billions of dollars. (Sound familiar?)

❑ In 1992, a group of genetically engineered "supermen" tried to seize control of the world.

❑ By the year 2033, the United States will have fifty-two states.

❑ By the year 2037, we will all be using hover-cars.

- ☐ Television will die out in the year 2040.
- ☐ The last year of professional baseball will be 2042, when only three hundred people turn up for the World Series.
- ☐ In the twenty-first century, all lawyers will be killed. Contrary to public opinion, this will not have a positive effect on society.

11

THE *STAR TREK* CONVENTION;

OR,

"IF WE DON'T LEAVE NOW, I'M GOING TO START CRYING"

In the course of every relationship there comes a reckoning. Be they friends, lovers, or spouses, every couple reaches a defining moment that captures the essence of the union. There is a limit to what people will sacrifice for one another. For the significant others of Trekkers, that limit is usually reached at a *Star Trek* convention.

Star Trek conventions are gatherings held periodically across the country. They can be found in every region and in several foreign countries. They are events that are designed for people to gather and talk about *Star Trek*, think about the future of *Star Trek*, and, most important, spend money on *Star Trek*. You will never see a greater collection of useless dust attractors (or tchotchkes, as my grandmother would say) for sale in your life.

During this book, you might have wondered: "What makes a Trekker a Trekker? I mean, if I watch the show, and enjoy it, does that make me a Trekker?" Not necessarily. I know lots of people who look forward to watching the show, but who are not close to being Trekkers. The dividing line between ordinary humans and true *Star Trek* fans is usually found on the floor of a *Star Trek* convention. That's what separates the amateurs from the professionals and the superstars from the professionals. Only true Trekkers can really appreciate a good convention.*

---

*By the way, Trekkers will also be cynical and critical of conventions, frequently saying things like "Boy, there were a lot of geeks there." Don't be fooled. The difference between Trekker and non-Trekker is that while they will both complain, the Trekker will go to the next one.

WHAT'S A CONVENTION?

Star Trek conventions are usually held in large hotels, in the ballrooms that they rent out to groups. A *Star Trek* fan committee or fan club will organize it, but far more often it will be put together by a professional organizer. Events will be held, such as trivia contests and raffles. Slide shows and trailers from upcoming episodes will be shown. Usually there is a guest speaker, and the bigger the convention, the more "central" to the *Trek* world the guest speaker will be. But the common denominator at every convention is the selling floor. Here the dozens of tables rented out by merchants make the place look like the Ferengi have taken over *Deep Space Nine*. You will find the following for sale:

- ❑ comic books
- ❑ novels
- ❑ movie posters
- ❑ toys
- ❑ reproductions of *Star Trek* props including Klingon knives that snap open and could gut a trout
- ❑ more toys
- ❑ starship models built to the precise dimensions of ships on the shows
- ❑ T-shirts that say things like PICARD/RIKER 2000: REAL LEADERSHIP FOR A CHANGE; KIRK/SPOCK 2000; ROMULANS MAKE BETTER LOVERS; and YOU WILL BE ASSIMILATED, BORG FOR PRESIDENT
- ❑ *Star Trek* episode videotapes
- ❑ more toys
- ❑ Hockey jerseys with the symbol of the Klingon Empire (one size only, extra-large)
- ❑ *Babylon-Five* episode videotapes
- ❑ models of starships that have been partially destroyed by phaser fire and whose decks have been exposed to the terrible vacuum of space
- ❑ Japanese pornographic *animé* (animation) videotapes (adults only)
- ❑ makeup kits, complete with molded plastic forehead ridges for all races

- ❏ $300 leather and woolen black baseball jackets with the *X-Files* slogan THE TRUTH IS OUT THERE tastefully embroidered in little letters that exactly match the type used in the credits of the television show
- ❏ tribbles

All of these items will be presented as if they were "one-of-a-kind-never-to-be-found-again-I-can't-believe-I'm-even-thinking-about-selling-you-this" artifacts. Sometimes they're right, because a lot of things sold there are painstakingly assembled by dedicated fans, such as the above-mentioned phaser-damaged ships. Paramount will sell lots of toy spaceship models in stores, but I guarantee you none of them have little dead plastic bodies floating out into deep space.

The big conventions, like the ones in New York City and Los Angeles, will have production staff on hand to speak to the faithful to give us cryptic updates and teasers about upcoming episodes. The Trekkers sit in velvet-carpeted ballrooms with their arms folded across their chests acting nonchalant and unimpressed. After all, they all know they could write better episodes than these "experts." Inside, though, they are thrilled to be there and are acting cool because they are so jealous of the writing staff it's all they can do to keep from pulling out a plasma rifle and vaporizing them on the spot.

If your Trekker asks you to go to one of these conventions, you might want to try it once. It's doubtful that you will enjoy most of the climate, but it's worth it to see two things: (1) the way people dress up and (2) the way the fans interact with the actors from the shows. I guarantee you will never forget it.

SECURITY

Like all events designed to make money, the organizers charge an admittance fee. To make sure you pays your money and takes your chances, a security staff is hired to work the door. These are not your typical roadies. To save money, the organizers let certain fans in for free, and these fans work as ushers to take money and keep order. To let you know they are security, they wear Starfleet uniforms, complete with phasers and communicator pins. (They look forward to this for weeks.) Some workers dress as Klingons, who are pretty intimidating with their "Security" tags pinned to their bandoliers. These Klingons will not smile, or joke, or laugh. They will conduct themselves as true humorless Klingon warriors, and will even speak Klingon to you. It's fun to interact with them if you know some rudimentary Klingon. My Klingon is pretty bad, but here are some phrases you might want to try on the doormen:*

Klingon Phrase	English Translation
Maj Po!	Good morning!
Nuqneh!	What do you want?
Huch?	Money?
Do'Ha'	Unfortunate
Heghlu'meH QaQ JajVam.	Today is a good day to die.
DaslIj tIn qIj.	Oh, your boots are big and black.
JlQos.	I'm sorry.
NaDev Huch.	Here is the money.
Hip pu'Hich Pagh Quch jiHlegh, gar'a?	Is that a disruptor pistol in your pocket or are you just happy to see me?
net'oy!	That hurt!

Inside, you will find people dressed as Ferengi, Borg, Bajorans (these are the easiest costumes: all you need is a weird earring and some nose ridges), Romulans, and any other alien race you can think of. Be careful not to go there with a hangover, because you will fear that you are suffering from alcohol poisoning like Ray Milland in *The Lost Weekend.* If they are showing a blooper reel, try to go see it. These will be humorous outtakes from the shows, with actors walking into doors that don't open automatically like they should, and people flubbing their technobabble lines. Trekkers get a big kick out of this.

---

*You can translate other neat phrases by using *The Klingon Dictionary* by Marc Okrand, from Pocket Books.

THE BIG SPEAKER

By all means, go and see the big speaker. A genuine star surrounded by the faithful provides an interesting scene and the actors are actually very nice to the *Trek* fans. (They know who butters their bread.) Finally, take a quick swing around the merchandise, and check out the handcrafted models created by *Trek* artisans. It's like a visit to the Galleria dell'Academia in Florence, except with Data instead of David.

Star Trek conventions have been reduced to a science. Each one is basically the same. They differ mainly in size and diversity. How did they get to be this way? Ever wonder what the first *Star Trek* convention was like?

THE FIRST CONVENTION

Well, I'm going to tell you anyway. I am one the lucky few who were at the first *Star Trek* convention in New York City in 1972. I was nine years old. I found out about it on television when I saw an ad telling all *Star Trek* fans to beam down to the Statler-Hilton Hotel near Penn Station in Manhattan. The entire crew of the *Enterprise* was going to be there, and you could get their autographs and meet them. It was a three-day convention, and tomorrow, Sunday, was the last day.

Star Trek was my favorite show. I watched every episode and knew some of the lines by heart. The idea of meeting the actors, of meeting Captain Kirk himself, seemed preposterous to me. But there it was, on television. Maybe there was a chance. Who knew when this type of opportunity would present itself again? For all I knew, I might never get a chance to see William Shatner in person again. (This turned out to be correct, but not nearly as undesirable as I thought it would be.)

I looked at my mother with a longing expression that I knew would prevail if I kept it up. She made a few feeble arguments against going, such as "It's the last day" and "It's probably expensive" and "You don't really want to go to that, do you?" But I just kept looking at my mother like one of those dogs in the black velvet paintings with the big, soulful eyes, and she sighed. Kids know that sigh, we wait for it like cheetahs wait for the sight of fuzzy little antelope ears sticking out above the grass of the savannah. It means we win.

Well, pity my poor mother, because she did not know what she was getting into. How could she? How could anyone? Even the cast was taken aback by the response. Where they expected a thousand people, five thousand showed up.

It was a madhouse. People stood in lines three deep to take a look at blinking *Star Trek*–type jewelry. (Remember the first LEDs? Incredible, weren't they?) Pictures of the actors were flying out the doors. My mother tried to be a good sport about it, taking me to the blooper reel show, and steering me clear of the merchandise. (Luckily, there weren't any models of the ships yet, or there would've been a withdrawal scene like Gene Hackman quitting smack in *French Connection II.*)

At the blooper reel show, we were reduced to sitting on the floor, and were lucky to get that, when people started craning their necks through the open doorway. We got to see Shatner walk into closed doors about twenty times, Spock crack up laughing, and Dr. McCoy ham it up during the coffee breaks. It was wondrous.

At this point, my mother needed a break. We fought our way to the coffee shop and grabbed two seats together at the counter. Next to my mother sat a man in his early twenties. He must've weighed about 120 pounds. He had long stringy hair, a long goatee, and he was wearing a denim jacket covered with *Star Trek* buttons: STAR TREK LIVES; I GROK SPOCK; BEAM ME UP, SCOTTY—the whole deal. And he was hitting on my mother. He kept telling her "He's going to be here" over and over, and really gave my mom the creeps. Leaping into action, I said to him what any nine-year-old in my situation would have said:

"Hey, where did you get all those cool buttons?"

ME AND WILLIAM SHATNER

The main event, "Meet the Cast," took place in the main ballroom. The entire cast except for Spock sat at a podium onstage. Roddenberry himself was there. Now, this was the third day of the convention, and they did seem a little irritable. They also seemed just a little amazed at the numbers of people filing into the ballroom. Thinking back on it now, the strongest feeling I have about them was that they seemed sad. Of course, at the time I wasn't paying attention to any of that. I was in a *Trek*-induced haze.

There must have been a thousand people filling the seats and the aisles. Each cast member spoke a little, and they each apologized for Nimoy's absence. You could feel the disappointment of the crowd. As the cast talked about the great response of the fans, what they were doing to try to get a new show on the air, there was strangely not much enthusiasm in their voices. You could feel the tension: the affection of all these science fiction fans pressing out toward these actors on the stage, and in return, a kind of defeated apathy from the cast, whose careers were dead in the water.

A microphone stood in the aisle halfway to the stage. Bill Shatner invited any kids who had questions to come up to the microphone and ask two questions only. Even though I almost drop-kicked some lady in the head while jumping out of my chair, four kids beat me to the mike.

The children asked Shatner questions like when would there be another show, how do you like being captain, you know, *normal questions*. Then it was my turn. Now, I had prepared the questions I most wanted answers to all day, just in case this opportunity came. I picked two and kept them front-loading in my mind.

Just when I got to the mike, Shatner spoke up. He said, "You know, everyone here is here to answer your questions and give you more information about the show. Gene, James, Nichelle, they all know more about *Star Trek* than I do. And they'd love to answer your questions. So when you come forward, just tell us who you want to talk to, okay?"

He pointed at me. "Now, who do *you* want to talk to?"

"You," I said.

The crowd laughed. "Okay," Shatner asked, "what's your question?"

I froze. I completely lost my train of thought. Shatner had thrown me off. The ballroom was silent. As I wracked my brain, he jumped in.

"My first question is… 'What's my question?'"

He got a few laughs.

Then I remembered. "Oh yeah," and the noise dimmed.

"According to Einstein's Theory of Relativity..." I began, and Shatner glanced around the room in bewilderment as the entire ballroom echoed with laughter. My mother rested her forehead in her palm. I was *nine years old.*

"According to Einstein's Theory of Relativity," I repeated, "no object can travel faster than the speed of light. How do you explain the *Enterprise* achieving speeds of warp 14.1?" You must understand, I was at an age where I could actually spend my time worrying about something like that.

Shatner looked back at Gene Roddenberry, who shrugged. Shatner thought about it, and said, "Well, you'll notice how slowly I walked out on stage."

This didn't make everyone laugh. I suspect I wasn't the only Trekker in the ballroom who wanted an answer to this question. Then I hit him with my second question, much more important to a nine-year-old boy.

"How come they don't use the phaser rifle more often?"

Shatner was now back to his dramatic form, pauses and sudden bursts of speech.

"Because..." he started. "They're afraid of it."

I left that convention floating on air. It didn't matter that I didn't have my questions answered or even taken seriously. What mattered was I wasn't alone. We had been given an outlet to express our need for heroes. So what if the actors didn't get it yet? We would keep the show alive ourselves if need be.

TIME TRAVEL

Flash forward twenty-four years. My friend Adam Shrager* asked me if I'd like to go to a *Star Trek* convention. It'd been years since I walked into one. "C'mon, it'll only be a few minutes," he said.

Once again, I walked into the Statler-Hilton Hotel (its name was

---

*The author of a great biography of the actors who starred in *Star Trek: The Next Generation.* Look for *The Finest Crew in the Fleet,* in bookstores now.

changed years ago, then changed again, but for most New Yorkers it's still the Statler-Hilton). We paid an outrageous fee and walked through.

"Hey, Sam, you want a Klingon knife for your birthday?" he asked.

"Nah," I said. I was tempted, though.

"Hey," Adam said. "Robert Duncan McNeill is speaking in five minutes. Want to see?" McNeill plays Tom Paris on *Voyager*.

What the hell.

This convention was smaller than usual, so the only big speaker they had was Robert McNeill. *Voyager* was the new show and we'd only seen one season, so he wasn't exactly a Trekker's dream.

But you should've seen him up there. What a difference twenty-four years make. Smiling broadly, he was relaxed and friendly. He had the easy mannerisms of a man who knows he will be taken care of. He'd made it into the *Star Trek* pantheon, and regardless of how well the show did, he knew he would live forever. We easily found two seats near the front.

A line formed at the microphone set up for people to ask questions. McNeill took his time with each one, talking about how much fun it was to do the show, and how genuinely happy he was that his career was safe. A teenager approached the mike.

"Robert, I don't know how much information you're privy to, and if you can't answer my question just say you can't answer and don't make anything up. We know that *Voyager* is lost in the Delta Quadrant. Now, it makes sense to me that the Borg must have taken over most of the Delta Quadrant because they already found their way to the Alpha Quadrant, and that's much farther for them than their own quadrant. So how come *Voyager* hasn't run into the Borg? And if you can answer that one, are there any plans to run into the Borg?"

When you're nine years old you can get away with that. When you're sixteen, people start groaning, which is what they did. Someone yelled, "Next!"

McNeill was cool. He thought about it while the room went silent, and then asked:

"What's the Borg?"

The crowd broke out laughing, and, surprisingly, I laughed with them. We haven't changed at all, we Trekkers. We still look at actors and writers for answers, for inspiration, for hope, but the actors have changed. Their outlook is different. They realize the gift bestowed upon them, and want to have fun with it, take it around the block a little. Oh, they still don't understand it; no one does—and Trekkers are just as demanding as always. But we're a little more relaxed now. We've got more room.

-12-

THE FUTURE;

OR,

"HONEY, THEY'RE JUST CHILDREN.
DON'T DRESS THEM LIKE THE BORG."

Every Trekker dreams of having a little information about the future of *Star Trek*. Since we're futurists, the future of the future holds a special attraction. It seems to get weirder and weirder. What direction will *Star Trek* go in?

Well, information like this is hard to come by. The best place to look for it is on the Web—and there are several locations that stand out as sources of information.

Star Trek: WWW (http://www.vol.it/luca/startrek)
   The mother of all *Star Trek* sites. This should be your first stop on the Web. Luca Sambucci's creation truly competes with official *Trek* Websites. He's done a lot of work, and it shows.

The Best of *Trek* (http://www.bestoftrek.com)
   Luca Sambucci regularly scans *Star Trek*–related Websites and picks the best ones for you to peruse.

Star Trek **Continuum** (http://startrek.msn.com)
   The official Paramount-sponsored site, a treasure trove of *Star Trek*–related material (for members of the Microsoft Network only).

Sev Trek (http://www.sev.com.au/toonzone/sevtrek)
   All the *Star Trek* cartoons and humor you could possibly want.

IFT Operations (http://www.iftcommand.com)
   Those of you wanting to "join" Starfleet can do it here. Not for the fainthearted.

❋ ❋ ❋

If you're wondering how long you're going to have to put up with your friend's "special little hobby," my guess is quite a while. Although *Deep Space Nine* and *Voyager* are not enjoying the same level of success that *Next Generation* did, they are still such solid performers that no one in his right mind would consider canceling. In addition, *Star Trek: First Contact* made a fortune and is continuing to make money overseas.*

You can expect a new *Star Trek* film once every three years. Although the *Next Generation* crew only contracted to do three films, making the next one the last, I've been told that that's standard in the industry and that it doesn't mean that they won't contract to do more. Even though the actors have moved on to other things, *Star Trek* is still the biggest phenomenon in their careers.†

Now that the Borg were resoundingly defeated in the Alpha Quadrant you probably will not see them in the movies. The most likely topic for the *Enterprise*-E crew to handle would be the mirror universe, which we have seen go through severe changes lately. Look for an evil Picard, and quite soon (on *Voyager,* perhaps) an evil Deanna Troi!

Much more up in the air is *Deep Space Nine*. At the time of this writing, the show is going into its sixth season. There have been rumors that the cast is less than pleased with the program. This may be the final season of *Deep Space Nine,* and as long as the *Enterprise*-E is still functioning on a movie screen it would be tough for the station to jump to the big screen.

Clearly the big issue is how *Deep Space Nine* will resolve the conflict with the Dominion. There is always the possibility that they will fall prey to someone stronger than themselves, the Borg, perhaps—but it is also likely that it is the station that will fall, a downfall that may be political. Some people feel that *Deep Space*

---

*On a recent trip to Rome, I saw the movie advertised as *Primo Contato.* Just imagine the Borg speaking Italian. "Hey, we're going to assimilate you. *Que coso fi?*" I'd be laughing so hard I'd say *"Prego"* (go right ahead).

†Patrick Stewart (Picard) is doing Shakespeare, while Brent Spiner (Data) has been in *Independence Day* and *Phenomenon.*

Nine will be handed over to the Bajoran people, and that they will continue to opt out of the Federation, becoming a far less benign presence. But my gut instincts tell me that the situation around the station will remain volatile after the show ends, so perhaps, occasionally, two-hour episodes would continue the *DS9* saga.

Much more promising is *Star Trek: Voyager.* Although it has, by far, been the weakest of the three programs (some Trekkers have stopped watching altogether), it has the characters and drama to become far greater. The summer cliffhanger involving Species 8472 and a possible Borg-*Voyager* alliance will keep college fans devising possible outcomes.

Fans have heard of whispers of a fifth *Star Trek* series, perhaps as a replacement for *Deep Space Nine. Star Trek: Starfleet Academy* would focus on a group of young cadets training on Earth to become Starfleet officers in the latter half of the twenty-fourth century. We know that Picard once turned down the position of head of Starfleet Academy, but that doesn't mean that somebody else (say, Benjamin Sisko) couldn't take a shot at it. In any event, the comic book for Starfleet Academy is already out, so someone is thinking very seriously about this idea.

THE GREATEST *STAR TREK* EPISODES OF ALL TIME

AND

WHY YOU'LL LIKE THEM

One of the fun things about being a Trekker is arguing about which episodes are the greatest. And if you are spending a lot of time with a Trekker, it's a sure bet he'll want you to watch his favorites with him.

Below are my picks for the ten best episodes in each series, and the order of quality of the movies. Although these reflect my personal taste, I have consulted with many "Treksperts." I have concluded that these picks come close to a Trekker "consensus of quality." I realize that I will probably get lots of letters threatening to assimilate me for leaving out someone's favorite, but here goes.

STAR TREK: THE ORIGINAL SHOW

10. "A Piece of the Action"
   This is the one where they find a planet patterned after a book on Chicago mobs. The crew has to act like Edward G. Robinson to get out of a jam.

9. "The Trouble With Tribbles"
   The cutesy episode. Furry little tribbles eat all the top-secret grain and multiply all over the ship. "Aye, and they're in the food replicators, too."

8. "The Immunity Syndrome"
   A giant bacterium invades our galaxy, and the *Enterprise* becomes the germ invading *its* body.

7. **"The Enterprise Incident"**

Kirk undergoes surgery and makes a great Romulan. We find out they don't have to wait seven years for sex.

6. **"The Devil in the Dark"**

A mining colony stumbles across a mother hen, only this hen can melt your arm off. Nimoy does a great acting job mind-melding to an injured creature. "Pain!"

5. **"Space Seed"**

Kirk thaws Khan Noonien Singh (Ricardo Montalban) out of deep sleep. Khan takes woman, then takes ship. Basis for *Star Trek II: The Wrath of Khan.*

4. **"Mirror, Mirror"**

Accidental crew exchange program with evil *Enterprise.* Spock is cool even when torturing people.

3. **"Amok Time"**

This is the one where Spock goes crazy because he hasn't had a date in seven years. So *that's* why his ears are pointy.

2. **"The City on the Edge of Forever"**

McCoy goes back in time and saves a peace activist, changing history. Kirk falls for her, but still has to let her die. This episode includes the first curse uttered in a drama on prime-time television, by a solemn Kirk at the end: "Let's get the hell out of here."

1. **"The Doomsday Machine"**

The *Enterprise* must stop an ancient planet-killing machine, the original Death Star. Spock is in command and almost loses his cool. Best quotes: "Vulcans never bluff," and "Mister Scott, Mis...ter Scott."

Star Trek: The Next Generation

10. **"Q Who?"**

Q introduces us to the Borg. Great fun watching Picard being polite to a Borg before they slice a chunk out of the ship. Oh, if he only knew.

9. "Darmok"

Picard has to learn how to communicate with an alien who only speaks in metaphors. The only single episode of a TV show to spawn an entire language.

8. "The Offspring"

Data creates a daughter, Lal, and loses her. Just try not crying when she says "Thank you for my life, Father."

7. "Reunion"

Worf has a son, but loses the mother. We really liked her, too.

6. "Tapestry"

Picard dies and Q lets him re-live his life a little more wisely. What a mistake. The message: Your mistakes make you stronger.

5. "Relics"

Scotty returns, and they find an actual Dyson sphere. Hard to believe the special-effects crew pulled it off, but they did. It looks better than *Star Wars*.

4. "The Inner Light"

Picard is zapped by an alien probe and lives out an entire life in thirty minutes. (I felt that way the last time I watched *Friends*.)

3. "I, Borg"

The *Enterprise* finds a wounded teenage Borg and bonds with him. Picard opts not to use this Borg to destroy the Collective. Trekkers everywhere scream, "Fool."

2. "The Best of Both Worlds, Part I and Part II"

The Borg invade Federation space, kidnap Picard, and turn him into Locutus. Riker creates the most nervewracking cliffhanger ever by uttering one word. You'll have to watch it to find out.

1. "Yesterday's *Enterprise*"

A tough call. Picard is now the captain of the Battleship *Enterprise*-D as the *Enterprise*-C is blown into the future. To save the Federation from the Klingons, *Enterprise*-C must return to the past and be destroyed. Drama, alternate universes, sequel episodes. What more could you want?

STAR TREK: DEEP SPACE NINE

10. "The Visitor"

Sisko disappears and it takes the rest of Jake's life to find him. We get to see Jake really old.

9. "The Sons of Mogh"

Worf's brother Kurn wants Worf to kill him. Worf doesn't even stop to think about it. Kurn lives, but as Rodek, a humble Klingon.

8. "The Ship"

A wrecked Jem'Hadar ship is fought over. People needlessly die. Sisko's guilt is overwhelming.

7. *"Defiant"*

Sisko gets a new starship, and man, she moves. New life in dull series.

6. "The House of Quark"

Klingon woman has her way with Quark. Quark likes it.

5. "Hard Time"

O'Brien serves twenty years for a crime, all in his head. Doesn't make it any less real.

4. "The Jem'Hadar"

A new enemy is found in the Gamma Quadrant and they can blow up a ship like the *Enterprise*-D. What are the chances they can be stopped?

3. "The Die Is Cast"

Cardassians and Romulans attack the Founders. The Founders were waiting for them. Bye-bye Tal Shiar, bye-bye Obsidian Order.

2. "Crossover"

We find out what happened to Spock in the mirror universe. He should never have listened to Kirk.

1. **"The Way of the Warrior"**

 The Klingon Empire attacks *Deep Space Nine*. Awesome battles, stalemate. Worf joins the crew. Hey, maybe we should watch this show.

STAR TREK: VOYAGER

10. **"Dreadnought"**

 A talking bomb from Torres's past won't divert its course from an innocent planet. Great tension as Torres outwits herself.

9. **"Investigations"**

 Paris quits *Voyager* to discover who the spy is. Well done. So he's not really a jerk.

8. **"Phage"**

 We meet the Vidiians, the doctors from hell. Hold onto your spleen.

7. **"Eye of the Needle"**

 We found a wormhole home! Too bad it takes you back twenty years, too.

6. **"Basics, Part II"**

 Suder takes out an entire load of Kazon, while the Doctor insults Seska.

5. **"Basics, Part I"**

 The Kazon smarten up and take *Voyager*. If only they could've kept it.

4. **"Future's End, Part II"**

 Voyager vs. evil Bill Gates. You have to love that.

3. **"Future's End, Part I"**

 Voyager goes back in time to L.A. in 1996. Couldn't they have gone back a little earlier and prevented the O. J. Simpson case?

2. **"Unity"**

 The Borg are back, but this time call them Borg Lite. Same collective consciousness, but without the malevolence. We'll see about that.

1. "Scorpion, Part I"

Species 8472 teaches *Voyager* the meaning of the phrase *"Curiosity killed the cat."* Janeway wants to team up with the Borg. Will they agree…?

THE MOVIES

Here, in descending order of quality, are all the *Star Trek* movies made to date:

Star Trek II: The Wrath of Khan
Star Trek: First Contact
Star Trek IV: The Voyage Home
Star Trek VI: The Undiscovered Country (tie)
Star Trek: Generations (tie)
Star Trek III: The Search for Spock
Star Trek: The Motion Picture
       and
Star Trek V: The Final Frontier

Please note: There has been much debate about which is the worse film: *Star Trek: The Motion Picture* or *Star Trek V: The Final Frontier.* In my opinion, there is no debate. *Star Trek V* stands apart as the very worst. At least *Star Trek: The Motion Picture* had an excuse; there hadn't been any *Star Trek* for ten years, so they were rusty. But *Star Trek V* was awful. Not only were the effects bad, and not only was the plot bad, but it was also borderline blasphemous (the crew goes to meet "God"). Also, Uhura does a naked sand dance that makes you wince. Also, it was unbelieveable that

ty
ssdefed
ckjchrvufhfj
msjsjs
snjj

I'm sorry, I hit the keyboard with my fist.

ABOUT THE AUTHOR

Sam Ramer, a lifelong fan of *Star Trek*, was born in Manhattan and raised in the Bronx. He has performed stand-up comedy in New York, Boston, and Los Angeles. He lives in Manhattan, where he is currently an assistant district attorney for the Special Narcotics Prosecutor's Office for the City of New York.